Kindly Bent to Ease Us

Klong-chen rab-'byams-pa

Part One: Mind
Sems-nyid ngal-gso

from

The Trilogy of Finding Comfort and Ease
Ngal-gso skor-gsum

Translated from the Tibetan and annotated by

Herbert V. Guenther

Dharma Publishing

TIBETAN TRANSLATION SERIES

Illustrations
Frontispiece: Padmasambhava, the Great Guru
who inspired Klong-chen rab-'byams-pa
Page 2: Klong-chen-rab-'byams-pa

ISBN: 0-913546-39-9; 0-913546-40-2 (pbk)
Library of Congress Catalogue Card Number: 75-29959

Typeset in Fototronic Elegante and
printed in the United States of America
by Dharma Press
9 8 7 6 5 4

To Tarthang Tulku Rinpoche

Contents

Foreword

Until now, there has been no authentic translation describing the Dzogchen teachings of the Nyingma school which are the most sophisticated and effective practices of Vajrayana Buddhism. So I am very grateful and happy that this introductory text is now available to all those interested in deepening their understanding of the Buddhist path.

The subject of this book is how to attain Enlightenment. By interweaving the teachings of the Sutras and Tantras, Longchenpa beautifully summarizes all Buddhist thought. Traditionally, each aspect of the Buddhist path has three parts: *tawa, gompa,* and *chodpa*—'view', 'meditation', and 'action'. 'View' means to investigate the nature of the Buddha's inner experience. This effort to see reality 'just as it is' inspired all Buddhist philosophy and intellectual development. Through meditation, we learn to be mindful each moment and to integrate this view in every situation. According to the Tantras, negative energies and subjective interpretations become subtly transformed and purified, like alchemy—everything is seen as naturally pure and completely perfect. When we learn to participate in this world fully, with all its joys, allurements, and sorrows, every situation is useful. The very bonds which attach us to samsara become the means to Enlightenment.

This knowledge already exists within our own experience, but we need to study, meditate, and practice properly. First we must understand both the text and the teachings and learn to magnify them within ourselves through our own direct experience. Longchenpa's presentation is very deep and meaningful, so read and study each word and sentence carefully. In the Nyingma view, philosophy and experience function simultaneously. Like water and wetness, one is not separate from the other.

The Nyingma lineage which we follow represents the living continuation of this inner realization, the link and the thread, the key to Enlightenment which has been passed on from teacher to student for many centuries. Following this lineage, we cannot accumulate any more negative karma. Once this realization becomes part of our inner nature, no questions or doubts remain. We share the same enlightened understanding of the living lineage which cannot die, cannot disappear, cannot be destroyed or lost. Traditionally it is said that 'Padmasambhava pointed to the door and Longchenpa opened it'. Through his omniscient insight and untiring compassion, he inspired many followers to practice the Dzogchen teachings and to attain Enlightenment in one lifetime.

The world today seems very dark, confused, and empty, so I sincerely hope that this book will, in a small way, bring the light of the Dharma to whoever is interested in the Buddhist path or wishes to improve himself. I am especially grateful to Dr. Guenther for helping to preserve these introductory Nyingma teachings. Longchenpa is such an important figure in this unbroken lineage that in the future we hope to publish many more volumes of his exceptional and illuminating work.

Founder, Nyingma Institute   Tarthang Tulku Rinpoche
Berkeley, California

Preface

There is depth, breadth, and magic in Nyingma (*rnying-ma*) thought and its charm grows the more one studies it. Klong-chen rab-'byams-pa Dri-med 'od-zer's presentation is lit with a mysterious light that radiates into and transfigures every aspect of man's life. For he is no mere pedant, content with parading passages from hallowed texts he has happened to have learned by heart. Rather, he is a person who has something to say because he can speak from experience, and he is quite explicit as to how he wants us to understand what he has to say. Therefore, in the notes to the translation of the text I have utilized his many other works in which he stipulates in greater detail his meanings for the terms he uses; and I have, precisely for this reason, refrained from resorting to Sanskrit words which are not only quite meaningless for an English-speaking reader but have very little, if any, significance to indigenous Tibetan works which have been written in Tibetan and not in Sanskrit. Only in the case of proper names have I employed the more familiar Sanskrit terms—provided they are available, which is not always the case.

Klong-chen rab-'byams-pa has structured each chapter of his work in a distinct manner. This I have indicated by the use of letters and numbers for each major section (e.g., A, B, C . . .) and for the many sub-sections (e.g., Ia, IIa, IIIaIai . . .) within larger sections. In the introductory passage to each chapter, I have also attempted to summarize the philosophical and psychological import of Klong-chen rab-'byams-pa's presentation.

Those familiar with the pungent writing of the good Dean Jonathan Swift will have little difficulty in recognizing the source of inspiration for the English title of Klong-chen rab-'byams-pa's work which points to the thrust towards Being as both source and fulfillment of man's ongoing quest for the meaning of his life. Since in this quest Mind and, in particular, the understanding of its working is of primary importance, the vast scope of mind is the subject of the first part of Klong-chen rab-'byams-pa's trilogy presented here. In the remaining two parts to be translated subsequently, he treats the subjects of contemplation and of detached vision capable of retaining the magic and vividness of experience.

The translation owes its impetus to my late friend Kathog Ontrul who introduced me into and guided me through the intricacies of the sNying-thig teachings, so important for Nyingma thought, and, above all, to my close friend Tarthang Tulku whose concern for keeping the Nyingma tradition alive I have shared from the moment we met, who has been over the years indefatigable in making available whatever was needed for such a project as undertaken here, whose knowledge of Nyingma thought is unparalleled, and whose enthusiasm for the Nyingma tradition is truly infectious.

A book of this nature is the outcome of so many experiences and so much help that it is impossible to make adequate acknowledgements. However, I am most grateful to my wife whose patience and encouragement played a significant role, and who not only typed and retyped the manuscript but also prepared the index.

I am also grateful to my colleagues, professors Keith Scott and Leslie Sumio Kawamura, for critical comments; to my graduate students Kennard Lipman and Leonard van der Kuijp for their assistance in proofreading.

Finally, my thanks are due to the members of the Nyingma Institute in Berkeley, California, and the editorial staff of Dharma Publishing, in particular, to Mr. Steven D. Goodman, Mr. Stephen Tainer, Mr. Paul Clemens and, last but not least, Miss Judy Robertson, for their careful editorial work on the typescript.

University of Saskatchewan   HERBERT V. GUENTHER
Saskatoon, Canada

Introduction

Kun-mkhyen (the 'all-knowing', 'all-understanding') Klong-chen rab-'byams-pa Dri-med 'od-zer, hailed as a second Buddha and certainly the greatest thinker in the Old Tradition (*rnying-ma-pa*), was born on the eighth day of the second lunar month of the Earth-Male-Ape year (i.e., Friday, 1st of March, 1308) at Gra-phu stod-grong in gYo-ru, the most eastern of the two parts into which dBus (Central Tibet) was originally divided. His father, the 'teacher' (*slob-dpon*) bTsan-pa-srung, could trace his ancestry back to Ye-shes dbang-po-srung of the Rog clan, who is counted as one of the 'seven chosen ones' (*sad-mi bdun*), intelligent men who had been selected from the nobility at about 779 to be ordained as monks by Śāntarakṣita, the renowned Indian paṇḍita, during his stay in Tibet. His mother, 'Brom-gza'-ma bsod-nams-rgyan, was a descendant of the 'Brom clan, to which 'Brom-ston rgyal-ba'i 'byung-gnas (1005–1064), the famous disciple of Atīśa, also known as Dīpankara Śrījñāna (982–1054), belonged.

In 1319, Klong-chen rab-'byams-pa took up ordination at

bSam-yas in the presence of the 'abbot' (*mkhan-po*) bSam-grub rin-chen and the 'teacher' (*slob-dpon*) Kun-dga' 'od-zer, when he was given the name Tshul-khrims blo-gros. The next years were spent in intensive studies under the most famous teachers of the time. Apart from studying under those belonging to his own tradition, the rNying-ma, he also was a student of Rang-byung rdo-rje (1284–1339), the Karma-pa bKa'-brgyud-pa hierarch, and of the Sa-skya-pa bla-ma Dam-pa bsod-nams rgyal-mtshan (1312–1375), both of them representing the 'New (*gsar-ma*) Tradition' (the dGe-lugs tradition originated after Klong-chen rab-'byams-pa's time). Because of his knowledge he became known as Ngag-gi dbang-po of bSam-yas and as Klong-chen rab-'byams-pa, and he used these titles as signatures to some of his works.

When he was in his late twenties two events occurred that were to be of decisive importance for his intellectual and spiritual development. The one was a vision of Padmasambhava and his consort Ye-shes mtsho-rgyal, which resulted in his adopting the names Dri-med 'od-zer, as given him by Padmasambhava, and rDo-rje gzi-brjid, as conferred upon him by Ye-shes mtsho-rgyal, in his vision. At this time—and one experience may have led to another—he became deeply attracted to and involved in the *mKha'-'gro snying-thig*, mystical teachings connected with Padmasambhava, which he then developed in his own *mKha'-'gro yang-tig*. He also conceived the plan of founding or restoring the monastic settlements of Lha-ring-brag, O-rgyan-rdzong, and Zhva'i lha-khang. The last named had been founded by Myang Ting-nge-'dzin bzang-po, who was an important personage during the reign of Khri-srong lde'u-btsan (755–797) and his successors, and had been a supporter of the growing Buddhist movement. It was for this reason that he was executed, after 836, under Glang dar-ma (who was opposed to Buddhist ideas). In this temple Myang Ting-nge-'dzin bzang-po had concealed the *sNying-thig* teachings of Vimalamitra who had been one of the earliest representatives of rDzogs-chen thought in Tibet.

The second decisive event in the life of Klong-chen rab-'byams-pa was his meeting with the great mystic (*phyam-rdal rig-'dzin chen-po*) Kumaradza (gZhon-nu rgyal-po, Kumārarāja, 1266–1343), a Tibetan, who is most often mentioned under his Indian name. Kumārarāja was particularly connected with the teachings of Vimalamitra, whose embodiment he is believed to have been.[1] Vimalamitra's teachings, summed up in the *Bi-ma snying-thig*, had been rediscovered by lDang-ma lhun-rgyal and in course of time transmitted by Me-long-rdo-rje (1243–1303) to Kumārarāja and by the latter to Klong-chen rab-'byams-pa, who elaborated these teachings into his *Bla-ma yang-tig* and then fused the teachings of both the *mKha'-'gro yang-tig* and the *Bla-ma yang-tig* into his most profound *Zab-mo yang-tig*.

An unfortunate incident seems to have provoked the hostility of the powerful Tai-si-tu Byang-chub rgyal-mtshan (1302–1364) of Phag-mo-gru who in 1358 had formally taken over power from Sa-skya and who, almost immediately afterwards, believed Klong-chen rab-'byams-pa to be an ally of 'Bri-khung. In 1359 one of the 'Bri-khung monks, a fanatic (*sgom-chen*) Kun-rin, staged a revolt. Klong-chen rab-'byams-pa tried to mediate, but his effort was considered a support of this revolt. He was forced into exile in Bhutan and stayed at the monastery of Thar-pa-gling near Bum-thang where he had been in 1355.[2] Eventually he was reconciled with Tai-si-tu Byang-chub rgyal-mtshan through the efforts of his lay patrons, prince Si-tu Shākya bzang-po of dBus-stod and prince rDo-rje rgyal-mtshan of Yar-'brog, and was allowed to return.

Klong-chen rab-'byams-pa died on the eighteenth day of the twelfth lunar month of the Water-Female-Hare year (i.e., Wednesday, the 24th of January, 1364) at O-rgyan-rdzong in Gangs-ri thod-kar, the place he had loved most during his many travels and periods of seclusion in various caves.

In his relatively short life Klong-chen rab-'byams-pa was able to write an enormous number of works. His biographer, Chos-grags bzang-po,[3] lists two hundred and seventy titles, unfortunately arranged according to subject-matter and not in chronological order so that we cannot trace Klong-chen rab-'byams-pa's intellectual development.[4] Another unfortunate circumstance is that quite a number of his works seem to have been lost. Throughout his major writings he presents a unitary account of Buddhist thought which, long before his time, had tended to proliferate into, and even become stagnant in, highly specialized areas. rDza dPal-sprul O-rgyan 'Jigs-med chos-kyi dbang-po (b. 1808) has well brought out this unifying character of Klong-chen rab-'byams-pa's writings, when he says:[5]

> They are *dBu-ma* (Mādhyamika), *Pha-rol-phyin-pa* (Pāramitā), *gCod-yul, Zhi-byed* (the calming of frustration and suffering), *Phyag-rgya-che* (Mahāmudrā),[6] and the very essence of *rDzogs-chen.*
> All these interpretations gather here, and still (Klong-chen rab-'byams-pa's writings) are superior to all of them.
> If you happen to be a follower of this all-knowing guru,
> You must never become separated from this his wholesome teaching;
> It will be enough if you make it your companion in all your thinking;
> There is nothing like this to let your mind realize its aim.

The major works, about which this eulogy was written, are the "Seven Treasures" (*mdzod bdun*), each of them indispensable for an understanding of the profound and intricate teaching which is termed *rDzogs-chen* ('absolutely complete'), and which is based so much on direct experience rather than on speculative and representational thought.[7] Of these "Seven Treasures," the *Theg-pa'i mchog rin-po-che'i mdzod* is the most comprehensive work, dealing with all aspects of the rDzogs-chen teaching in twenty-five chapters; the remaining six "Treasures" take up specific points.

Thus, the *gNas-lugs rin-po-che'i mdzod*, consisting of a short basic text in verse form and its detailed commentary, the *sDe-gsum snying-po'i don-'grel gnas-lugs rin-po-che'i mdzod*, discusses the four vectorial connections in what may be termed the 'experience of Being'—its ineffability, coherence, spontaneity and solitariness—as well as the person to whom this teaching can and may be imparted.

The *Man-ngag rin-po-che'i mdzod* is a summary in verse form of the essentials for practicing and understanding the tenets of Buddhism, and, through understanding, growing into the fullness of Being. It is arranged in sets of six topics.

The *Grub-pa'i mtha' rin-po-che'i mdzod*, in eight chapters, is the most exhaustive and critical treatment of Buddhist philosophy. The work begins with the history of the Buddha as both a spiritual and cultural phenomenon, then deals with the compilation and transmission of the teaching and the beginnings of the early schools after the demise of the Buddha. After a detailed presentation and trenchant critique of the tenets of the traditional four schools—Vaibhāṣika, Sautrāntika, Yogācāra and Mādhyamika—Klong-chen rab-'byams-pa elucidates the 'existential' experience culminating in 'absolute completeness' (*rdzogs-chen*).

The *Yid-bzhin rin-po-che'i mdzod*, in twenty-two chapters, consists of a relatively short basic text in verse form and a very lengthy and exhaustive commentary, the *Padma dkar-po*, and covers the whole of the Buddhist world-view with man as an integral part. It first considers the origin of the world in philosophical perspective, and then treats ontology (the problem of Being, not of some kind of being), cosmology (the rich unfolding of Being, as envisaged in the Avataṃsaka teaching, and not the more or less static arrangement of objects around us, as presented in the Abhidharmakośa),[8] and anthropology (man as an open-ended task, not an essence or ego). It then turns to the spiritual growth of man in his predicament of being man, to his need for friends to help him along in developing ethically, and to the relationship between teacher and disciple. This is followed by a detailed account of the various philosophical systems that had evolved in both Buddhist and non-Buddhist circles. The discussion aims at clarifying the student's task of coming to an awareness and understanding of Being, rather than remaining bound in mere doctrinal postulations.[9]

The *Tshig-don rin-po-che'i mdzod*, in eleven chapters, sums up the essentials of rDzogs-chen thought—the seeming loss of Being in the state of a human being, a loss which always presents itself as a challenge to find Being, and the inner experiences with their symbols through which man's development towards Being manifests itself. This work is intimately related to the *sNying-thig* teachings.

The *Chos-dbyings-rin-po-che'i mdzod*, consisting of a short basic text in verse form and a detailed commentary, the *Lung-gi gter-mdzod*, in thirteen chapters, deals with the primordial experience of the meaningfulness of Being. Essentially, it is an account of experience as experience, not of a particular experience of something.

In all these works Klong-chen rab-'byams-pa quotes from the vast literature that had developed during the early phase of Buddhism in Tibet, in support of his own brilliant exposition of a living and lived-through experience. He uses these quotations in an interpretative rather than dogmatic fashion. Thus throughout his works he reveals himself as an independent and original thinker.

Although the "Seven Treasures" are counted as Klong-chen rab-'byams-pa's crowning achievement, this does not mean that his other works are less important. As a matter of fact, Klong-chen rab-'byams-pa is so unique that a distinction between more important and less important works is not only not possible, but even meaningless. The "Seven Treasures" are as indispensable for understanding his other works as his other works are for the "Seven Treasures". Especially important in this respect are his two trilogies, the *Ngal-gso skor-gsum*, "The Trilogy of Finding Comfort and

Ease," and the *Rang-grol skor-gsum*, "The Trilogy of Freedom as Freedom."[10] The fact that Klong-chen rab-'byams-pa himself seems to have considered these trilogies of primary importance may be gleaned from the number of works he wrote to bring out their significance in making Buddhist ideas a living experience.

The *Ngal-gso skor-gsum* consists of the following works:

A 1. *rDzogs-pa chen-po Sems-nyid ngal-gso*, the basic work, written in verses and consisting of thirteen chapters, intricately interwoven as to content and practical guidance as to the meaning and significance of Mind-as-such.

 2. *rDzogs-pa chen-po Sems-nyid ngal-gso'i 'grel-pa Shing-rta chen-po*, a detailed commentary on the above work.

 3. *rDzogs-pa chen-po Sems-nyid ngal-gso'i 'grel-pa Shing-rta chen-po'i bsdus-don-gyi gnas rgya-cher dbye-ba Padma dkar-po'i phreng-ba*, a structural analysis of each of the thirteen chapters.[11]

 4. *rDzogs-pa chen-po Sems-nyid ngal-gso'i gnas-gsum dge-ba gsum-gyi don-khrid Byang-chub lam-bzang*, an analysis of the basic work into one hundred and forty-one contemplative topics, of which ninety-two belong to the common form of Mahāyāna, twenty-two to the Vajrayāna, and twenty-seven to the rDzogs-chen.

B 1. *rDzogs-pa chen-po bSam-gtan ngal-gso*, the basic work, written in verses and consisting of only three chapters, dealing with the suitable places for contemplative attentiveness, the person engaging in this activity, and the process and purpose of contemplative attentiveness.

 2. *rDzogs-pa chen-po bSam-gtan ngal-gso'i bsdus-don Puṇḍarīka'i phreng-ba*, a structural analysis of the above work.

3. *rDzogs-pa chen-po bSam-gtan ngal-gso'i 'grel-pa Shing-rta rnam-par dag-pa*, a detailed commentary on the basic work.

4. *rDzogs-pa chen-po bSam-gtan ngal-gso'i don-khrid snying-po bcud-bsdus*, a short guidance to contemplative experience.

C 1. *rDzogs-pa chen-po sGyu-ma ngal-gso*, the basic work, written in verses and consisting of eight chapters, each of them dealing with the apparitional, fleeting, dreamlike character of what is usually believed to be steady and reliable.

2. *rDzogs-pa chen-po sGyu-ma ngal-gso'i bsdus-don Māndarava'i phreng-ba*, a structural analysis of each of the eight chapters of the basic work.

3. *rDzogs-pa chen-po sGyu-ma ngal-gso'i 'grel-pa Shing-rta bzang-po*, a detailed commentary on the basic work.

4. *rDzogs-pa chen-po sGyu-ma ngal-gso'i don-khrid Yid-bzhin nor-bu*, a short guidance to practice.

The arrangement of the basic works together with their commentaries in this order A, B, C, is explained by Klong-chen rab-'byams-pa in his *Ngal-gso skor-gsum-gyi spyi-don legs-bshad rgya-mtsho*. There[12] he says that, if a person is to set out on his quest for life's meaning, he must already have a conviction that life holds meaning and have a vision of its meaningfulness. At the same time meaningfulness is somehow a clue pointing back to the fundamental stratum on which the pursuit of meaningfulness is founded. The explication of this fundamental stratum is found in the *Sems-nyid ngal-gso*. Once this fundamental stratum has been understood one can 'travel the road' towards meaningfulness through attending to representational and non-representational forms of thinking. This is the theme of the *bSam-gtan ngal-gso*. Lastly, we tend to reify the contents into inflexible objects, into constant patterns somewhere 'out there' into which we locate 'ourselves' as a new object—the ego. To prevent experience from turning into an objectified event and to safeguard the unique moment of knowing and valuing, perceiving and conceiving, before all this again congeals into rigid categories of representational thinking, some aid is needed. This aid is offered by the *sGyu-ma ngal-gso*. In other words, the first work explicates that all that is is the source material that serves as the highway towards life's meaning; the second, that all that is is spontaneously present in sheer lucency; and the third, that all that is is self-presenting without ever being something 'concretely' real.[13]

Throughout these three works experience is and remains the central theme. But experience is not an object nor a fact alongside other objects or facts. Therefore experience must never be confused with sentimentality and its attendant 'mannerisms'. These mannerisms are made possible through the projective character of experience which brings about the objectification of the emerging content and entails the loss of the dynamic aspect of experience. Experience as experience is a more ultimate factor, broader in range and scope and prior to even a 'mind'. And yet, without mind there would be no meaning to experience. However, mind (*sems*) as a noetic-noematic complex, determining the 'meaning' of world, of being, of experience and of whatever it takes notice, is a coming-into-presence made possible through the open and projective presence of Mind-as-such (*sems-nyid*), which is irreducible to object and fact, while constituting their configurative location.

The importance of experience as the seed from which perception, cognition, and valuation grow and as the upsurge that occasions its actualization, is emphasized by Klong-chen rab-'byams-pa in the analysis of the title *rDzogs-pa chen-po Sems-nyid ngal-gso*. He says:[14]

> *rDzogs-pa* ('complete') indicates the whole of Saṃsāra and Nirvāṇa. And when is this completeness found? From the very beginning it is complete in (or as) absolute (*chen-po*)

self-existing pristine cognition, and from it everything ('all meanings') originate. As is stated in the *Kun-byed*:[15]

> One—complete; two—complete; as mind—complete;
> Since (its) acts are excellent—bliss.

And in the Dohā:[16]

> Mind-as-such alone is the seed of all;
> From it the world of fictions and the world of quiescence
>   grow forth.
> Praise to the mind which like the Wish-fulfilling Gem
> Grants whatever one desires.

Mind-as-such (*sems-nyid*), in the narrower sense of the word, is the complex of the mind and the mental events (*sems* and *sems-byung*). Relaxation in comfort and ease (*ngal-gso*) is to indicate that in self-existing pristine cognition propositions no longer obtain. In a fundamental sense, Mind-as-such is, in its actuality, a sheer lucency; relaxation in comfort and ease is to indicate that proliferating reflective thinking has come to rest.

The distinction Klong-chen rab-'byams-pa draws between Mind-as-such (*sems-nyid*) and the noetic-noematic complex of the mind and its events (*sems* and *sems-byung*), clearly shows that he was well aware of the fact that experience has both a prereflective-nonthematic aspect (termed 'Mind-as-such' *sems-nyid*) and a reflective-thematic movement (termed 'mind', *sems*), and that the two structural features are so intricately interwoven that the one is not temporally prior or posterior to the other. This is important to note because it is merely our language that introduces a seeming serial time sequence by making use of the prefix 'pre'- in prereflective.[17] Klong-chen rab-'byams-pa is spared this potential misunderstanding: Mind-as-such (*sems-nyid*) *is* mind (*sems*) and their distinctness is inseparable. To illustrate what this may mean, we may consider the image of a traveler. A traveler is a person who may proceed on his road and who may rest from time to time without losing his identity as a traveler. It is this image that Klong-chen rab-'byams-pa uses in defense of the title of his work against an imaginary opponent (who may not have been quite so imaginary, because there are always literalists impervious to 'meaning' due to the fact that they are unable to recognize the meaning to be dynamic, vibrant with life, and not fossil-like). Thus he writes:[18]

> Calling your treatise 'Relaxation in Comfort and Ease by Mind-as-such' is inadmissible, because Mind-as-such has nothing to do with relaxation or exhaustion. — Now, the term 'Mind-as-such' can be taken in a narrower sense and in a more fundamental sense. In the narrower sense, it is quite appropriate to speak of 'Relaxation in Comfort and Ease by Mind-as-such'; since the whole of mind and mental events are the concepts that set up the triple world which is the cause of Saṃsāra, they must come to rest in the continuum of experience into which no fictions enter. . . . Therefore, since the fictions due to mind and mental events are again and again wearing themselves out and grow tired in Saṃsāra which is their domain, they must relax on their walking-stick, a conceptless pristine cognition, the continuum of meaningfulness, the other shore reached by appreciative discrimination, the coming to rest of all propositions. For this reason I have deliberately used this title for the treatise about finding comfort and ease while proceeding on the road to the primordial experience of Being. . . . Also, in a more fundamental sense it is appropriate to speak of 'Relaxation in Comfort and Ease by Mind-as-such'. The host of concepts, the travelers who have become tired through having run around in circles (Saṃsāra) while for a long time having engaged in the deceptive appearance conjured up by the mind, simply sit down in the reach and range in which all propositions have come to rest and which is the resting-place of Mind-as-such relaxed in comfort and ease. Travelers who are exhausted and tired simply lean on their walking-stick and let body, speech, and mind come to rest, and this is like relaxing in comfort and ease. Therefore, when the escapades of the mind, having become tired by Saṃsāra kept up by actions in body, speech, and mind, have ceased on Mind-as-such which is relaxation in comfort and ease, this relaxation in comfort and ease is the entrance into real freedom.

Klong-chen rab-'byams-pa never loses sight of the dual character of experience. He notices that experience is directed towards what is then reflected on in experience, but he sees the latter taking place in experience and this avoids creating a gap between Mind-as-such and the mind of the experiencer—and he explores how this happens. Therefore, each chapter is based on a 'how'-question, not on a 'what'-question. 'How' is it that man finds himself in his predicament of being man, and 'how' is man to go about solving the problem he is? Klong-chen rab-'byams-pa does not quantify objectifiable features of experience: he interprets, and in his interpretations he opens up ways towards understanding —'how' man can understand himself and, in understanding himself, understand his world.

This explains why Klong-chen rab-'byams-pa is so careful in his diction, taking account of the 'weights' and overtones which he then takes up in his commentaries. *byang-chub* is a common word in Tibetan Buddhist writings and corresponds to the Sanskrit word *bodhi*, which is usually translated by 'enlightenment'. But Klong-chen rab-'byams-pa breaks this word down into its components *byang*, 'limpid clearness', and *chub*, 'consummate perspicacity', and gives it a very specific, dynamic meaning. And this he does with every other term. Klong-chen rab-'byams-pa is concerned with the exploration of lived-through experience, not with an intellectual parlor game of quantifications of fetish-words that have no longer any meaning because they have become divorced from experience.

Since Klong-chen rab-'byams-pa's primary concern is lived-through experience and its interpretation in terms of 'meanings' and 'values', many, if not the majority, of his works are written in poetry. A poem is a peculiar entity or occurrence that simultaneously embodies a world of its own and transports the reader or listener into its special world, enabling him to experience, whether in imagination or in real life, a state of being which may otherwise have remained unknown to him.

In conclusion it may be stated that Klong-chen rab-'byams-pa exerted a tremendous influence on his successors, who had no hesitation in imitating him. Thus, 'Jigs-med gling-pa's (1729 or 30–1798) *Yon-tan rin-po-che'i mdzod dga'-ba'i char* is in every respect modeled after Klong-chen rab-'byams-pa's *Sems-nyid ngal-gso* and incorporates whole passages from it.

Kindly Bent to Ease Us

CHAPTER ONE

A Unique Occasion
and the Right Juncture

*T*raditional philosophy has been dominated by the con-
trasting ideas of essence and existence. Essence is said
to be that factor in finite entities which determines
them and marks them off from others, while existence is the
act that makes them actual and separates them from nothing.
As the determinate whatness of finite entities, essence was
further conceived to be something universal, timeless, and
inactive, and the various essences of the multiplicity of finite
entities were held together by necessary logical relationships. All this led to the construction of conceptual systems,
and to the assumption that essence preceded existence in the
case of man determining his nature, which remained fixed
for all times. Similarly existence was tied up with particular
entities. When in more recent times it was claimed that
existence preceded essence and that in the act of existence
man determined his own essence, this existential reversal of
the essentialist trend did not change the basic conceptualism.

Whether we give precedence to essence or to existence,
we deal with an abstraction, and this means that we have

taken something smaller from something greater. It is a fact that the greater can never be caught by or reduced to the smaller. It cannot even be pointed out. Attempts to do so are more often than not attempts to dwell on elements which are merely ingredients, aspects of rationalization upon which the construction of a conceptual system rests, but which leave out the most important factor of all, which in a work of art is known as beauty and in a life situation as Being.

While we cannot point out beauty or Being, we can point *to* it and this pointing may help people to experience for themselves this something greater. Such pointing is indicated by the use of word 'Being' which is the most universal of concepts, for it covers anything and everything —even 'nothing' which, in the sense that it is spoken or thought, *is* something. Beyond the domain of this concept there is, in the strictest sense of the word, nothing more on which 'Being' could rest and on the basis of which it could be more specifically determined. This is tantamount to saying that the more comprehensive a concept is the more indeterminate and 'empty' is its content. There is 'nothing' of either essence or of existence in it, and yet there is the awareness and feeling of 'Being' in the sense that 'Being' is awareness and awareness is feeling.

Of course, terms like 'awareness' and 'feeling' are quite inadequate. We have the tendency to say that we are aware of something and we tacitly assume that this something is always something finite, as is the awareness itself. The same applies to feeling, as when I say that I feel happy or comfortable, unhappy or uncomfortable. What we have done in all these cases is that we have made up a concept and, in our efforts to bring the something greater under the concept, we have attempted to make it something smaller and have quite literally strayed away from *it* into fictions of our own making —whether we call these 'essences', 'existences', or 'minds'. It is as if, and it seems almost inevitable to do so, we were desperate to fill nothingness, the 'emptiness' of Being, with 'essences', fundamental characteristics, and to replace pure awareness by distinct acts of cognitions. However, rather than to say that we 'fill' nothingness it seems more correct to say that we tend to 'falsify' 'Being' into some sort of 'existent' which we then further split up into essence and existence, and to 'falsify' Mind (as a pointer to the awareness that is Being) into 'some' mind which also is split up into a mind and mental events. Thus the openness of Being is lost, its sheer lucency becomes dimmer and dimmer until it is as dull as the 'existents', the objects it deals with as *a* mind.

This falsification, however, makes us uneasy. This uneasiness not only signals the fact that something, somewhere, sometime has gone wrong, and that something has to be done about it, it also makes clear that what is at stake is man's humanity which cannot be defined in terms of 'essences' but is inseparable from, if not identical with, Being, to which, in the context of man's being human, the name 'Buddha nature' is given.

Insofar as Being operates through a human existence which illustrates this working of Being as the rediscovery of Being by itself, a human existence is a 'unique occasion' and 'right juncture'. To the extent that Being is allowed to penetrate man's 'existence' and to return it to 'Being', to heal the wounds of fragmentation and to restore the wholeness of Being, a human existence is precious. This means neither more nor less than that the presence of something already there, and the direction and scope of the question (and the quest) of being human, are determined by the question and the quest of Being, which aims at making the meaning of Being explicit through its immediate experience.

Homage to Śrī Samantabhadra[1]

omage to the beginningless primordial Lord,[2]   A1
an ocean great and full of capabilities;[3]
Whose range of intuition[4] and depth of
    tenderness[5] cannot be fathomed,
Who is the birthplace of the Wish-fulfilling Gem, the
    Buddhas and their spiritual sons, and
From whom cloudbanks of prosperity and bliss arise.

Sheer lucency,[6] founding stratum of meaning,[7]   A2
    immaculate, man's Buddha-nature,[8]
Through ego-centered apprehensions following the loss
    of pure awareness,[9] strays into fictitious being.[10]
Wearied and weakened in the deserts of
Karmic actions and turbulent emotions[11] may Mind[12]
    today find comfort and ease.

Friends, a precious human body, being a unique   BI
    occasion and the right juncture,
Is very hard to find within the six life-forms.
As delighted as a blind man who has stumbled on a
    precious hoard,
Use this body for prosperity and bliss.

What is meant by a unique occasion and the right   BII1
    juncture?[13]
I am a person beyond the eight unfavorable
    conditions:[14]
My mind has not been born in the realms of hells, of
    hungry spirits,
And of animals, I am not dumb, and I am not one of the
    long-living gods, nor one of the savages, and

I do not harbor wrong views, and do not live in a period
in which there are no Buddhas;
And I represent the right juncture: five events affecting
me directly by being complete in me—[15]
I have become a human being, I live in the central
country, and I possess all senses,
I do not revert to inexpiable evil deeds, and I have
confidence in the foundation of spiritual life; and
Five events affecting me indirectly:[16]
The coming of a Buddha, his having taught the
doctrine, the presence of his teaching now,
The following so that it continues, and the loving
guidance by others.
These are the eighteen facets of a unique occasion and
the right juncture.
While they are thus complete,
Thoroughly exert yourself and realize deliverance.

BII2   If in this lifetime you do not make good use (of your
existence)
You will in the hereafter not even hear the word 'happy
life-form',
But for a long time will roam about in evil forms of life.
Not knowing what is to be rejected and what to be
accepted, and so going the wrong way,
You cannot but drift about in Saṃsāra that has no
beginning nor end.

BII3   Therefore, while you still have the power now,
Apply yourself to the accumulation of inexhaustible
positive qualities,
In view of the fact that you are the juncture for the path
to happiness,
And pass beyond the stronghold of fictitious being.

BII4   But if I dare not cross this endless ocean of Saṃsāra,
Although I have a precious boat,

What shall I do when forever
Emotional reactions and frustrations are raging in
    tumultuous waves?

Then quickly don the armor of perseverance   BII5
And, in order to let the turbid state of mind and mental
    events[17] be cleared,
Set out on the path of sheer lucency, of immaculate
    pristine cognitions,[18]
And let no obstacles impede the road to limpid
    clearness and consummate perspicacity.[19]

He who has become the foundation for bliss and   BII6
    happiness
And has found a precious and clean vessel,
But does not gather the refreshing rain of the
    nectar-like doctrine,
Will let himself be crushed by the swelter of Saṃsāra.

The downpour of (the Buddha's) truth, the refreshing   BII7
    water of pristine cognitions
With clouds of glorious bliss and happiness and
    prosperity,
Will fall on the pure mind of living beings, the fertile
    soil of a unique occasion and the right juncture.
Therefore, with joy and from your heart engage in the
    quest for the real meaning of life.[20]

It is easier for a tortoise to put its neck into the hole   BII8
Of a yoke tossed about in the middle of the ocean
Than to find a human existence—the teacher of men
    and gods has said.
How much more difficult is it to find a precious body
    that is a unique occasion and the right juncture!
Therefore, from today onwards you just have to make
    efforts.

BIII1   Thus there are those who have a mere human existence,
A special one, and a precious one.
In this order, (first) there is the ordinary human
existence, complete with all senses,
But not knowing good and evil, and acting
objectionably;
Though being born in the world of civilized men, one is
found among the savages and barbarians.

BIII2   (The second type) are those who have not gone into the
teachings and are confused about good and evil,
In their concern with this life only they are enamored of
its bustle,
Impudent and easy-going they put off the hereafter,
Not caring for deliverance, even if they hear (the
Buddha's) message.
They do not represent a superior existence, but merely
mediocrity.
Occasionally they will set their mind on something
positive,
But mostly their mental vision is obscured by evil.
Having only adopted the marks (of a human existence),
what use are they to themselves and others?
They may assume the appearance of a householder or
of a mendicant, and
Only because they are slightly better than those in evil
forms of life,
They are called 'special human beings' by the Buddha.

BIII3   The supreme person, immaculate, a worthy vessel for
the teaching,
Will apply himself to the meaning of what he has heard
and thought about,
And disciplining himself he will establish others in the
wholesome—
An unshakeable mountain of realization,

A royal banner of saintliness. These, whether
They be householders or recluses,
Represent the preciousness of human existence—so our
    teacher has said.

Therefore, hear the teaching from worthy persons and,
In order to realize accordingly (life's meaning), stay
    with the teaching,
Remain with those who live by it and, stopping what is
    objectionable,
Realize the meaning of (the Buddha's) message and
    abide by it.

Do not wait any longer, but cross over the ocean of
    fictitious being
And quickly travel to the island of peace, where you
    will have passed beyond suffering.

There is none more stupid than the one
Who, having become a human being, does not practice
    what is wholesome;
Like a person who returns empty-handed from the
    island of jewels,
He merely wastes his unique occasion and right
    juncture.
Therefore, always engage in the quest for life's meaning
    which is (inner) peace.

The quest for life's meaning depends on the mind, and
    the mind
On a unique occasion and the right juncture, and both
    occur in functional dependence.
When at this time the many causes and conditions have
    combined,
The most important thing to do is to cultivate the mind.

C2   When, in the endless cycle of existences frightened by
          death,
      Poverty and frustration pour down like rain,
          (know that)
      They come from making light of a unique occasion and
          the right juncture.
      Therefore, since higher forms of life and ultimate
          deliverance
      Come from thinking about the difficulty of finding the
          unique occasion and right juncture,
      Set your heart on them by not slackening in your efforts
          day and night.

C3   Since it is meaningful to see the leader (of mankind),
      And since it is meaningful to study and to realize,
          and since
      A meaningful life here and all its subsequent results
      Stem from this existence being a unique occasion and
          the right juncture,
      Joyfully contemplate this over and over again.

C4   Since even the arrival at the citadel of the nectar of
          deathlessness
      By the Lord surrounded by his sons, the Śrāvakas and
          Pratyekabuddhas—
      The most exalted being in this world with its gods—
      Has been due to the most precious existence as a
          human body,
      Unique occasion and right juncture are renowned as an
          existence superior to that of a god.
      Therefore set your heart on winning this human
          existence.

C5   The place of the pristine cognitions, which see truth
          with no notions (distorting it),

Is easy to reach when from among gods and men you
    have become a human being.
Even the profound reality of the Vajrayāna path,
The ultimate in having a human existence, is easily
    realized.
Therefore the basis of life's meaning in both the
    Mahāyāna and the Hīnayāna
Is said to be the most sublime human existence as
    unique occasion and right juncture.

In the same way as a destitute person having found a   C6
    precious jewel
Is afraid and apprehensive that it is but a dream,
You should joyfully and longingly think about this
    unique occasion and right juncture,
Whereby true prosperity and bliss here and hereafter
    are attained.

When by the nectar of hearing this good news of   D
    happiness
The infatuation with the futility (of concern for this life
    only) has been stilled,
All beings may wish to go into the solitude of forests.
May Mind wearied and weakened by the wilderness of
    the emotions today find comfort and ease.

CHAPTER TWO

Impermanence and Death

*T*he preciousness of a human existence as a unique occasion and the right juncture for the quest for the meaning which life may have for man, is, strange to say, underlined by the fact that at every moment it is overshadowed by death. We may try to postpone it and we may even succeed in so doing for a time, but in the end we can do nothing about it. It is because of its inexorable presence that, as a rule, we try to deal with it in terms of observed phenomena such as stoppage of the heartbeat, loss of consciousness, lowering of the rate of respiration, and a host of similar phenomena along with the generalizations based on them. This, however, is merely an observation from the outside and has little significance for understanding the harsh fact of death being ever present. It merely induces me to dismiss it callously as something universal. Still, death concerns me as an individual.

It would be quite wrong to try to evade and to suppress the thought of death, and it would be quite morbid to brood over this inescapable fact. Death is not the end of Being; it may be the end of some sort of being. Being remains un-affected by death; only that which is fictitious, sham, is continuously dying. Hence the thought of death is rather a powerful stimulus that brings me back to myself as the unique occasion for the search for the meaning of life, and it makes me recognize the importance of this very moment, as it highlights the real possibilities that are still before me. It is in the light of death that I am prompted to act in such a way that, should death strike, my life may have had some total significance. The thought of death prevents me from losing myself in the fictions with which I tend to surround myself in order to escape from Being, so much more so as it reveals the uncanny instability, if not the absurdity, of what we call the world.

A   Even if this unique occasion so difficult to
     find has been won,
     It will not last a moment but break any time.
And if you scrutinize it, it turns out to have nothing
     to it.
And since you cannot trust what is like a bubble,
You should all day and night keep in mind the certainty
     of death.

B1   Although this body that is the foundation of all
          frustrations and unhappiness,
     The great birthplace of the emotions,
     May be decked with clothes, jewelry and
          flower-garlands,
     Or be pleased and gratified with delicious food and
          drink,
     Finally you have to part with it because it is transitory
          and fragile.
     Dismiss the thoughts that prize what is food for foxes,
          vultures, and jackals;
     Hold the body to last forever and to be impeccable.
     From now on engage in the quest for the real meaning
          in life.

B2   Brahma, Śiva, Sūrya and the powerful overlords
     Being the mainspring of all the wealth in the three
          regions,[1]
     Though they may shine in the splendor of fame and
          merits,
     Have no chance of escaping from the domain of the
          Lord of Death,
     Even if you may last through meditation for an aeon,

Once your karma has been exhausted you are back in
    the realm of death.
Gods, demigods, saints and sorcerers,
Rulers and commoners, however many there may be,
Are caught in the endless rounds of birth terrified
    by death.

In the drifting rain-clouds of life's impermanence   B3
Dances the Lord of Death with flashes of lightning.
Day and night the rain of the changing seasons
Drenches all the sproutings in the three worlds.

When the impermanent world with its beings, in the   B4
    cycle of origination and destruction of the world
    spheres,
Is consumed by fire seven times, drowned by water
    once and scattered by wind,
Even Mount Meru with its four walls consisting of four
    precious jewels and metals,[2] and
Surrounded by the outer wall of the world, the world
    oceans, the continents and mountain ranges, is
    impermanent.
Think of the fact that everything will turn into (the
    emptiness of) space,
And from your heart engage in the quest for the
    meaning of life.

Even the leaders of the world, the Pratyekabuddhas, the   B5
    crowds of disciples,
Our Lord Buddha surrounded by his disciples,
Like the moon in the clear sky,
Surrounded by galaxies of stars and planets,
Although so radiant, clear, and brilliant,[3]
Demonstrated impermanence by passing into Nirvāṇa.
Look how even the precious teaching as boundless as
    the sun
Has declined from generation to generation.

Why should our own bodily existence, like a plantain[4]
   with no substance to it,
And like a phantom house, not break up?

B6   Therefore while it is certain that we have to die, but
   Uncertain when and where and whereby we are going
      to die,
   And since our life-span is not going to increase, but
      steadily decreases,
   And the conditions for death are many and the chances
      of living very slim,
   Without wasting your time, but rather confining your
      mind to the basic problem,
   It stands to reason that you should strive for a
      meaningful life from today onwards.

B7   Although sentient beings, (which are like) a bower
      formed by the elemental forces,[5]
   May be embellished by moving thoughts, its occupants,
   (This combination) has come into existence under
      certain conditions and will break up because of its
      compositeness.
   Quickly engage in the quest for the real meaning of life
   Since (everything) is impermanent like a city that has
      grown old.

B8   Since we shall not last long but certainly are to die,
   When suddenly we are smitten by the fierce conditions
      of death,
   Just like a flame in a strong gale
   Flickering and unstable every moment,
   Now, indeed, engage in the quest for the real meaning
      of life.

B9   Since there is no refuge other than a meaningful life,
   When we have to go alone after having left behind
   All our relatives, pleasures, friends,

Beauty, youth, power and status,
And are followed by our good and evil deeds until they
    have been exhausted,
Why should we not exert ourselves now?

Thus think of the existence of former and later worlds: B10
The countless people of former generations have
    passed away,
And even the majority of those living now
Will certainly not last for a hundred years,
And future generations will follow them in the
    same way.
Look at the old and the young, sharing the same fate.
Keeping the certainty of death in mind, (which means)
That I am certainly not different from them,
Engage in the quest for the meaning of life.

In the three regions of the world from the lowest hell to   B11
    its highest peak,
There is no escape from the domain of the Lord of
    Death,
Everything is impermanent, changing, and has nothing
    to it.
Nothing can be trusted and everything is (rolling on)
    like a wagon-wheel.
Particularly in the world of man there are many
    afflictions:
Being the place for many diseases, harmful influences
    by demons,
Weapons, fire, abysses, wild animals, poisons,
Kings, enemies, thieves and others,
Whatever valuables one has brought together in one's
    life are destroyed by them.

Even if there are no afflictions, a person's life is passing   B12
With every minute or second; day and night

It moves closer to the domain of the Lord of Death
Just like the water of a waterfall flowing into the ocean,
Or the sun setting behind the mountain.

B13   Since the valuable conditions for life, including food,
Are an occasion for creating suffering, like poison,
Why should these valuables not break up, there being
    so many contrary influences?
Therefore, as there is nothing that does not become a
    cause of death,
And as you do not know where and when and by what
    means you are going to die,
Renounce the things of the world which are fraught
    with futility
And from your heart realize (the meaning of)
    impermanence and death.

C1   If I make no effort to cross the river of frustration
While having the boat of unique occasion and right
    juncture
With its captain, the Guru's instructions,
There is nothing else for me but to be deceived, and
    to be carried away by this river.

C2   If you do not hold to this right juncture, good for
    yourself and for others,
While you have this vessel highly praised by the
    Teacher as
Eradicating all evil,
You will but chain yourself in the prison of Saṃsāra.

C3   Ah! Like a person chained to a rock, while
Thinking about the world in general, let your disgust
    with it grow.
Will I ever be useful to a person who,
If he is taught something does not understand it, and if
    something is explained to him, does not grasp it;

Who, even if he were to die tomorrow, will believe that
    life lasts and is permanent;
Who will not be weary of Saṃsāra and has not the
    slightest inclination to get out of it;
Who consciously is proud of it and knowingly makes
    errors;
Who is enamored with its bustle and drenched by the
    rain of emotions?

He who wants to cross the ocean of evil   D
And realize the wondrous qualities of the positive
Must now keep in mind the certainty of death,
And all day and night contemplate impermanence
    alone,
And ever and again develop a desire to get out of
    (Saṃsāra) and a feeling of disgust with it.

When thus with firm resolve he strives to realize what   D1
Is the meaning of prosperity and bliss here and
    hereafter, and
Dismisses this life from his mind, the mistaken belief in
    a self breaks down.
In brief, confine the mind to the basic nature of all that
    is, impermanence,
Which is the cause of true deliverance where all evil has
    been eradicated
And all positive qualities have been realized.

By the sound of this profound and melodious   E
    instruction in what is truly helpful,
Coming from the thunder of meaningfulness,
May Mind wearied and weakened by the excitement,
    the emotions, and the belief in permanence of
    all beings,
Today find comfort and ease.

CHAPTER THREE

Frustration and Suffering

Impermanence and death are inescapable facts and implacably confront us at all times. We may try to avoid facing up to them or we may struggle against them, but in the end we are shattered by them. Moreover, we are not so much the passive targets of shifting forces; rather we ourselves are a system of shifting, active, and tendential forces, comparable to a magnetic field with its vectors of magnetic flux density and magnetic field intensity. Hence we are not merely *in* a world, but *are* our world of ever changing situations that limit us and hem us in. The mood or feeling tone of this total pattern or field is one of frustration and suffering, which may assume many forms. Apart from coloring the total situation, frustration and suffering are ever present in the changes that are going on continuously, whether we observe them in the so-called external world or feel them to happen within ourselves. Most important, we bring ourselves into situations in the sense that, in attempting to solve or to escape from a situation, we bring about, and find ourselves in, another situation. Therefore, frustration and suffering are not so much passive feelings but active forces. They represent the tension that is inherent in every situation, as well as the instability and changeability that go with every situation because of the tension in it, and the active formulation of new situations which present further complicated tensions.

At every moment we *are* and thereby bring about a situation which wholly absorbs and necessarily hems us in. This limitation applies to us as living beings on every level or layer of our existence which we indicate by such terms as 'body', 'speech', and 'mind'. Each of these layers has its own domain or range over which it roams as a force. These ranges are termed 'realms of sensuous desires, of aesthetic forms, and of formlessness', while their limiting character is aptly indicated by the image of a stronghold, and the extent of the area controlled from a stronghold may be readily apparent or invisible. Thus we have

> body: realm of sensuous projects-at-hand as a readily apparent area controlled from a stronghold,
> speech: realm of aesthetic form as a semi-apparent area controlled from a stronghold,
> mind: realm of formlessness as an invisible (non-apparent) area controlled from a stronghold.

This triad of body, speech, and mind must be seen as a unity, not as disjunct, juxtaposed entities. In talking about the body we must be aware of it as an animate organism which, because of its being animated and alive, and constituting a live situation, embodies—and also is—the site of psychical life. The body therefore is both an 'expression' and 'what is expressed'. In other words, something 'invisible, not readily apparent', manifests (expresses) itself in (and as) the body and is manifested (expressed) by the body. My gestures, postures, movements embody my thoughts and feelings: the sparkle of my eyes *is* my joy, but the 'is' here is not that of identity, nor is there any inference from something presented and manifested (the sparkling of the eyes) to something not presented and non-manifest (the joy of the mind). Hence we also do not find a mind or 'the' mind anywhere as a demonstrable something because that which orders and defines a field or situation (the animate or live organism) cannot itself be an object within the same field, since it is that by virtue of which there is a field or situation. On the other hand, the live body is the center of its particular milieu, the perceived things of the world as 'projects-at-hand', dealt with by bodily activities and organized around the body as an orientational point with many sub-points, the individual senses. My eyes are the orientational or zero-point for the visual field or sphere, my ears that for the audible sphere, and so on.

But what about speech, which is said to range over the realm of aesthetic forms as a semi-apparent stronghold? Is speech only a system of sounds—or something else besides? If it were only the former it would have been wholly included in the audible, sensuous sphere, and it would never have been listed as something apart. Speech is halfway between the non-apparent and the readily apparent. It is a re-creation of an experience which the speaker wants to communicate and which through its formulation we recognize as our own. Speech is not so clear-cut as what we perceive with our eyes or take in by the other senses. That is why speech lends itself so freely to abuse as a means of blunting perceptivity: it may cease to be the expression of an experience and become the worthless currency of platitudes, the ceaseless chatter that communicates nothing. This is, unfortunately, though certainly, one aspect of speech, but it is not valid, as a rule, for poetry, in which language is, on the whole, not separable from experience. The experience that creates the language of poetry is aesthetic experience and can only be appreciated within its own terms of reference. Speech is a link between the visible and the invisible, but not, on any account, a mediator. It does not start from ideas, but from an inner hidden structure, which is the shaping of the experience the speaker happens to translate into perceptual images. If one

e to start from pre-existing ideas, one would be merely a
lgarizer, never an artist.

Body, speech, and mind with their realms of projects-
at-hand, aesthetic experience, and the indeterminate (form-
less) readiness to formulate the world—the world of men in
our case—are thus the indubitable 'boundary situations'.

These boundaries, however, are not fixed properties,
certain determinative traits (essences) of something immu-
table, but are tendential phases which involve awareness and
being. This opens up the possibility of looking at the 'world'
(including ourselves) both epistemologically and ontologi-
cally. In both cases we have to start with the initial, immediately apprehended fact of an all-embracing field, which,
more exactly, is a 'presence', an 'appearance' not *of* something but *as* something, and which is termed 'object-appearance' (*yul-snang*). Terms like 'appearance' and 'presence' sug-
gest something static, but in rDzogs-chen philosophy they
are always understood as dynamic processes of 'appearing' and 'presentation' and 'disclosure'. The field character
of the initial situation implies that the perception of the 'object-appearance' is not something going on outside the field
but is a part, and a distinct phase, of the initial situation.

Perception is both a process and a product: I become
aware of a colored patch, a shape, a sound, or I feel the breeze
of the wind (process), and my awareness and feeling become
vaguely yet formally identified with what I feel or am aware
of (product), but this does not mean that my eyes or ears turn
into colored patches or sounds, or my skin into air. All that is
involved is an aspect of an existential differentiation (process). This complex phase is termed *rnam-par shes-pa* which
for want of an exactly corresponding or suitable term we
shall render as 'perception'.[1] However, within the complexity of the initial field situation other factors can be distinguished. When in my everyday living in a concrete sensuous
perception of a state of affairs I visually perceive a green tree,
I usually experience an object as a more or less determined

type ('*di*) against a background or horizon of equally more or
less determinate, typical objects. The tree, in this example,
stands out from this unquestioned (but always questionable)
background for further activities in terms of my particular
project-at-hand prevailing at this particular time. This stand-
ing-out is inseparable from my interest at the moment
or from what is relevant to my project-at-hand.

This aspect within the complexity of the perceptual process and the 'object-appearance diversity' is termed *sems*,
which has been traditionally translated by 'mind', but which
is more exactly to be rendered as an 'intentiveness', delin-
eating the noetic-noematic structure of representational
thinking in its first phase of a 'bestowing attention to'
something, and nothing more. It certainly is not an explicit
predicative activity. As a matter of fact, *what* specific object I
am attending to in any particular perceptual situation depends upon my interests and upon what is relevant to my
particular project-at-hand. This elaboration and explication
phase is termed *yid* and, as a mental event (*sems-byung*), is
co-constituted simultaneously with *sems* in a temporal process. Thus *yid* indicates and points to my particular 'interest'
which involves cognitions and feelings (as well as other
facets of my becoming ever more involved in my projects-
at-hand), and these determine what object shall be in the
'foreground', how I am going to feel about it, and furthermore, how I am going to deal with it. Thus I may perceive
my wife against the familiar background of my home and
love her—my perception of and love for her are simultaneous, but the latter could not occur without the former. Or,
I may perceive an obnoxious person against the equally familiar public scene and hate him; or, I may perceive a
wall, a river, a highway, a tree, or any person against the
background of a familiar landscape and feel nothing for
or about them. The whole process referred to by the terms
sems and, more specifically, *yid*, is necessarily an 'ego-act'.
Such an 'act' does not support the assumption of an 'ego'

within or outside the process, and extends from its lowest level of 'bestowing attention' to its explicit predication involving a judgment of existence. Hence, *this* (outstanding, typically and habitually familiar 'object') *girl* (conceptual and emotional elaboration and explication involving possible action) *is* (object-appearance as a field including those elements that are irrelevant to my prevailing project-at-hand).

The unity of knowing and being, which reverberates in such a statement as 'I *am* aware', has, more often than not throughout the history of philosophy, given rise to wrong conclusions. The fact that awareness *is* does not imply that the being of awareness is something over and above or behind awareness. On the other hand, awareness, insofar as it is, implies an awareness of something, which means that awareness intends something as an object, that it has or posits something before it to which its intention applies. It is this intentionality that leads at once, and imperceptibly, into the domain of epistemology, the discipline that deals with the manner in which we know, and consequently the ever-present ontological problem is blurred over. Ontology deals with the question of Being, not of some sort of being which is the realm of speculative thought. But because of the epistemological concern, Being is confused and equated with the intentionality of knowing, which is summed up in the term 'mind' (*sems*) which we have seen to be a low-level 'ego-act' involving an 'intentiveness' and a 'bestowing attention' to something selected and outstanding within a field. Hence, the confusion of epistemology with ontology leads to the subjectivism of mentalistic philosophies, the so-called objective idealism being no less a form of subjective speculation. One other significant feature of this intentionality is that it is an indication as well as a movement, referred to as a loss of awareness (*ma-rig-pa*), a straying away from Being-Awareness into fictitious, 'intended' being. In this movement the ground is lost and we drift helplessly into a state of seeming being which in a sense is not, and yet has us captured.

It is by this intentionality, this having before itself something seemingly 'other', that the universe of objects (*yul*) is present and presented as a milieu (*gnas*) structured in terms of particular intentions or projects-at-hand. In this milieu of a surrounding world, by the same process of intentionality, my body (*lus*) is singled out as being the most significant and value-constituted pivot for all dealings with the world of objects (*don*). Thus my body becomes the site (*rten*) for the perception of the surrounding world and the means by which there are sensuously perceivable things (objects) in the world, and which is now experienced by the mind (*sems*) as its own animate organism (*my* body). Furthermore, all actions issue from this '*me*-here-and-now', and 'every thing' is oriented to this same '*me*-here-and-now' as '*mine*', and evaluated in the light of my projects-at-hand. The mind is thus the root (*rtsa-ba*) of all frustration and suffering, which far outweighs pleasure. Becoming more and more engrossed in our projects-at-hand we set up standards of good and evil. Whatever furthers my projects-at-hand is considered 'wholesome' and 'good', and whatever obstructs them is 'unwholesome' or 'evil'. The 'good' and 'wholesome', thus defined, belong to what may be called 'conventional ethics' which is the subject-matter of the following chapter.

All speculative philosophy comes to nought because of its inability to grasp the difference between the absoluteness of Being and the mere absolutization of something which is then contrasted with and placed over and above the rest of all that is, as well as because of its urge to explain that which is as issuing from or being dependent upon the alleged absolute. Being is not in need of explanation; at best it may be explicated. The absoluteness of Being means that it is not dependent upon anything, is not subject to change, and neither increases nor decreases. (Only that which is some thing or other may undergo changes, but even then its Being is not affected by them.) If there is change in any relevant sense, it can only involve a shift from seeming, postulated being to real Being—a change which, by virtue of its being, is identical with the absoluteness of Being. The change-over (*gnas-'gyur*)[2] is never a change *in* or *of* Being, but is a return to or, rather, the reinstatement of the awareness of the unchangeability of Being in and as its absoluteness. This understanding or awareness has nothing to do with the *form* or *content* of knowledge. Again, it is the ontological consideration that reveals the distinction that has to be realized between Awareness since time out of mind—pristine cognition (*ye-shes*) or Mind(-as-such, *sems-nyid*)—and mind (*sems*)[3] as a distinct form of 'existence', engrossed in its ego-related projects-at-hand. This being engrossed in seeming, fictitious being is a constant source of frustration and suffering which, of course, do not touch Being. Frustration and suffering are 'existential' in the sense that they are the form of 'existence' as the limited and limiting horizon that is 'mind' (*sems*).

Frustration and suffering have a spatio-temporal character which is different from what science understands by space and time. Geometrical space does not lie around a vital center and is not oriented with respect to vital directions. But the space of man's life-world is oriented and represents the limiting horizon of his understanding of his life. Similarly, man's lived (experienced) time is quite different from clock-time to which we nevertheless refer when we attempt to measure his lived time. We say 'I have been waiting for ages', while maybe only five minutes clock-time have passed. Lived-time is a function of a person's milieu, and it is in this sense that the duration of suffering in the various life-forms discussed in the text is to be understood. Clock-time is a convenient, consensual agreement within the milieu of being-human such that one can organize and coordinate various projects-at-hand. Thus, clock-time 'is' only as it is used. This is not to say that suffering 'really' only lasts for a short span of clock-time, for the text is not invoking a clock-time standard at all.

A1   Thus in its impermanence the whole of Saṃsāra
        extending over three realms[4]
         Is thoroughly frustrating because of its
        changeability.
    How terribly exhausted become all the beings in the six
        strongholds (of their life-forms)
    Through frustration, change, and the tendency to bring
        about further suffering.

A2   If you were in a blaze or attacked by wild animals or
        savages,
    Or had been put into prison by the king
    And were tormented by frustration upon frustration,
    Disgust with the fact that there is no chance to find
        deliverance now would grow.

A3   Although there may be the desire and intent to find
        bliss and to be free from frustration,
    Frustration rushes on you, being both cause and effect.
    You are deceived by your addiction to and desire for
        sensuous objects,
    As is the moth by the flame of a lamp,
    Or, likewise, deer, bees, fish, and buffaloes[5]
    By sound, fragrance, flavor, and touch.
    Look how people are deceived by the five sensuous
        objects,
    Never finding bliss but only misery.

A4   For these six kinds of beings—gods, demigods,
        denizens of hell, spirits, men, and beasts of
        burden—
    There is endless suffering.

It goes on and on like the buckets of a water-mill, one
    coming up after the other.

Each and every sentient being in the course of countless   A5
    generations
Has carried the burden of having been a friend, an
    enemy, or a neutral,
And the times he has provided happiness and sorrow,
    help or harm, cannot be counted.
There is no certainty as to when a father has been a
    mother and she a sister,
Or a sister a brother.
There is also no certainty as to when a friend will
    become an enemy.

If you have thought about previous and later actions in   A6
    this world,
Your disgust with them should be more than just
    ordinary disgust.
If you were to bring together and pile into one heap
All the bodies you have carried, be they of the size of
    an ant,
This heap would be higher than Mount Meru made up
    of four precious metals,
And all the tears you have shed would be more (than
    the water) in the four oceans,
And the amount of molten metal, foul blood, and
    excrements
You have consumed when your mind had become a
    denizen of hell or a spirit,
Would not be matched by the rivers flowing to the end
    of the world.
And there are countless other sufferings as wide as
    the sky.
All the atoms in the world will not make up a fraction
Of the number of times your head or limbs have been
    cut off because of your desires.

A7   Beasts of burden, demons, goblins, snakes and others
      Have experienced countless joys and sorrows belonging
            to the realm of living beings.
      Brahma, Indra, those in meditation[6] and those in the
            world of formlessness,
      The rulers of men enjoying their seven jewels,[7] and the
            earth,
      Although they had attained exquisite splendor,
      Had to suffer greatly after having fallen into evil forms
            of life.

A8   Those exalted beings that in this life had enjoyed
            infinite wealth,
      Once they had departed,
      Were tormented by poverty and even became servants.
      It is all like the wealth in a dream that is no more when
            you wake up.
      When you earnestly think about this frustration of
            changeability (in which) happiness and sorrow are
            impermanent,
      Let your disgust grow ever stronger.
      Therefore the beings in the three strongholds (of their
            limitation)
      Should strive for limpid clearness and consummate
            perspicacity
      Where there is no attachment to the pleasures of
            Saṃsāra.

BI1   Body, speech, and mind are the realm of sensuous
            desires, of aesthetic forms, and of formlessness;
      In the stronghold of appearance, semi-appearance,
            and non-appearance,
      They are afflicted by frustration, change, and the
            tendency to bring about further suffering.
      Through the spread of perceptual readiness,
            (conceptual and emotional) elaboration, and distinct
            judgments of perception,

The continuity of the deceptive round of objects
   engendering happiness and sorrow, remains
   unbroken.

The process of expansion from a stratum-bound   BI2
   perceptivity[8] through a (conceptual and emotional)
   elaboration, to the perception by means of the five
   senses (with the accompanying judgments of
   perception),
Is also the expansion of this process.
From this comes the frustration of fictitious being, that
   is both cause and effect.
The basic factor is the loss of awareness that takes on
   the deceptiveness of subject and object.
Through the belief in an 'I' and a 'mine',
Owing to the tendency (of hardening into) a universe of
   objects, a pivot (from which to deal with it), and a
   mind (dealing with it in terms of its
   projects-at-hand), Saṃsāra is established.

Even Mind-as-such, the unchanging Absolute, the   BII1
   founding stratum of meaning,
Through habituation to the postulates[9] that come with
   appropriating (perception) in the wake of the loss of
   awareness,
Takes on the deceptiveness of the seeming-presence of
   the impure relativity (of the phenomenal world).[10]
And the dualistic manifestation of a universe of objects
   and the pivot (from which to deal with it in terms
   of) the 'I' and the 'other' are taken as two (separate)
   entities.
As a result of this, unfathomable frustration sets in
   spontaneously.
Once you understand the meaning of the unchanging
   Absolute, Mind-as-such,
You travel the path of the incontrovertible Absolute[11]

And easily reach the realm of the pure relativity (of the
　　visionary world)
And are relieved of the weariness and exhaustion
　　(which belong to) the stronghold of fictitious being.

BII2　Ah, the frustration that comes with the fatigue of
　　traveling the road of fictitious being,
　　The endless realms of Saṃsāra so difficult to look
　　through,
　　Is such that there is no happiness whatsoever, wherever
　　you are born,
　　And the effect brought about by unwholesome (actions)
　　is unbearable.
　　What the six kinds of beings individually experience,
　　Like a dream, by misunderstanding the
　　self-manifestation (of Reality)
　　Is immeasurable suffering because what is not, is
　　mistaken for a presence.
　　Listen to a short summary of the tradition.

BIII1a1　On top of glowing iron filings there is the 'Hell of
　　Revival'.
　　When those there meet, they kill each other with
　　weapons.
　　By the sound 'come to life again', (they are revived) and
　　as before they suffer.
　　They cannot but undergo this suffering until their
　　karma is exhausted.
　　Fifty years of a man's life
　　Are but one day in the life of the Four Great World
　　Kings.
　　Thirty such days form one month and twelve months
　　a year.
　　Since five hundred such years are one day for those (in
　　this hell)
　　They must suffer for five hundred years of their own.

This detailed calculation, according to the Sūtras,
Is in human time one hundred and sixty-two thousand
   times ten million years.

In the 'Black Thread Hell' they suffer very much   BIII1a2
As a result of being sawn up and stitched together and
   then sawn up again.
A thousand years of what in human terms is one
   hundred years, and thirty-three days being one day,
Is for them one day.
A thousand years for them is according to the Teacher's
   words
Twelve times one hundred thousand ten million
   years and
Ninety-six thousand times ten million years.

In the 'Hell of Crushing Pain' they are crushed to   BIII1a3
   powder in between
Mountains that are like a horse and a yak, a tiger and
   a lion,
And when these mountains draw apart they come to life
   as before.
In iron mortars they are ground to powder by pestles
And in this process of grinding, streams of blood flow
   down.
Two hundred years are one day of the Aviha gods, and
Two thousand years of the Yāma gods are one day in
   the 'Hell of Crushing Pain',
Where they suffer for two thousand years.
In human time this is ten million times ten million years
   and three hundred and ninety-eight thousand times
   ten million years.

In the 'Hell of Howling Noises', they are burnt by a   BIII1a4
   blazing fire and utter terrifying cries.

They suffer by being boiled in iron cauldrons.
Four hundred human years are one day of the
    Tuṣita gods.
Four thousand such years are one day in the 'Hell of
    Howling Noises'.
There they suffer for five thousand years.
In human years this is eight million times ten million
    years
And ten million times ten million years
And nine hundred and forty-four thousand times ten
    million years.

BIII1a5   In the 'Hell of Loud Howling' in a flaming iron house
They are burnt in a blazing fire and cut to pieces by
    Yama.[12]
Eight hundred human years are one day of the
    Nirmāṇarati gods,
Eight thousand years among them are one day in the
    'Hell of Loud Howling'.
The suffering there for eight thousand years
Is in human time six hundred and sixty times ten
    million years
And three million times ten million years
And five hundred and fifty-two thousand times ten
    million years.

BIII1a6   In the 'Hell of Heat' the skulls of those who have
    entered an iron house
Are cleft open with a short spear and hammered with a
    cudgel.
Blazing flames burn the within and the without.
One thousand six hundred human years are one day of
    the Paranirmitavaśavartin gods.
Sixteen thousand years among them is one day in the
    'Hell of Heat'.

Sixteen thousand such years
Is in human time five hundred ten million times ten
    million years
And three hundred million times ten million years
And eight million times ten million years
And four hundred thousand times ten million years and
    sixteen thousand times ten million years.

In the 'Hell of Intense Heat' they are pierced through   BIII1a7
    with three-spoked weapons
And burnt by a blazing fire in between rows of iron
    houses.
The head and the two shoulders are torn open and tied
    with bandages,
And they suffer by being thrown into cauldrons of
    molten copper.
Their life there is half an antaḥkalpa.[13]
It cannot be counted in terms of human years:
The period of the world originating, staying, decaying,
    and being annihilated are four 'small kalpas' or one
    antaḥkalpa.
Eighty kalpas form one 'great kalpa'.

In the 'Hell of Uninterrupted Pain' in the blazing fire of   BIII1a8
    iron houses,
Apart from the howling and wailing of those in there,
You cannot see the fire and the beings separately.
Just as a burning flame clings to its center,
A mere spark of life remains in the center of the fire.
For the time of one antaḥkalpa they have to suffer,
Since there is no other or greater suffering,
This hell is called the one of 'Uninterrupted Pain'.

All these hells that have been mentioned   BIII1a9
Increase in heat seven times one after the other,
And the suffering is more the lower they lie.
Until one's karma is exhausted, one has to suffer.

BIII1a10i
The 'Ephemeral Hells' are so called because
Those there are tormented by respective frustration
When for a while, or in crowds, or singly they live
In mountains, under trees, in the sky, or
In rocks or in fire or in water, as the case may be.

BIII1a10ii
There are some who hold the mistaken belief that the
    name 'ephemeral' is due
To the fact that life there is short or that only a few go
    there.
But it has been said that the life of scorpions among the
    rocks is quite long and
That five hundred Śrāvakas having gathered at
    dinnertime
Were fighting each other with weapons.

BIII1a11i
The 'Neighboring Hells' are situated at the four cardinal
    points of the 'Hell of Uninterrupted Pain'.
They are the 'fire pit of live coals', 'the dirty pond of
    putrefactions',
'The steppe of weapons', and 'the river of ashes'—in all
    sixteen such hells.

BIII1a11iia
The moment they have gone where they have seen
    shady places with running water,
When they run out of the 'Hell of Uninterrupted Pain'
    in the belief that its ten million gates have opened,
They sink into a swamp of burning fire up to their
    knees.
And when they climb out, all their flesh has been burnt
    away and only their bones as white as a lotus,
    are left.
Having come to life again they suffer terribly.

BIII1a11iib
The moment they enter the cool ponds they have seen,
They submerge in this swamp of decomposing corpses
    and evil-smelling rotting matter.

They are attacked by worms having mouths of iron,
  copper, and gold.

Or the moment they come to pleasant openings they   BIII1a11i
  have seen,
They suffer by being cut to pieces with flashing daggers.

Having gone to a grove under pleasant leaves,   BIII1a11i
They are crushed by being assailed by a storm of their
  karma in the forest of swords.

Having passed on, from the peak of a lovely mountain,   BIII1a11i
They see their former homeland and, going in that
  direction, as if called,
Their flesh and blood is scraped away with sharp-edged
  spoons.
When they climb up, vultures crack their skulls;
When, intending to escape from this mountain, as if
  called away,
They descend, they are scraped with spoons in the
  other direction.
Where the mountain joins the steppe they suffer
  terribly
By being embraced by men and women who have
  flaming, sharp teeth,
And are eaten by many dogs and jackals.

Or, having seen rivers with cool water   BIII1a11i
They joyfully go there, and the moment they have
  stepped into them,
They sink into hot ashes up to their waist, and their
  flesh and bones are burnt.
They see themselves being prevented from stepping out
  by the helpers of Yama on both banks.
There they suffer for many thousands of years.

BIII1a12   If someone is able not to be frightened by these hells,
But knows what this endless suffering is,
He has the means to pass beyond it.

BIII1b1   There are eight afflictions by cold:
In very cold places where ice and snow is piled up,
Their bodies are ravished by storms of whistling snow
    in deep darkness.
In the Arbuda, Nirarbuda, Aṭaṭa, Mahava,
Huhuva, Utpala, Padma, and in the Mahāpadma,
They are eaten by creatures that have flaming sharp
    beaks,
And they suffer terribly and shiver until their karma
    has come to an end.

BIII1b2   Their span of life in Arbuda is as long as
It would take to empty a sesame store
In the country of Kosala, holding eighty bushels and
    being crammed full,
By taking out a single grain every hundred years.
In the other hells it is twenty times as long.

BIII1b3   If only sensible people were to develop the strength
    of effort
To overcome fully these worlds of hells that are (their
    own) mind!

BIII2a   The spirits that stay in the spirit world and roam over
    its reaches
Have big bodies, small hands and feet, and swollen
    bellies.
Their necks are thin and their mouths are tiny as the
    eye of a needle.
They are consumed by burning pangs of hunger and
    thirst.

Medicinal herbs, trees, and flowers wither when they
    look at them.
Outwardly they eat what is unpleasant, bad, or has
    been vomited.
Even if they see food and drink they seem to be
    prevented from taking it.
Those who are disturbed from within feel their bodies
    burning and
Smoky flames issuing from their mouths.
According to the general obscurations (that go with this
    state) they are tormented by poverty and terror, and
In places of dread they suffer the misery of loneliness.

The spirits that live in the air and space, the imps,   BIII2b
Goblins, gnomes, demons, kings and others,
Go everywhere unhindered by the magic of their
    actions
And set up various forms of harm.
They send diseases, steal a person's health and
    endanger his life.
As to their span of life, one month among men is one
    day for them.
Their five hundred years equal fifty thousand
    human years.
So they suffer in the world of Yama.

A man, true to his real nature, having seen   BIII2c
This disgusting state of affairs, should banish all
    thoughts
That delight in this fictitious being in order to realize
    deliverance.
Then he certainly will find peace, the real meaning
    of life.

In the animal kingdom those that live in the depths of   BIII3a
    the four oceans

Suffer immeasurable misery in the process of devouring
    one another.
Even hidden in the seas in the darkness of the
    continents
They are afraid of suffering from heat or cold, hunger
    or thirst, and being eaten.
Those scattered over the human world, birds and deer
    and others,
Are endangered, primarily, by hunters, and by each
    other.
Horses, buffaloes, yaks, sheep, donkeys and others
Suffer immensely by carrying loads and being beaten,
And by dying for the sake of their meat, skin, and
    bones.
Not realizing the natural misery of their state,
The snakes suffer the pleasures and pains of the
    midday and the midnight,
The pleasures and pain of early morning and late
    afternoon.
In some places sandstorms rage,
In others they are alone, friendless, destitute.
They encounter many kinds of suffering,
Mostly through fear of stupid people and birds of prey.
Their life is not certain, sometimes only a day;
Takṣaka ('Jog-pa)[14] and others are said to live a kalpa.

BIII3b   Those who, having thought about them, want
        deliverance
    From the world of animals, in order to realize
        prosperity and bliss,
    Should set out on the highway to superior forms of life
        and to the ultimate good,
    And day and night strenuously apply themselves to
        what is wholesome.

BIII4a   Also among men there is no chance for happiness:

Troubles, sorrow, wars and so on
Are his basic frustration, one coming on top of the
    other.
There are the changes that come over him by having
    eaten food and other things mixed with poison,
And there are the further frustrations that come with
    diseases
When food, clothing, and his way of life have
    deteriorated.
Frustration is immeasurable because of its eight
    varieties:
In addition to three kinds of frustration,
There is birth, old age, disease, and death, meeting with
    unfavorable persons, and
Separation from beloved ones, not getting what you
    want, and having to put up with what you have.

The cognitive capacity (in its state of) loss of awareness   BIII4b
    as motility and intentionality[15] concentrates in the
    creative fluids,
And within seven weeks the body is formed passing
    through the stages
Of an oval, oblong, lumpish, hardy, roundish, fish-like
    and tortoise-like form.
It suffers tremendously even when the mother feels
    only a little
Fatigue and weariness, hunger and thirst, heat and cold,
And it must endure unbearable suffering of being
    restricted to stay
In darkness, in narrowness and unpleasant
    horribleness.
Within the span of the seventh and twenty-sixth week
Its sense organs, limbs, hair and so on are established,
And until the thirty-sixth week
It grows in vigor and begins to move.
Thereafter when it is about to be pressed out through
    the bone-structure (of the mother's pelvis),

Its karmic motility turns it head down and lets it
    be born.
It is as if all the misery of approaching death had come
    to destroy it.
When it is touched after having been born it feels as if
    it were flayed,
And when bathed it feels as if its down were shaved.

BIII4c   The misery of having grown old is hard to bear.
Since youth has gone, nothing pleases anymore.
Unable to raise any part of the body you lean on a stick,
And since the body's warmth is failing, digesting food
    becomes difficult.
And since your strength is ebbing it becomes difficult to
    walk or sit or move or hurry.
You become a walking skeleton unable to reach the
    place you want to go.
Since the senses are failing the eyes become dim and no
    longer see.
You no longer hear, nor smell nor taste nor feel.
Memory becomes confused and is submerged in dark
    sleep.
Since the enjoyment of things has weakened there is
    little interest.
Even delicious food and drink seem to be the opposite.
As life declines you grow afraid of death and your
    thoughts become upset.
Like a child, you cannot bear anything anymore since
    patience has grown thin.
Quickly you pass away, like a lamp with no more oil.

BIII4d   The misery of being ill is very difficult to bear.
The body's constitution changes and the mind is
    unhappy.
Enjoyment of things becomes unpleasant,
And the worry and fear of losing your life grow.
You wail and whimper about this unbearable suffering.

The misery of dying is even greater: BIII4e
Food, clothes, talk, and sleep are for the last time.
You leave behind your life and body, your attendants,
     relatives and wealth,
And you are afraid to go alone, not being able to
     remain.

The misery of meeting undesirable persons   BIII4f
Carries the danger and fear of being painfully harmed
     and injured.

To be separated from your beloved and from your   BIII4g
     pleasant country
Is ground for lamenting and unhappiness.
Remembering their qualities you are tormented by
     longing.

The misery of being deprived of what you have and   BIII4h
     want,
And of not achieving your aim, causes your mind to be
     in agony.
Exhausted by poverty you are like the hungry and
     thirsty spirits.

The five psychosomatic constituents we have,   BIII4i
Form, feeling, conception, motivation and perception,
Are said to be, because of their fragility,
The place, foundation, vessel, and origin of all
     frustrations.

Thus in this wide human world   BIII4j
There is no happiness because frustration rules as cause
     and effect.
In order to be delivered from it, think about that which
     is positive,
And you have the means to find deliverance from
     Saṃsāra.

BIII5a   Also among the demigods there is no chance for
            happiness.
            There is hatred in senseless quarrels, strifes and wars,
            And envy which is unable to endure the splendor of
            the gods.
            There cannot but be hundreds of frustrations on their
            side of their army.

BIII5b   Therefore those who are about to go to happiness and
            peace
            Should quickly practice that which leads to deliverance.

BIII6a   Among the gods of the world of desire, frustration is
            immeasurable.
            Carelessness, intoxication by desire, passing and falling
            from their state in death, (marked by)
            The fading of flowers, discontent with their thrones,
            Being forsaken by their friends and becoming fearful of
            their next status—
            These intolerable feelings appear within seven days
            among the gods.

BIII6b   The gods of the meditational realms such as Brahma
            and the others
            Fall down into lower realms of fictitious being when
            their karma is exhausted.
            Seeing the misery involved in this change they suffer.
            Having glimpsed the calm of the formless world where
            karma is suspended
            They suffer by their intention about a future fictitious
            world.
            Since you cannot rely on these higher forms of life,
            even if you have reached them,
            Fortunate people should realize deliverance.

BIII6c   All those who are attached to the pleasures of Saṃsāra
            Are afflicted by being consumed in its fire-pit.

The teacher of men and gods has said that
Deliverance depends on ourselves and so does the
    means to it.
There is no chance that others will deliver us
    incidentally,
Just as nobody can stop the dream of a person asleep.
If this were possible, Saṃsāra would already have been
    emptied
By the rays of compassion radiating from the Buddha
    and his sons.
Therefore, you yourself must put on the armor of effort.
The time to exert yourself and to set out on the road to
    deliverance has come.

Think of it: people like myself who have not done
    anything about remedying this state of affairs,
As was done by the countless Buddhas of the past,
Will have to drift about in the solitude of fictitious
    being, evil in itself;
And if, as in the past, we do not exert ourselves,
We will suffer again and again in the six forms of life.

If you put up with the misery of Saṃsāra as vast as
    the sky
And as unbearable as fire and as varied as the objects of
    the world,
You stay in low places that are no place for you.
Where is then a possibility of receiving (the Buddha's)
    compassion
When you have no self-respect and no decorum?
The charismatic action of Him who is well-versed in
    appropriate means
Is said to depend on the karmic conditions of those to
    be affected by them.
Therefore, recognize your own shortcomings.
Set out on the path to peace

So that I and all the others may be delivered from
    worldliness
By being alert to and mindful of the misery of Saṃsāra.

BIII6d4   If you cannot bear the little suffering you experience
    now,
How will you bear the whole intolerable misery of
    fictitious being?
If I am not moved a little, having been told all this,
My heart must be of solid iron
Or like stone, and obviously must have no feeling.

C   Who would add to fictitious being when he knows
    the mind
To be the source of the many forms
Of the emotions, the proximate emotions and the
    overall emotionality
That is the unbearable misery of Saṃsāra?
Therefore, quickly conquer this fictitious being.

D   Thus through this feast of life's meaning, the source of
    bliss,
May all the living beings in the three strongholds
Live longer in happiness and joy, and may Mind,
Wearied and weakened by various frustrations, today
    find comfort and ease.

CHAPTER FOUR

Ethics and Self-growth

*T*he status of the world in which we live depends as much upon how we see it as upon how we deal with it. Both our perception of and dealings with the world go on in terms of meanings which tie in with our interests and projects-at-hand. Whatever furthers these is automatically evaluated as 'good' and whatever hinders them as 'evil' and the resultant situation, the world in which we find ourselves by our own actions, is accordingly termed a 'happy' or an 'evil' form of life, each of which again constitutes a specific milieu for further dealings with this world in what generally turns out to be a vicious circle (Saṃsāra).

Man's being-in-the-world, which is more precisely his being-his-world, is a system in the specific sense of a system-from-within which is the integral unity of that about which a thinking person thinks. This system cannot be derived from pre-established axioms. Rather, as the inner demand to seek and to find himself, that is, his (if ever this possessive pronoun is applicable) Being, it is both man's motivating force and guide. As there is nothing predetermined or pre-established, the quest for Being can go astray and turn into a sort of flight from Being, into an unending search for solutions to problems which pose but new problems that are as disquieting and frustrating as the old ones.

The problem of man's being is peculiarly difficult because man is not just an object among other objects—just like anything else. Rather, in experiencing himself (as object) he is intended as being reflexively related to himself (as subject) in a double manner: sense-perceptively and in action. Not only do actions, in the broadest sense of the word, issue from him as a here-and-now, but all things perceived are orientated to this same here-and-now, which turns out to be a highly complex system. Every sense is an orientation point for specific performances and for specific objects; my eyes are the zero-point for the visual field, my ears that for the auditory field, and so on. But all of them are relative to a more fundamental ground which, in the narrower sense, is man's body, and this again is relative to man's concrete existence. This existence itself seems to be relativized as a ground with respect to another, even more fundamental, ground. This most fundamental ground is termed 'the stratum of all and everything' (*kun-gzhi*),[1] and what occurs on it are not properties of it as a 'thing', but *actional* properties, properties of the stratum's activity. These actional properties occur *if* circumstances warrant, *when* time permits, *there where* they are manifested, and *through* certain regularities which tend to grow and to lead to a progressive construction of a 'world' with an equally progressive separation of 'subject' from 'object'. The way in which these regularities are concretely lived is precisely their causal efficacy.

Thus, this 'stratum of all things' (*kun-gzhi*) acts as a force of unification by virtue of which data of the most diverse kind are held together and intended by its actional properties as pertaining to one identical state of affairs and intended back to one and the same ground. This is to say that the first actional property to go into action is a cognitive phase so intimately grounded in this 'stratum' that it derives its name from it: *kun-gzhi'i rnam-par shes-pa,* 'stratum-bound perceptivity'. This delineates a certain milieu for possible perceptions and possible ways of action before any stimulation whatsoever has occurred. Only on this basis do distinct perceptions and their evaluation in terms of specific projects-at-hand take place. To give an example, I see an expanse of water, hear it (lapping), taste it (to be sweet), smell it (to be fresh), touch it (to be cool), and judge it to be useful for serving my immediate interest in, say, quenching my thirst. The 'it' is not only intended in all cases as one and the same object, but is also intended back to one and the same ground, which is my body with its sensory activities. Since the body is itself a sensory activity, as a 'stratum' it is also referred to as *kun-gzhi,* which unifies the actional properties. As such it is termed *bag-chags sna-tshogs-kyi kun-gzhi,* 'the (unifying) stratum or force for a variety (of operations) due to ingrained tendencies' which are the cognitive processes with all their elaboration.[2]

Throughout, this 'stratum' remains in its state of identity with itself and is, in all the various perceptual adumbrations, co-intended as being identical with itself and indeterminate, and as the 'stratum' of the actional perceptual and apperceptional processes. So also it remains as it becomes involved in the various situational alterations that are being experienced. In its aspect of becoming involved, yet remaining identical with itself and indeterminate, it is termed *sbyor-ba don-gyi kun-gzhi,* 'the stratum (remaining self-identical) in concrete situations with which it becomes involved', each of us individually being the 'pivot' (*don*) of the involvement. These situations are primarily the heights and depths of our 'world' ranging from the lowest 'hells' to the loftiest imaginings of heavenly worlds and pleasures. Still, we have to return from them, and so all of these situations are in the end frustrating. The best they can do is to urge on us the necessity of searching for Being rather than for forms of being.

It is of utmost importance not only to bear in mind the distinction between Being and forms of being, but also to refrain from confusing the absoluteness of Being with an absolutized form of being. Absoluteness of Being is also absoluteness of awareness, which means that it is not dependent upon any possible content. Awareness, however, is not so much a static quality as an act of being cognizant. In this activity the possibility of its malfunctioning is ever present. It is therefore as beginningless as the proper functioning of awareness. The proper functioning is termed 'pure awareness' (*rig-pa*), and its malfunctioning, 'cognate loss of pure awareness' (*lhan-cig-skyes-pa'i ma-rig-pa*) which still is cognizant, but in a dim, obscure, and faintly luminous manner and, for this reason, tends to 'go astray' into what it thinks about or intends Being to be. In this process of malfunctioning, Being is not affected at all; it remains Being and is present as a challenge to do something about the malfunctioning. More often than not, however, nothing is done about this malfunctioning, and it continues 'going astray' into the ordinary perceptual processes and those 'ideas' about Being which lead to the 'stratum of all and everything' (*kun-gzhi*).

It follows that 'loss of awareness' (*ma-rig-pa*) and 'stratum of all and everything' (*kun-gzhi*) are identical, the former emphasizing the 'cognitive' aspect, the latter the 'existential' one. This 'stratum', inseparable from the malfunctioning of 'pure awareness', presents itself as the 'stratum of concrete situations that has been there since time without beginning' (*ye don-gyi kun-gzhi*).[3] But in responding to the challenge of Being, the involvement takes a different turn. Instead of gliding off into the habitual 'perceptions' fed by the residua and sediments of fictitious being, the process enters upon a 'path' that leads to the experience of Being and frees Being from fictions about it. This process takes place nowhere else than on the 'stratum of all and everything' which is, as it were, Being in disguise. Through this process the very ground is consumed as is, in the end, the process itself.

In the same way as a flame, depending on its wick, consumes itself, or as a fire, depending on the fire-wood, so the path of the two accumulations (of knowledge and merits), depending on the ground of all and everything (for its existence), effects the self-purification of the tendencies leading to Saṃsāra and removes the impurities of (man's) affinity with or constitution of Being. Since (this process) first brings to light the limpid clearness and consummate perspicacity that directly reveals Being as a presence, it is termed 'a pure condition'; later on (this process) consumes even that which aids the purification, because it is the positive and wholesome (belonging to) the postulates that are tagged on to (the process) by the intellect.[4]

The upshot of this matter is that, since Being is nowhere else than in the stratum of all and everything, although the latter is the malfunctioning of Being, the stratum of all and everything is also the stratum on which the malfunctioning takes place and results in fictitious being with all its frustrations, and also the stratum on which the 'repair work' takes place, but it is never the ground of Being. Being is not grounded in anything, although all that is, is grounded in Being.

In the specific case of man, the presence of Being within him as a challenge to find himself is termed his 'affinity with Being',[5] which is both absolute inasmuch as it is also the absoluteness of Being, and relative inasmuch as it is seen to grow and to unfold, relative to the waning of the strength of the fictions that dominate man's life. In its absoluteness it is an absolute, not an arbitrarily assigned, value and is likened to a precious jewel. Moreover since 'absoluteness' denies the possibility of being relative to something—if it were, it would no longer be absolute—it is also unchanging, like the sky which remains the sky whether or not clouds are drifting through it. Since Being is nowhere else than in what there is (in this case man, who is relative to other men but not to Being), it is like water that moistens and pervades everything that is put into it. Thus man is steeped in Being.[6]

There is also always a cognitive side to Being and this is

'sheer lucency', which is faintly present even in the murkiness of the mind with its fictions about Being. It is the presence of this lucency that is termed 'affinity with Being' as
long as it is shrouded in the mind's fictions and merely
remains a challenge. It is termed 'limpid clearness and consummate perspicacity' when the fictions have gone and the
absolute value of Being is present in all its richness. The
relationship between these two is not one of cause and effect,
the one setting up something new and different from it, but
one of low intensity and maximum or optimum intensity.
The reference to 'sheer lucency' clearly reflects the observable fact that a person can 'glow with pleasure' or 'shine with
joy'. Pleasure, joy and happiness are certainly more 'wholesome' and, hence, healthy, and health is basic, while illness is
a disturbance and a sign that 'something has gone wrong'.
But if health, pleasure, and Being were not basic, no attempts
would ever be made to get rid of disease, to avoid all that is
unpleasant, and 'to be'. In this sense Being is a challenge
eliciting a response:

> If this affinity with Being were not in those who are alive,
> there would never occur any disgust with suffering and frus-
> tration; there also would never arise the idea of doing away
> with Saṃsāra and attaining Nirvāṇa, and there could never in
> one's mind arise the desire for deliverance. Yet there is pity
> for the suffering of others, without this having to be pointed
> out by someone, and there is the struggle to get away from
> the suffering and frustration that is experienced. All this is the
> power of the wholesomeness of the absoluteness of Being
> since time without beginning.[7]

Needless to say, this challenge is not identical with meeting
the challenge.

The 'path', by which the 'traveling' of the path is meant,
leads man out of the confines of fictitious being to Being, and
so also frees him from the cause-effect relationship of his
actions performed in the dim light of the loss of awareness.

Specifically this means that actions, as usually understood in terms of ethical behavior, belong to the realm of fictitious being which is broadly divided into 'happy' and 'evil' forms of life. The latter are due to 'evil' actions which actually do, and are meant to, increase the general unsatisfactoriness and suffering of our existence. 'Good' actions are those which insure 'happy' forms of life and which make for better relationships among living beings. But, still, these are mostly of a conventionally accepted and socially acceptable nature. Certainly, killing, stealing, philandering, lying, slandering, talk for talk's sake, abusive language, covetousness, malice, and ideological fanaticism, do not make for happiness—but neither does refraining from them indicate growth or maturity. Whether 'good' or 'evil', these actions do not allow man to grow beyond his self-made 'hells' or his self-induced 'heavens'. Hence, even the positive, the good and wholesome actions are 'low-level' ones and only those actions that are sustained by the 'path' involving sustained intellectual effort, discrimination, and appreciation are truly wholesome and good.[8] The more I learn and know, the more appropriate my actions become. Ready-made answers (the conventional 'good' or 'evil') to questions that have never been asked, are worthless.

We act in the manner in which we see the world, but our seeing is also influenced by our actions. Yet we cannot help seeing and acting. How is it then possible to free ourselves from this vicious circle? It is possible to see in a disinterested way and thereby to avoid planting the seeds of frustration, which are the 'three poisons' of desire and attachment, aversion and hatred, and indifference and obtuseness (the prevailing mood of 'I couldn't care less'), and which cloud our vision and distinctly poison the atmosphere.

A   The Buddha has declared that pleasures and
sorrows, the heights and depths
of fictitious being,
Have come from previously accumulated karma.

BIa   The actions that initiate Saṃsāra are black and white;
And as wholesome and unwholesome they have ten
varieties each.

BIb1a   The foundation for the site of their activity is an
indeterminate stratum of all and everything,
Similar to a mirror. Since its surface, undisturbed by
any (conceptual) division
Allows a cognitive capacity, lucent, but as yet not
conceptually determined and divided as to content,
To rise, it is like the brightness of the mirror.
From this (capacity) there come the five sense
perceptions that apprehend their respective objects
as color-form and so on.
In themselves they are not (conceptually) determined
and (subject-object) divided, but are like the images
in a mirror.
Afterwards come the ego-centered cognitive processes
that widen the gap between the apprehendable
(objects) and the apprehending (subject).
In a series of successive moments there is apprehension
and non-apprehension,
Conceptualization and non-conceptualization,
emotionally toned cognition and mere cognition of
content.

BIb1b   Moreover, the tendencies that initiate the world of
sensuous desires,

By way of good and evil as the hardening of the
   (conceptual) division (suffused by) passion, depend
   on the stratum of all and everything.
A lucent presence, undivided as yet by concepts,
   initiates the world of pure aesthetic forms.
(The state of) being focussed (on itself), undivided by
   any concepts, depends on the tendencies towards
   the world of formlessness.
The two incidental obscurations[9] that are the nature of
   Saṃsāra
Are at all times close by.

When the cognitive capacity is without any concept,   BIb1c
   and in the presence of distraction
Does not apprehend as object that which is present, but
   remains focussed (on itself), this is the time of the
   'stratum of all and everything'.
When whatever is luminously present is not
   (subjectively) taken to be 'this is that', this is the
   unmoving, lucent 'stratum-bound perceptivity'.
When through the subject-object structure (of
   representational thought) with its negation and
   affirmation, as well as through the objects before the
   five senses,
The seven patterns (of the cognitive process) develop
   into coarse concepts about objects,
The term 'seven perception patterns'[10] is used.

When through habituation to them you drift into   BIb1d
   fictitious being comprising these three realms,[11]
Actions done by body, speech, and mind initiate
   frustration and suffering.

Moreover, in the world of sensuous desires, seven   BIb1e
   cognitive patterns are predominant;
In the world of pure aesthetic forms the 'stratum-bound
   perceptivity' is predominant;

And in the world of formlessness there is only the
　　'stratum of all and everything'.
(Wherever one set is dominant), the two others are
　　latent in attendance.
Know this to be the case on each level.

BIb1f　Thus, when in the world of sensuous desires you go to
　　　　rest at night,
The perceptions dealing with the five sense objects
　　gradually submerge in a plain 'ego-act'.
When this submerges in the 'stratum-bound
　　perceptivity', there is (for a moment the state of)
　　conceptlessness.
This very state which is (one in which mind is) focussed
　　upon itself and in which any presence before it is *dreamless sleep?*
　　not turned into any object,
Submerges in the continuum that is pure experience of
　　meaningfulness,[12] and its actuality is divested of all
　　propositions.
When there comes again the process of unfolding, from
　　the 'stratum-bound perceptivity'
There arises an 'ego-act' alone, which, as the
　　dream-mind,
Engages in negation and affirmation of its various
　　images and lets be present what is nothing.
When this process spreads further there comes the
　　awakening from sleep and the reinstatement of six
　　cognitive patterns which
Become involved in their respective objects and initiate
　　karmic consequences.
And at all times, day and night, there is thus this
　　self-manifestation (of psychic life).

BIb1g　The cognitive processes at the level of the realm of pure
　　　　aesthetic forms are the four meditation stages,
Which stay in the reach and range of the
　　'stratum-bound perceptivity',

And while occasionally subtle apprehensions of objects
    may occur,
Generally they are in abeyance because of the fact that
    a holistic primordial experience[13] has become
    habitual.

The cognitive processes at the level of the realm of   BIb1h
    formlessness are the reach and range of the 'stratum
    of all and everything'.
Since its four infinity feelings are close to the state of
    utter calmness in which (the mind) is focussed upon
    itself, and since
The noetic-noematic complex resting on the
    conglomerate of the quaternity of
Very subtle feeling, ideas, motivations, and perception,
    has become dormant,
You may not wake up for an aeon from this state of
    utter calmness in which (the mind) is focussed upon
    itself;
And there is no planting of the seeds of the wholesome
    which involves discriminating judgments.

Thus even the mind in the states of meditation and in   BIb1i
    the realm of formlessness
Is the result of a previous operation; when its power is
    exhausted, it parts from these states.
You have to find deliverance from it because it over and
    over again
Sets up deceptive cause-effect relationships in Saṃsāra,
    and
Simply because of its murkiness it is an indeterminate
    process.

However because the mind of the world of sensuous   BIb1ji
    desires is
What it accustoms itself to, it also provides the reason
    for deliverance from its heights and depths.

BIb1jii   During daytime usually the seven cognitive patterns are
            dominant
            And the other two are peripheral.
            Take visual perception of color-form by the eye:
            Its lucent, yet concept-free component is the
                'stratum-bound perceptivity',
            And the concept-free component is the 'stratum' itself.
            The same holds good for the other six patterns.

BIb1jiii   In sleep (the mind) is focussed upon itself, and when
                you wake up from a dream
            There comes the time when the 'stratum of all and
                everything', the 'stratum-bound perceptivity', the
                'plain ego-act' and
            The six cognitive patterns, in this order, exist as one or
                two, or one,
            And all together as one fact.

BIb2a   The root of karmic activity is the loss of pure
                awareness.
            It is made up of cupidity, aversion, delusion.
            That which is engendered by them are the black and
                white (deeds) initiating fictitious being.

BIb2b1   Because you may rise to the heights and fall into the
                depths of Saṃsāra, the unwholesome (actions)
            Appear in ten different forms.
            These unwholesome actions divide into
            Three by body, four by speech, and three by mind, in
                this order.

BIb2b2i   Killing is the premeditated taking of another's life,
            Related to it is endangering life by beating, cudgelling
                and so on.
            Theft is stealing another's property;
            Related to it is obtaining things by deceit.
            Adultery is to have intercourse with another's wife;

Related to it is seducing those who are taboo.

Telling lies is to utter words to change a person's   Blb2b2ii
    opinion;
Related to it is deceiving others by insinuation.
Slander is to speak words that will bring about a rift;
Related to it is speaking this way here and that way
    there.
Idle talk is propounding bad doctrines and mere
    verbiage;
Related to it are incoherent and indecent talks.
Abuse is to use harsh words and to chide others;
Related to it are unfriendly words which are used to
    humiliate someone.

Covetousness is being unable to bear someone's wealth   Blb2b2iii
    and to make it your own;
Related to it is the desire to have someone's qualities
    like learning and so on.
Malice is hatred that does harm and damage to others;
Related to it is anger that is averse to what is profitable.
Wrong views are eternalism *a parte ante* and eternalism
    a parte post[14] and the denial of cause and effect;
Related to these are such perversions as speculative
    imputations and detractions.

The consequences of indulging in the ten unwholesome   Blb2b3i
    actions
Are fourfold inasmuch as their performance involves
    content, consequences, intent, and execution:
(General) maturation, compatibility (with their cause),
    dominance, and over-all effectiveness.

These ten actions, if light, mature into a status of an   Blb2b3iia
    animal,
If medium, into that of spirits, and
If strong, into the suffering of hell.

BIb2b3iib1   Compatibility with the cause is said to be twofold:
To be born in that situation which you have brought
about, and the bringing about of this situation.

BIb2b3biib2   Even if you have reached heaven, your life there is short
and diseases are many.
The necessities of life are wanting and become your
enemies:
You get an ugly spouse, and people become your
enemies.
Abuses are many and you are cheated by others.
Your servants are rebellious and you have bad servants.
You have to hear unpleasant words and there are
altercations.
Your words are not heeded and you venture on
uncertain things.
You are incontinent and desires become excessive.
You do not look for what is profitable and you are
liable to be harmed by others.
You cherish wrong views and are full of deceit.
The ten unwholesome actions have, in this order, two
aspects
Which are well said to be the results compatible to the
cause, and which you have to experience.

BIb2b3iic   The dominant effect takes place in the outside world.
Here where you are at the mercy of other factors,
On account of murder committed, the environment
is drab;
Herbs, trees, leaves, fruits, flowers, food, drink, and
so on,
Have little nourishing value, are difficult to digest, and
endanger your life.
On account of theft crops do not ripen,
And you are born in a region that is awful because of its
coldness, its hailstorms and its famine.
On account of adultery you are born in places

That are pits of excrements and urine,
Places of dirty, evil-smelling filth,
Narrow, depressing, and unenjoyable.
On account of telling lies you are born in hostile and
    terrifying places
Where your wealth is insecure and you are swindled by
    others.
On account of slander you are born in places
That are difficult to traverse, are high and low,
Are eroded, have precipices, narrow passages and
    so on,
And when touched are quite unpleasant.
On account of abuse you are born in places with
    stumps of trees, large and small stones, and thorns,
Dust, sediment, coarse and bad fruits,
Saline places and so on.
On account of idle talk you are born in places where
    crops do not ripen,
Where the seasons are in disorder, and where you
    cannot live because there is no stability for long.
On account of covetousness you are born where grains
    are few and chaff aplenty,
And where pleasant seasons turn bad.
On account of malice you are born in regions that by
    nature provide much harm
Due to crops and fruits being spicy and bitter,
And to there being kings, robbers, thieves, savages,
    snakes and so on.
On account of wrong views you are born where there is
    no refuge and where there are no helpers,
No natural resources, and where
Herbs, trees, flowers, and fruits are few.

The over-all effect is that any unwholesome action   B1b2b3iid
    whatsoever done by you

Will create suffering by proliferation.

BIb2b3iii   In brief, the ten unwholesome actions by themselves
Are like poison, and he who engages in them
Had better try to shun them like an enemy,
Because whether they are heavy, medium, or light, they
    produce great suffering.

BIb3a   The ten wholesome actions that lead to higher
    existences
Are the wholesomeness of the intention to shun the ten
    unwholesome ones:
Not to kill, not to steal,
Not to commit adultery, not to tell lies, and not to
    slander,
Not to abuse and not to engage in idle talk, not to be
    covetous,
Not to bear malice and not to entertain wrong views.

BIb3b   Through such actions, even if their scale is but small or
    moderate, you become a man or a god in the world
    of sensuous desires;
If it is great, you reach the concentrations that belong to
    the worlds of meditation and formlessness,
And they make you retain the pleasures of the higher
    spheres.
There are four results, and by inverting the previous
    ones
You can know the result of the ten wholesome actions
    to be higher forms of existence.

BIb3c   Thus the ten wholesome actions by virtue of their
    meritoriousness
Lead to happy forms of life, while the ten unwholesome
    ones

Lead to evil forms of life. To accept and reject
     respectively the
Blackness and whiteness of cause and effect is the
     positive worldly way,
The road to the status of gods or men. Thus the Buddha
     has said.
Therefore, if in the hereafter you have established a
     happy form of life,
You have laid the foundation for deliverance.
Such fortunate people should attend to this.

The sublime wholesomeness of deliverance puts   BIIa
     Saṃsāra far away.
Moreover, the unfailing cause in what is conducive to
     deliverance,
Leading to the peace that is beyond black and white
     actions that
Initiate the heights and depths of fictitious being,
Is summed up by the five paths that (comprise)
The ten wholesome actions, the meditational and
     formless states of experience, the six transcending
     functions[15] and so on.
When in working for the benefit of beings, without
     staying in either your fictitious being or in passive
     quietude,
By means of the wholesomeness of the unity of
     appropriate action and appreciative discrimination,
Once you have understood that neither a self nor any
     other entity of the world has an ontological status,
You have reached the vast citadel of Buddhahood, and
A wholesome communion with Being[16] (lets) you pass
     beyond all the worlds.

Further, that which has an objective reference is the   BIIb
     accumulation of merits;

That which has no such reference is the accumulation
    of pristine cognitions, and through the unity of
    these accumulations

The two obscurations[17] are cleared away and the two
    founding strata of meaning[18] are brought to light.

Moreover, through the cultivation of concentrative and
    post-concentrative states which are tenuously held
    by ordinary people, but are stable with superior
    people,

In this order, deliverance will be obtained.

BIIc   The site for the wholesomeness of deliverance is your
    affinity with Being:

As the sheer lucency of Mind

It is (your) undefiled existentiality and naturally
    'present' affinity with Being;

Its presentational presence, the two founding strata of
    meaning described by nine analogies,

As compassionate spirituality has been there since all
    beginning,

And this, the Buddha has said, is the 'growing'
    affinity.[19]

While its root is the sheer lucency of pristine cognitions
    that come from pure awareness,

Its very facticity is wholesomeness because the three
    poisons are not present.

BIId   When by the arousal of these two affinities[20] two
    processes[21] are generated,

The manifest enactment of compassion is the
    accumulation of merits in the conventional sense,

And represents the pure Developing Stage comprising
    three empowerments[22] as by jar and so on.

The openness (of appreciativeness) is the accumulation
    of pristine cognitions in the true sense,

Representing the fourth empowerment, the Fulfillment
    Stage and the Mahāmudrā.
When you properly attend to these processes and let
    both Stages grow,
The emotions change over to pristine cognitions,
    wholesomeness increases even further,
The obscurations of your existentiality are cleared up,
And you see the sun of the stainless founding strata of
    meaning in their Being and their manifestation.

The ten wholesome actions, which are the best things in   BIIe1
    the world,
And the experience of the stages of meditation and the
    formless realms are accumulations that belong to
    the 'manifest'.
That which is beyond the world and inaccessible to
    propositions
Is the accumulation of the 'absolutely real' pristine
    cognitions.
By practicing them in the unity of concentrative and
    post-concentrative states,
Everything positive is realized.

Positive actions, regardless of whether they initiate   BIIe2
    fictitious being
Or passive quietude, are called karmic actions.
Since by these (specific positive engagements) you may
    pass beyond fictitious being, they are the
    deliverance from karmic actions.

The result of the ten wholesome actions by him who   BIIe3a
    has set out on the path, comprises
Maturation, compatibility with the cause, dominance,
    and over-all effectiveness.

According to their degree of low, medium, or great   BIIeb3bi
    intensity

You will, incidentally, become a god or a human being,
  and, ultimately, realize the highest good.

BIIe3bii   Compatibility with the cause means that you apply
  yourself naturally to what is wholesome,
And the actual experience is a long life, great wealth,
An agreeable consort, no enemies.
There are no abuses heaped on you, friends are helpful,
Your words are heeded, and all like to listen to you.
You are content, possess kindness, and entertain good
  views.

BIIe3biii   The dominant effect is that you are born in pleasant and
  rich countries,
That food and drink and medicinal herbs are easily
  digestible and nourishing,
That you are born in clean places with sweet-smelling
  herbs.
You are not cheated by others, you live without fear
  and there is no harm and danger to your life.
People are friendly and you are happy and intelligent.
The seasons are pleasant and the crops are plenty.
You live in level places with cool lakes and wells,
And you find that flowers and fruits are plentiful and
  increase in flavor.
Leaves, fruits, medicinal herbs have the most pleasant
  taste and flavor,
The natural resources are good and there are protectors.

BIIeb3iv   The over-all effect is that there is an increase in
  wholesomeness
And all positive thoughts are implemented easily.

BIIe3bv   Moreover, through generosity enjoyment is attained,
  and through discipline, happiness,

Through patience, beauty, and through diligence,
   splendor,
Through concentration, peace of mind, and through
   intelligence you reach freedom.

Through kindness you become loveable, through   BIIeb3bvi
   compassion you are a helper (to others),
Through joy you become distinguished, and through
   equanimity untroubled.
In brief, the result of a supreme accumulation of merits
   and pristine cognition
Is that, incidentally, you win higher states of being and,
   ultimately, the supreme good.
This is the good and positive road, the way of
   Mahāyāna.
It makes you realize the excellence of the Buddhas of
   the three times.

Thus the actions that initiate fictitious being as well as   BIIeb3bvii
   passive quietude
Depend on the mind, and the mind as such is sheer
   lucency,
Like the sky, no agent is observed and no propositions
   apply.
The meaning of the two realities lies in functional
   correlation.[23]

From the very beginning karma, though nothing in   BIIeb3bvii
   itself, is there manifesting itself
And is like an artist creating everything.
It accompanies you, like the shadow following your
   body, and
Does not change place but is there as the body's
   pleasure and pain.
Difficult to turn away, it is like a waterfall.

Making beings rise and fall, it is like a ruler over all that
is alive.
Very wide it is like the expanse of the sky.
Black and white, not changing (into the one or the
other), it is as distinct as a white or a blue lotus
flower.

BIIeb3bix   If you examine actions they may not have anything
to them,
But like a dream they bring about the variety of
happiness and sorrow.
Apart from being interpretations they have no qualities.
The profound functional correlation, infallible as cause
and effect,
Is not a duality, nor is it something existent or
non-existent.
Actions mature in the same way as they are performed.
This the Omniscient One has aptly termed
The vision of what there is and of how it is interrelated.

BIIf1   He who denies the cause-effect relationship of actions
Is an adherent of the view of eternalism *a parte post* and
goes from bad to worse.
These people who have started on a bad journey will
never find
Deliverance from evil situations, and will drive happy
existences farther and farther away.

BIIf2   Those who in their childishness consider cause and
effect,
Compassion and the accumulation of merits as
suggestive, will never awaken to Buddhahood,
And what kind of meditation is that of those great yogis
who think the real meaning is as insubstantial and
useless as thin air?

Holding a negativistic view lower than negativism,
They go from lower places to still lower ones.
How marvelous to claim a result but to deny its cause!

If (this good) is just empty space, what is the point of   BIIf3
   pondering over it,
And if it is not, you only go for exercises in futility.
If by pondering over absolute nothingness deliverance
   is found,
Then those who have a completely blank mind should
   become Buddhas.
And when they accept this as meditation, cause and
   effect is reintroduced.
Therefore, discard such bad ways.

The proper way is the interdependence of cause and   BIIf4
   effect.
The spontaneous unity of appropriate action and
   appreciative discrimination
Through the relationship that exists between cause and
   effect, apparent though nothing as such,
And through pursuing a path, apparent though nothing
   as such,
The goal is achieved, apparent though nothing as such.
Acting for the sentient beings, apparent though nothing
   in themselves
In a manner apparent though nothing as such,
Is the profound interrelationship of pure cause and
   effect.
Therefore the quintessence of the Sūtras and Tantras
   dealing with the real meaning
Is the quick realization of perfect Buddhahood
Through the unity of the two accumulations and the
   two stages of development and fulfillment.

Having thoroughly given up cause and effect with   C
   all their

Sidelines which initiate fictitious being,
Apply yourself earnestly to the cause and effect that
    ensures deliverance
And you will quickly realize the highest positive good,
    limpid clearness and consummate perspicacity.

D   Thus through this refreshing rain of life's meaning,
    bliss supreme,
May the two accumulations luxuriously grow in the
    soil, the mind of those who are alive,
And may Mind, wearied and weakened
In this fictitious being so full of karmic actions and
    emotions, today find comfort and ease.

CHAPTER FIVE

Teachers and Friends

It is not enough to be reminded of the preciousness of human existence, of its impermanence, of frustration and suffering, and of the significance our actions have in determining the life which we will have to live. Much more important is that we learn how to live a life that in retrospect may be deemed to have been worth living. There can, however, be no learning without there also being some teaching. Learning is not merely the memorizing of isolated facts but rather a perennial search for values relevant to the learner's existence. Similarly, teaching is not merely the presentation of bits and pieces of information and, when the person's concrete existence is at stake, the offering up of 'normative standards' to fixate on, but the explication of the human situation and of what this holds for him who is willing to learn. The common bond between teacher and disciple is the experience of an obligation which implies the recognition of a value relevant to the existence of both teacher and disciple. There are, as everybody knows, teachers and teachers and, if anything goes wrong in the precarious teacher-disciple relationship, it is customary—and often the impression is gained that there is a compulsive urge—to blame the teacher and to exonerate the student, contrary to all evidence. Yet it is equally true that there are students and students, and that some are willing to learn while others inertly exist without thought.

Although the relationship between a teacher who is able to teach because he has gone through the arduous process of learning, and a student who is willing to learn because he feels the need to be taught, is of paramount importance, this relationship does not occur in a vacuum. Rather it is a complex phenomenon having a private and a public sector. The public sector is represented by 'friends' who determine the milieu in which the learning process takes place and who aid this process by setting an example.

In the vast flux of human history there have always been personalities who have been able to arouse us to our Being, and in the end it is Being itself that becomes the real teacher so that, even at the danger of being accused of introducing a subjectivistic note, we can say that we learn by ourselves in encountering ourselves in and through another. In this sense, then, the 'friend' is Buddhahood (Being) manifest in the other, while, on the other hand, Buddhahood is nowhere else than in us and is the 'teacher' who guides us to our Being. This is the private sector, a response to Being, not an involvement in extraneous matters and the irrelevance of mass propaganda. The response itself involves labor and what is effected by it as a further means to growth. In a certain sense growth is a world-shattering experience, for the world is our horizon of meaning that may suddenly lose its comforting familiarity. In particular, it is our own ego that is being uprooted and as it had merely usurped a place that did not belong to it, it is made to pay the price for the mischief it has created. It is offered as ransom for man's Being.

*T*hus the proper path with its infallibility   A
    of the cause-effect relationship
    Starts from attaching yourself to worthy persons.

The realization of the three kinds of limpid clearness   B
    and consummate perspicacity (as represented)
By the Buddhas of the three times with their spiritual
    sons, the Śrāvakas and Pratyekabuddhas, comes
    through spiritual friends.
Even the higher life-forms in fictitious being, and
    whatever happiness there may be in them,
Come from attaching yourself to worthy people.
Therefore you should attach yourself to worthy
    persons.

By attaching yourself to worthy people you yourself   CI
    become worthy
As a creeper (assumes the fragrance of the) sandalwood
    tree, while
By attaching yourself to evil people you yourself
    become evil
As the kusa grass growing in a dirty swamp.
Therefore endeavor to attach yourself to worthy
    persons
And to reject evil friends.

What are the characteristics of worthy people?   CII1
They are like all others insofar as they are leaders
    of the world;
They are different from all others insofar as they go
    beyond the world;

And they are superior to all others through their
behavior in body, speech, and mind.

CIIa2　　Their bodily presence inspires calmness and their
behavior is pure and faultless.
They are wise in dispelling doubts and their words are
pleasant and clear.
Their mind is very calm and a veritable treasure of
omniscience.
Their qualities are immeasurable, they are learned and
compassionate,
Their profound intelligence and their spiritual horizon
is like the sky.
Their charismatic activity has no limits and its efficacy
is meaningful.
In their kindness they are never lazy but always
diligent
And they apply themselves to raising mankind.

CIIa3　　In particular the characteristics of the Mantra-guru are
as follows:
He has and keeps pure the empowerments, obligations,
and commitments.
He has reached the other shore of the ocean of
instructions concerning the meaning of the Tantras,
He has mastery over the charismatic activities that go
with the ritual and its effectiveness.
He has this warmth of feeling at its height as it comes
with the experience and the understanding through
vision, through attending to and cultivating the
vision, through its enactment, and through the
culmination (of all these three) in the fullness of
Being.
He is very kind and wise in appropriate actions and he
sets the aspirant on the path to maturation and
freedom.

He is a lingering cloud of continuous spiritual
    sustenance.
Attach yourself to such an illustrious *guru* who is both
    wise and accomplished.

If someone were to praise only partially such a person   CIIa4
    who is a helper of living beings
And whose qualities are so vast (he would have to say):
As he makes them cross safely over the ocean of
    fictitious being he is a steersman,
An incomparable leader of those who have started their
    journey.
He is the Wish-fulfilling Jewel as he removes poverty.
He is the water of nectar extinguishing the fire of karma
    and the emotions.
He is the excellent raincloud pouring down the cool
    rain of the meaningfulness of life.
He is the thunder that delights sentient beings.
He is the king of physicians curing the disease of the
    three poisons.[1]
He is the bright lamp dispelling the darkness of loss of
    pure awareness.
He is the wish-granting tree from which comes the
    happiness of all who are alive.
He is the auspicious jewel by which all desires are
    spontaneously fulfilled.
He is the countless rays of the sun of great kindness.
He is the moon with its white light of prosperity and
    happiness, removing afflictions.

Because of his vast spiritual horizon he resembles the   CIIa5
    spotless sky;
Because of the brilliance of his integration he resembles
    the spontaneous (luster) of the stars;
His sensitivity and kindness resemble the unfathomable
    depths of the ocean;

The billows of his compassion in their ceaseless
   movement resemble a river.
His unshakeability by distractions resembles the
   splendor of a snow-mountain.
His absolute steadiness resembles Mount Meru.
His not being defiled by living in the world of fictitious
   being resembles the lotus flower growing in mud.
His equanimity and kindness extending to all beings
   resemble a father and a mother.
His vast qualities resemble a jewel mine.
Since he is a leader of the world he resembles a
   powerful king.

CIIa6   Wherever such illustrious gurus, masters of life's
   meaning
Live, they are like the Buddhas.
To see, listen to, remember, touch them banishes
   Saṃsāra,
And their wave-like charismatic activities carrying a
   heavy load
Are like this great earth, the foundation for all who
   are alive.

CIIa7   This Guru-Buddha is the Fourth Jewel,
The lord of the maṇḍala, Heruka-śrī;
Since he acts on behalf of the beings in this evil age,
As far as they are concerned he is superior to all the
   Buddhas.
Bow to this Vajra-teacher, the root of all achievements
And let your actions by body, speech, and mind be
   honest and pure.

CIIa8   He ensures prosperity and bliss by blocking the way to
   evil forms of life
And setting us on the steps to happy forms of life, here
   and hereafter.

He shows the real meaning and he gives spiritual
    sustenance to the mind.
Since in this life here he sets us on the path to maturity
    and freedom,
Attach yourself to him at all times diligently
In firm and unchanging trust.

Just as a patient is in need of a physician,   CIIb1
People of a ruler, a lonely traveler of an escort,
A merchant of a guild-master, a boatman of a boat,
So in order to calm the emotions, to make evil
    harmless,
To overcome birth and death, to have the bitendential
    value of Being[2] spontaneously present, and
To cross the ocean of fictitious being, you must rely on
    a teacher.

Do so with four positive ideas in mind,   CIIb2
Since in so doing all other methods are outweighted:
The teacher is the physician, his instruction the
    medicine,
You yourself the patient,
Your effort the application of the medicine,
And peace and happiness, the result of having got rid of
    the illness.

By way of contrast, unworthy disciples are the   CIIc1a
    foundation of all evil:
Without faith, self-respect and decorum, with little
    compassion,
By background and by nature their behavior is
    ill-suited.
In their intentions and actions and emotions the five
    poisons are rampant,
They are confused about what is meaningful and what
    is not, what is good and evil.

They do not care for their obligations and commitments
    and do nothing against their shortcomings.
They are thoroughly infatuated, of little intelligence,
    but difficult to satisfy,
In them anger and angry words increase and multiply.
Such disciples attach themselves to a teacher with five
    wrong motives:
The teacher is the deer, the teaching the musk,
He himself the hunter, his efforts the arrow,
And the result he gets is to be sold somewhere else.
Being without principles, they will suffer here and in
    the hereafter.

CIIc1b   First, without proper examination, they rush into a
    teacher-disciple relationship:
In the novelty of this relationship there is fulsome
    praise, but afterwards comes calumny.
In other cases there is a mixture, and in private and in
    public through subtle meanness and cunning,
They disgrace those around the teacher.
The result is just plain hell.

CIIc2a   The worthy students, trustful and highly discerning,
Diligent, conscientious, circumspect and
    knowledgeable,
Not going beyond (the teacher's) word, observing their
    obligations and commitments,
Controlled in body, speech, and mind, compassionate
    and deeply concerned about others' well-being,
Accommodating, patient, generous, and visionary,
Steady and deeply devoted, will

CIIc2b   Always be mindful of the teacher's qualities.
They will not look for faults and, even if they see them,
    will consider them as (hidden) qualities.
By thinking from the bottom of their heart that these

faults are certainly their own (mistaken) views and
not existing in (the teacher),
They use admission (of their own shortcomings) and
self-restraint as counteragents (to their error).

They reject everything that may displease the teacher   CIIc2c
And they make every effort to please him.
They never go against the teacher's word
And treat those around the teacher, even if they are on
good terms with them, as the teacher.
They do not take the teacher's servants as their
disciples
But will rather ask them for explanations and
initiations.

In the presence of the teacher they restrain themselves   CIIc2d
in body, speech, and mind,
They sit with their legs tucked under and do not turn
their backs to him.
They show a smiling face and do not cast angry glances
nor frown upon him.

They will not speak rashly, neither will they tell lies nor   CIIc2e
slander,
Neither will they tell others' faults nor will they use
unpleasant harsh words,
Neither will they speak thoughtlessly nor at random.

They will not covet the teacher's utensils,   CIIc2f
And they will dismiss all kinds of harmful thoughts that
are like claws.
They will not judge as wrong and mistaken
The teacher's various actions and devices because that
which is openly done seems to belie the hidden
intention.
They renounce erroneous views that carry with them

the evil and defect of finding fault with everything,
    be it ever so small,
Thinking that this is inappropriate, but he is certainly
    going to do it.

CIIc2g   When they are cross with their teacher
They will certainly examine their own faults, admit
    them, and restrain themselves, and
Bowing their head they will sincerely offer their
    apologies.
Thereby they will please him and quickly achieve
    their aim.

CIIc2h   When they see their teacher, they will get up and greet
    him,
When he is about to sit down, they will offer him a
    comfortable seat and so on.
They will praise him with a pleasant voice and keep
    their hands folded.
When he walks about they will follow him in
    attendance and show him respect.

CIIc2i   Always mindful and conscientious and concerned,
Devotedly and meekly in awe they will stay with him.
When near the teacher, they will be bashful in body,
    speech, and mind like a young bride,
Not strutting about or being indolent,
Not taking sides, not flattering,
Not deceitful, not hypocritical,
Neither publicly nor privately showing affection or
    aversion to his near and distant relatives.

CIIc2j   If they are wealthy they will make gifts to the teacher, or
By body and speech will serve him, honor him, respect
    him; or
Dismissing their preoccupations with this life from

their minds they will please him by their individual
achievements.

If others speak evil of him, they will refute their   CIIc2k
   allegations.
If they are unable to do so, they will again and again
   think of his qualities,
Close their ears and in compassion give him help.
They will not use words that do not approve of him.

Thereby they gain prosperity in all generations;   CIIc2l
They will meet worthy persons and hear meaningful
   things,
They will be replete with wealth and qualities (that
   come)
With the paths and levels, with health and spiritual
   integration.
And they share this feat of peace and happiness with
   the living.

Thus by properly attaching yourself to worthy persons   DI
You should reject evil persons and friends of evil.
Moreover, a teacher who does not have the qualities
   mentioned above,
But has many bad faults, flouts his obligations and
   commitments,
Has little kindness, compassion and intelligence,
Is lazy, indolent, ignorant and very proud,
Full of violent hatred, in whom the five poisons of the
   emotions are very strong,
Who is concerned only with this life and has banished
   far away thoughts about the hereafter,
Teaches what seems to be the meaning of life, but
   upholds what is meaningless and hypocritical—
Such a teacher is like a dunghill
Driving away the bees of students, however many they
   may be.

Since he leads those who are trusting on the wrong road
    to evil forms of life,
Those who are eager for the path to deliverance should
    never attach themselves to him.

DII   Also friends of evil should be rejected.
To the extent that they befriend you, evil spreads,
The wholesome diminishes and the rain of emotions
    falls.
Happy forms of life are blocked and evil forms come
    out and dominate.
Friends of evil revile worthy people and hate bright
    qualities;
They praise the bad and rely on the dark.
They speak highly of those who share in their evil
    deeds.
Since they always lead a person the wrong way and into
    evil forms of life,
An intelligent person with eyes in his head should keep
    them far away.

DIII   By keeping evil friends and their accomplices away,
Happiness and good qualities grow here and hereafter.
The wholesome increases constantly and the profound
    path to deliverance is firmly trod.
You will never see evil persons,
But you will see the spiritual levels occupied by the
    Buddha's spiritual sons who are
Thinking of us and sustaining us spiritually.
Leading a life in happiness you will go to happy forms
    of life
And have such qualities which thoughts cannot
    encompass.

DIV   You should always attach yourself to worthy friends of
    the good;
Through them wholesome actions increase,

Bad actions and the emotions decrease and evil is
    stopped.
You reach the end of fictitious being and realize higher
    forms of life and ultimate good.
In this life you find happiness and in the hereafter its
    culmination,
And you become an effective leader of gods and men.

By attaching yourself to friends of the good and their   DV
    associates,
The wholesome increases and the result is realization of
    happiness.
In the world of fictitious being you are not afraid, and
    immeasurable prosperity and bliss is found,
And you have the immense wealth of fulfilling the
    bitendential value of Being among those who are
    alive.
The spiritual friend is the manifestation of the
    Victorious One, the leader (of mankind),
Who appears in this form during this degenerate age.
You should attach yourself to worthy persons
Until you have attained through them the very
    quintessence of limpid clearness and consummate
    perspicacity.

Thereby unrestricted pure visions will arise,   DVI
Kindness and compassion and cultivation of the mind
    reach their climax,
Feeling and understanding grow in intensity,
And the unlimited welfare of others in whichever way
    you may think of it, is appropriately assured.

The manner in which you have to think about and pray   EI
    to him is (as follows):
Constantly accumulating merits and knowledge and
    cleansing the obscurations,

You must during the day on the crown of your head, at
   night in your heart,
Mentally revere and petition
The basic Guru who is identical with the tutelary deity
   you have chosen,
And with the host of Ḍākas and Ḍākinīs,[3] adorned with
   the major and minor marks, as well as
The Gurus of your tradition, surrounded by the
   spiritual heroes and Ḍāka-Ḍākinīs.

EII   You should invoke his name in Sanskrit prefixing it
         with the syllable Oṃ
       And letting it end with Āḥ or Hūṃ, and then add the
         appropriate phrase for the work you want to
         perform.

EIII1   If you want diseases, affliction, evil, obscurations to
           subside,
         You must think that you attain the desired realization in
           which everything that is contrary to it has subsided,
         By emitting white rays into all directions.

EIII2   If you want wide-ranging action in regard to life,
           splendor, wealth,
         You must think of a yellow rain of desired good falling
           down.

EIII3   As to powers such as those which overpower and
           subdue,
         Everything is to be of red rays and in the shape of
           hooks.

EIII4   If you are to engage in eradicating hindrances and evil
           forces,
         You must think that everywhere weapons of blue-black
           rays emerge

And that everything is conquered by a firewheel with a
    thousand spikes.

You must imagine the three thousand worlds to shake,   EIII5
    quiver, tremble, agitate, by the sound of the mantra,
And you must go through the developing stages leading
    to the realization of the actions (you want to
    perform).

Afterwards you have to gather (all these images) and let   EIII6
    them easily and in a single moment
Fade into the sphere that is non-objectifiable and utterly
    open and transfer the good and wholesome (thus
    realized) to (a state of) limpid clearness and
    consummate perspicacity.

With each of these actions there are specific indications   EIII7
    (of success).
This, indeed, is the profound path, the ocean of bliss
    supreme.

In particular, when there are illness, evil influences,   EIV1
    obstacles, and foretokens of death,
You should think of your spiritual teacher, inseparable
    from Buddhahood, smiling and resplendent, as he is
    sitting, in front of you, in the sky,
On a lion throne symbolizing his intrepidities,
Surrounded by the teachers in your tradition, the
    Bodhisattvas and Ḍāka-Ḍākinīs, and
Below him the Lord of Compassion sensitive to the
    misfortunes of the six kinds of beings,
And of the sentient beings in Saṃsāra who through the
    three aspects of time have been your father and
    mother.

EIV2   From the symbol Hūṃ which is your own mind there
            emerges in the crown of your head (a white) Hero
        Holding a skull and a dagger, and
        Cutting up your body from the center of the eyebrows.
        The inside of the skull resting on a tripod
        Is filled with your body's flesh, blood, and bones.
        From above falls a rain of nectar and from below a fire
            blazes forth,
        And the skull becomes brimful with nectar enough to
            satisfy three thousand worlds.

EIV3   It is your own mind that in its manifestation of
            countless heroes
        Dispenses the nectar to all simultaneously from the
            skull.
        When the guests (symbolizing the life forms) of
            fictitious being have been satisfied, the adversities
            (that have beset you) since beginningless time
            are over;
        And when, in particular, the demons causing harm have
            been satisfied, all obstacles cease.
        When the rays of the light which is the satisfaction of
            all enter you,
        Disease is assuaged, evil influences cease, and obstacles
            dissolve;
        Death has been thwarted and you have gained the
            rewards of your labor.

EIV4   Afterwards, rest in a state of composure in the
            continuum of Being, absolute, Mind-as-such,
        The very range of your mind where everything has
            become absolute,
        And let everything return to this pure sphere from
            which it has come out as if it were an apparition.

Thereby all opposing conditions come to rest,   EIV5
The two accumulations are complete and the two
    obscurations[4] are removed.
There is no limit to spiritual sustenance and a deep
    understanding is born within it.
No longer is there the belief in a self, and you have
    narrowed your scope to deliverance.
Whatever you wanted has come about and the whole
    phenomenal world rises as your teacher.
There is no impediment to the essentials of life and the
    clear light of death has come.
You have become free in the intermediate state[5] and the
    bitendential value of Being is realized in its
    excellence.
Therefore make efforts to realize the Guru.

It has been said that to see the Guru for a moment   EIV6
Is better than practicing the Development Stage for
    an aeon.

He who wants this rain of real nectar in the three   EV1
    regions
With the clouds of prosperity and happiness, replete
    with all qualities,
Which are the basis for real wealth,
Should attach himself to persons having put their trust
    in compassionate spirituality.

In order to soothe the affliction caused by the emotions   EV2
    filling the subjective mind (which is as vast as) the
    sky, and which
Has been accustomed to these afflictions since
    beginningless time,
You must dismiss weariness and attach yourself to
    friends aiding you in what is wholesome,
In your search for the meaningfulness of life, as was
    done by Maṇibhadra and Sadāprarudita.[6]

F   Wearied and weakened by following a wrong path that
          is worse
Than a surrender to the sweet sound
Of the thousand-stringed lute of the ruler of the gods
          inviting us to indulge in the objects,
May Mind today find comfort and ease.

CHAPTER SIX

Refuge and the Way

eachers and friends can do little more than rouse us by their example from our passivity and lethargy. The venture of setting out on the path towards Being and ourselves must be undertaken by each of us individually. Since this seems to be fraught with vicissitudes, difficulties, and conflicts, it is only natural that we feel frightened and look for persons or things that promise to be of help and to come to the rescue if and when we run into trouble. It is only a feeling of shelteredness that emboldens us to risk the first steps. However, this feeling of shelteredness and that from which it stems is not something that holds uniformly under all circumstances. It varies with different individuals, and it not only reflects the scope of their aims but also directs their projected actions and sustains them till their very end.

Feeling secure poses a rather complex problem. We may want to set out with it as something providing us with a safe-conduct on our way to ourselves, or we may begin by taking it as a feeling of inner strength which is cumulative inasmuch as each action that contains something of this strength makes greater strength available for the next action. In the latter case, the pattern and the style in which we are going to live our lives is uniquely ours, while in the former case of dependence on safeguards we receive our motives and directions from elsewhere. This is the 'common' way of doing things, and even if, as turns out to be the case on closer inspection, the end (goal) is intentionally present before the mind, the realization of the goal will take place at some later time, and is aided and restrained by 'externals' which are, specifically, the teacher pointing out the way, the words he utters as the guidelines of our pursuit, and the milieu, the persons who uphold and assist us in finding what is accepted (received) as life's meaning. Hence it seems that we move from a 'cause' to an 'effect'.

The 'specific' pursuit, by way of contrast, is said to be 'goal-sustained'. It begins with the feeling of inner strength as it is first revealed in a vision which can pierce through conventions, habits, and desires which, by means of their inherent conceptualism, obscure our true Being. This vision is grounded in existential reality unfolding and developing according to its inner structure and, instead of slipping into a barren conceptualism desperately searching for life where it cannot be found, is aided and sustained and constantly enriched by further inner visions and images.

The goal-sustained refuge does not imply that the effect is made the cause. It rather points out and emphasizes that the 'goal' is the true fountainhead of human existence and gives birth to concepts and notions that turn into transmissible data (handed down from teacher to disciple, from generation to generation). These may be rationalistic, empiricistic, or positivistic, explicitly or implicitly replacing— if not denying—Being by substituting for it their own abstractions and conventional signs. In other words, the 'goal-sustained' shelteredness is existential rather than postulational. It is therefore more complete, and less one-sided, because it is not there as something intended to fit within the categories of a barren rationalism, but as a reality that has the power to bring to life new and fresher experiences.

In terms of the 'teacher' (Buddha), the founding stratum of embodiments of meaning (*sprul-pa'i sku*), operative in the intuitive apprehension and expression of an inner vision, must not be confused with its transmutation into a perceptual sign that has nearly lost all its symbolic value. In terms of the community (Sangha), the host of Ḍākas and Ḍākinīs, who aid the person in his spiritual growth, also belongs to this world of creative imagination. They are a symbolic presentation (rather than re-presentation) of experiences, and so must not be confused with their conceptual interpretations.

However important the contribution by the 'teacher' and the 'spiritual friends' to our feeling of shelteredness may be, the decisive problem is the quest for life's meaning (Dharma) which, precisely because of its meaningfulness, offers long-lasting shelteredness. It can, of course, be treated as something 'external', specifically, the codified texts that have come down to us. But as 'externals' which can be dealt with in terms of form, style, and other linguistic matters, they can offer only a sentimental feeling of shelteredness. An enduring feeling of shelteredness goes hand in hand with an understanding of the purport of the texts. In understanding them I become aware of 'significances' that spread, and in attempting to reach out to them and to take hold of them I am already on the way which is my very going and growing. The going involves the stages of the path I am passing through, and the growing is the rising to even higher levels.

There are five major stages. The first is the preparatory stage (*tshogs-lam*) on which the necessary prerequisites for the journey are made ready. It divides into three sections of increasing complexity, reflecting appreciative discrimination, sustained effort, and a heightened sense of integration, respectively. The first section, marking the very beginning of the path, consists of the application of four kinds of inspection which is the attempt to keep the perceptual situation as constant as possible, to see *its* objective constituent as like itself as possible, and to learn as much as possible about *its* nature—not moving from one perceptual situation to another, or from one objective constituent to another. However, the fourth kind of inspection is precisely this moving from one situation to another.

The first situation and its objective constituent relate to the 'body', which is used as a shorthand term for the physical world including the animate (my own and other persons' bodies) as well as the inanimate domains. Apart from making us aware of the transitoriness of physicality, it also serves to break our body-oriented preoccupation, which is based on a distorted image that deludes us into believing the body to be what it is not and never can be. The second situation refers to the world of feelings, and the inspection of them reveals a disquieting quality inasmuch as their instability is frustrating. The third situation deals with the mind and mental events, and does away with the assumption of an existent center, which is usually believed to be a Pure Ego or Self, by making us aware of the fact that a number of contemporary events, having their own specific characteristics, are directly related in specific ways. The fourth situation refers to the world of concepts and volitions that play a part in the construction of what we consider to be our intelligible world.

Inasmuch as inspection of the determinate objective constituents of any situation serves to break our preoccupation with them—which is to treat them as if they were something other than what they actually are and to see them as the sole end of human existence—it also paves the way for a healthier attitude towards life. This, in turn, generates the effort not to succumb again to the debilitating and, hence, evil influences which have made us miserable for such a long time. This effort dominates the second section of the preparatory stage, which comprises the four attempts: not to let that which is unwholesome or unhealthy and evil come into existence, and, if it has, to stop its continuation; to let all that which is wholesome and good come into existence and, if it has, to develop it further. The effort involved in achieving these four objectives takes on the character of a trust in our ability to decide between health (and what furthers it) and illness (and what makes it worse and worse). Then, when we have made a commitment to health, being both physical and mental, we make a further effort to abide by our commitment. This involves still another effort, to avoid both overdoing things and being remiss in doing them. In order to avoid these pitfalls it helps to let the mind hold to that which is cheerful, while at the same time keeping it in check so that it is not carried away by an excessive cheerfulness which has the tendency of letting things appear other than they really are.

This sustained effort provides footholds for dealing effectively with such phenomena as multiple personality, telepathic communication, and other supernormal facts which can occur, but are not to be sought after. On this third section of the preparatory path there are four 'footholds'. These involve and reflect a holistic feeling as it is present in the trust and interest in what is to become the releasing vision of life's meaning, and is operative in and through the factors which counteract the obstacles impeding progress along the path. The second holistic feeling is pervaded by sustained effort. The third comes with the focussing of the mind on itself, and the fourth is an alert scrutiny of any fluctuations which may once again fragment the hard-won wholeness.

The complexity of the preparatory stage, including the exercise of appreciative discrimination, and through sustained effort leading to holistic feelings, passes over into the stage of application (*sbyor-lam*) which eventually will link up with the stage of seeing reality as it really is. This stage of application has four phases. The first is termed 'warmth' because we quite literally (and figuratively) 'warm up' to our task. Warmth then reaches a certain 'peak', which leads into an 'acceptance' of the facts of our reality, and as a consequence then comes the 'supreme' moment in which we are able to rise above parts and to perceive the whole of Being. It is this last or 'supreme' moment that actually links up with the stage called the path of seeing. In the first two phases it remains uncertain whether we shall reach this stage of seeing reality as it is or not, while in the third phase it is just a matter of time when it will come, and at the 'supreme' moment the link-up is definitively effected. On the first two phases five 'inner controls' come into play which on the next two phases recur as 'inner strengths'. They are thus arranged in an integrated hierarchy, not dichotomously. They rest one upon another and lead from one to another. The 'controls' assist in the emergence of the positive forces and values that have to be developed still further, and as 'inner strength' they minimize or even render ineffective the growth-inhibiting factors and forces. The five 'controls' and 'strengths' are confidence, sustained effort, attentive inspection, the growing feeling of a state of wholeness or integratedness, and appreciative discrimination.

The 'supreme' moment still belongs to 'this world', the site where everything crumbles. But unlike the other moments in this stage, it is on the verge of merging into a pristine cognition that is not only free from concepts (which by their nature inevitably introduce a split into and lead to a further fragmentation of pure experience or awareness), but also is 'out of this world'. By this latter phrase we attempt to describe the experience in which one feels himself to be out of space and time. This is the stage of 'seeing' (*mthong-lam*) reality as it really is. It is receptive in the sense that it can 'let be', not only at the very moment of seeing, but also subsequently. It is an experience that surpasses everything that went before it, and its emotional quality is one of pure joy. Hence, the 'path of seeing' is also the first 'spiritual level' (*sa*) a person has reached. This element of pure joy distinguishes the receptivity of seeing from a passive state of just being resigned to the harsh facts of frustration that mark ordinary being. Although 'seeing' as it occurs at this stage is without judgment and is non-interfering, it is not inoperative. Rather it is an incentive to act appropriately. The conceptless pristine cognition is more astute—by virtue of its ability to perceive the whole and rise above parts—than any cognition that is channelled through conceptual categories, and can therefore more easily concentrate and select values intrinsic to Being and independent of arbitrary judgments. It is never an undiscriminating acceptance but a limpid clearness and consummate perspicacity, occurring not in isolation but as a structure. Its seven structural elements are attentive inspection, appreciative discrimination, sustained effort, joy, the capacity for making a person physically and mentally fit, a state of wholeness, and equanimity.

The vision that occurs when the 'supreme' moment belonging to 'this world' gives way to and fuses with a 'moment' that is 'out of this world', 'beyond this world', has three phases, each of them being a stage or a path. One does away with the emotional and intellectual obscurations and impediments that can be eliminated by the 'vision' and hence do not require the specific effort that comes only with the stage of cultivation, and that eliminates the more deeply ingrained and less accessible tendencies. The second assures the freedom from these hindrances, and the third makes the continuation of this experience possible. At the same time the vision is also the first moment in the 'stage of cultivation' (*bsgom-lam*) which is itself not something isolated, but a complex structure. Its structural elements are eight operations summed up under the term 'the noble eightfold path'. Here, the term 'noble' is again indicative of the fact that these operations are not of 'this world', but obtain their content and objectives from the 'vision'. For the same reason, the eight operations are specified as 'perfect' or 'right'. Not only is the initial vision perfect, complete, right (it is as good as it should be), but all actions inspired and sustained by it cannot but be perfect and right. However, this 'perfectness' and 'rightness' can easily be misinterpreted as implying an intolerable demand to live up to perfectionistic expectations. Such expectations derive from mistaken perceptions and, by turning into fanatical righteousness, become the breeding ground of all varieties of mental sickness.

Cultivation of the vision and of what it implies is a process, a 'path' that reaches every aspect of human activity involving man's body, speech, and mind. This is evident from the list of eight operations: 'right vision', which is to see in a non-classificatory, non-fragmentizing way; 'right concept', which is to think in terms of a 'whole' rather than in terms of 'parts', each percept, whether this be a person or a thing or an idea, being a unique instance; 'right speech', which is to communicate and means that our words can become the starting point for the mental operations of others in partially re-thinking our thoughts and partially re-feeling our feelings, but does not refer to an indulgence in meaningless babblings; 'right action', which is to be concerned with existential values; 'right living', which is to resort to whatever is conducive to health; 'right effort', which is to see to it that we do not slip from whatever level we may have reached through cultivating the vision; 'right inspection', which is to be fully aware of whatever may endanger the calmness and perspicacity that have been won; and 'right integratedness', which is not a static absorption in a trance- or stupor-like state of mental darkness or blankness, but a continual strengthening of our potential.

This stage of cultivation involves growth as a continual rising above the ordinary. This is indicated by reference to the 'spiritual levels' (*sa*) which are gradually scaled; each subsequent level lets us pass beyond previous limitations and increases our inner strength. While the first level of 'pure joy' is the moment of vision and identical with the 'stage of seeing', the remaining nine levels belong to this stage of

cultivation, each of them active in eliminating whatever obstacles and obscurations there may be and, at the same time,
allowing further qualities to grow and to enrich our lives.
The names of these levels are not so much descriptions as
symbols meant to evoke in us the circumstances, emotions,
sensations, and perceptions which went into the making of
the symbols.

All that has been stated so far belongs to the process of
learning which, at some time or other, climaxes in a stage of
no-more learning (*mi-slob lam*), when all human capacities are
well developed and fully functioning. This is the level of a
Buddha—every obscuration and every impediment has gone
(*sangs*) and every quality is at its fullest (*rgyas*). Inasmuch as
the 'path' from beginning to end—the end not being a dead
end—is, in concrete terms, man's growing-up, it may be
paraphrased by saying that in growing up to be a human
specimen it is important to become and be a good specimen,
not a poor one. The qualities that are allowed to grow are not
naturally exclusive, separate or distinct, but fuse with each
other because they are facets of Being, not detachable parts
to be looked at in isolation. It is the experience of this
wholeness that provides an abiding 'refuge' from the fear of
disintegration. Beyond that, these qualities are the means by
which, if a person is able and willing, he may find himself
and be a Buddha.

A   Once you have attached yourself to spiritual friends,
You have to learn step by step the stages on the
road to deliverance.

BIa   The foundation of all paths is the taking refuge:
The inferior person does so out of fear of evil forms
      of life.
The two mediocre types are afraid of fictitious being,
      and the superior type,
Having seen the sordid state of Saṃsāra in all its
      ramifications,
Is unable to bear the misery of others and is afraid of
      peace and happiness (for himself).
In order to set out on the great spiritual pursuit of the
      Buddha's sons,
There are thus three ways of taking refuge and three
      kinds of intention,
A general, an excellent, and an unsurpassable one.

BIb   The duration (of taking refuge) is determined by the
      intentions: the inferior type
Does so until he enjoys happiness in the hereafter.
The two mediocre types do so for the time being, as
      long as they live, and
Finally, until they have reached their goal of being a
      Śrāvaka or a Pratyekabuddha.
The superior one does so continually until he has
      realized limpid clearness and consummate
      perspicacity
Or has the inconceivable and imponderable pristine
      awareness (of Buddhahood).

The area of refuge has two aspects: a common or   BIb1
    'cause'-dominated one and
A specific or 'goal'-sustained one.
This axiom about a 'cause' and a 'goal'
Is established by the difference between
The cause-dominated spiritual pursuit, claiming that
    the goal will be reached at some future time,
And the Vajrayāna which emphasizes the goal which is
    already present now and is our mind.
Since the discussion of this topic in philosophically
    orientated pursuits
Has only the name in common, it must be considered as
    one-sided.

The area of the cause-dominated pursuit is the concrete   BIb2a
    Three Jewels:[1]
The Buddha in his supreme manifestation exhibiting
    the major and minor marks.
The Dharma is twofold: the pure message
And the meaning of the various spiritual pursuits as
    indicated in the Sūtras and Tantras as well as
The discourses as they appear in written form.

The discourses are of twelve kinds:[2]   BIb2bia
Sūtra, Geya, Vyākaraṇa, Gāthā,
Udāna, Nidāna, Avadāna, Ityukta,
Jātaka, Vaipulya, Adbhutadharma and Upadeśa.

The Tantras comprise the Kriyā-, Caryā- and   BIb2b
    Yoga-tantras as the exoteric pursuits;
Appropriate action, appreciative discrimination, and
    their unity (being the hallmark of the so-called)
    Father-, Mother-, and Non-dual Tantras as the
    esoteric pursuits of Mahāyoga, and
Their written forms as the volumes of scripture and
    so on.

BIb2biia   The real understanding is the spiritual levels and the
paths, the Developing and Fulfillment Stages.
Their efficacy is unlimited, as they are the actuality of
compassionate spirituality[3]
Which has as its quintessence spiritual sustenance,
holistic realizations, and pristine cognitions.

BIb2biib   The spiritual levels are the Joyful One, the Stainless
One, the Illumining One,
The Flaming One, the One Difficult to Conquer, the
One Immediately Present, the One Going Far,
The Unshakeable One, the One having Good
Understanding, and the Cloud of Meaningfulness.

BIb2biic   The eleventh level (which comes after the) ten levels of
the learning process is the level of 'Light
Everywhere',
The level of the founding stratum of embodiments of
meanings, recognized by the cause-dominated
pursuit.
In the Vajrayāna according to qualities and
life-patterns,
There are a twelfth level and countless others.[4]

BIb2biid   The five paths of preparation, application, vision,
cultivation (of the vision), no-more learning,
And the profoundness of the two Stages and so on are
the domain of mind,
The spotless light of the sun of the true meaning of life.

BIb2c   The Sangha is the Śrāvakas, Pratyekabuddhas, the four
pairs of aspirants,[5]
And those on the level of the Buddha's spiritual sons
are the exoteric circle;
The Ḍāka-Ḍākinīs and the Mantra-masters are the
mystical inspirations.[6]

These are the concrete personages of your refuge and   BIc1
    you should envisage them (in front of you) in
    the sky;
In particular, you should attach greatest importance
    (outwardly) to the Buddha and (internally) to the
    Guru.

Venerating them materially, mentally, and mystically,   BIc2
    (you should say):
"With folded hands and full of joy, I and all others
Take refuge in the Guru-Buddha, the Dharma, and the
    Sangha
For the sake of others until we are in a state of limpid
    clearness and consummate perspicacity."
So you should do over and over again from the depth of
    your heart and bones.

You should think that through such joy and its   BIc3
    radiation
The obscurations of your own and others' actions by
    body, speech, and mind are cleared away, and the
    rewards of your labor are obtained.
Thereby the accumulation of merits is complete and the
    founding strata of apprehendable meanings are
    realized.

The ultimate and goal-sustained area of refuge is the   BIIa
    experience of the founding stratum of meaning
Which is your own mind, lucent, beyond all
    propositions,
The divine[7] as the core of what is Buddha, Dharma,
    Sangha.

To make (this experience) the way is the taking   BIIb
    refuge.

BIIc   Everything, insofar as the cause itself and its
            consequences are concerned, is your mind.
        Since actually there is no duality between the going and
            the goer,
        You are in a state of composure in Being as such.
        If you hold the content and the mind to be two entities,
            there is no ultimacy.
        The goal-sustained refuge has no desire (outside itself).

BIId   Thereby the accumulation of pristine cognitions is
            complete and the founding stratum of meaning
            realized.
        What appears as the consequences, treat as if it were a
            dream or an apparition.

BIIe1a Of these two kinds of learning, the one in the
            cause-dominated area of refuge is
        Not to renounce the Guru and the Three Jewels
        In order to have joy in life and in dealing with the
            world;

BIIe1b Having taken refuge in them as the Guru, not to cheat
            those who observe respect,
        And not to revile worthy people,

BIIe1c Having taken refuge in the Buddha, not to revere other
            gods;
        Having taken refuge in the Dharma, not to harm others;
        Having taken refuge in the Sangha, not to associate with
            extremists;

BIIe1d To revere (the Guru and Three Jewels), even if they be
            mere statues, and
        To think of them day and night and always to take
            refuge in them.

The learning in the goal-sustained area of refuge is to   BIIe2a
    make efforts in (realizing) sameness,[8]
Not to think of good or evil, neither of acceptance nor
    rejection;
Not to rely on propositions, but to deal with genuine
    meaningfulness;
To act (out of a feeling) that everything is a single
    maṇḍala of spontaneity and perfection.

He who understands figuratively the phrase, 'it has to   BIIe2b
    be given up', goes beyond (the literalist's
    imbecility);
But he who takes the phrase literally, harbors a wrong
    view.[9]
Failing in what you have to learn and practice you
    fall low;
You have to distinguish between acceptance and
    rejection by being concerned and cautious.

He who has seen other refuges to be deceptive   BIIIa
And who trusts in the Compassionate One in particular
Will be protected and be without fear in all lives.
How could there be a greater promoter of prosperity
    and bliss?

When the soil of trust that is a pure mind   BIIIb
Is well soaked by the rain of merits and pristine
    cognitions,
The sprouts of the wholesome and healthy in the world
    grow large
And the crop of the excellence of the Victorious One
    ripens.

There are many accumulations of qualities such as the   BIIIc
    meaningfully wholesome,
Self-respect and decorum, concern and mindfulness.

The sun of pristine cognitions rises in your mind from
　　behind the clouds of mantras.
Even in dreams you see yourself not deprived of them
And you remember them over generations and you are
　　beautiful by virtue of status and wealth.

BIIId　When all beings rejoice, the bitendential value of Being
　　　is spontaneously present.
　　In the end you yourself become the refuge for all
　　　embodied beings;
　　By being a helper you possess the wealth of the three
　　　founding strata of meaning.[10]

BIIIe　If the qualities of having taken refuge could be given
　　　concrete form,
　　They would be wider than the sky and their merits
　　　would be even vaster.

BIIIf　Which intelligent person would not rely on
　　What is the foundation of all positive qualities?

BIIIg　I bow my head in faith
　　To the helper of all beings who, renouncing evil, go to
　　　inner peace.
　　And I take refuge in the excellent leader who is the
　　　wish-granting tree of the merits in the three realms
　　And the origin of prosperity and happiness.

C　Through applying itself to a way of action as behooves
　　　worthy people,
　　Since bliss supreme has been declared to be the most
　　　sublime,
　　May Mind, wearied and weakened by having resorted
　　To bad things that grow worse, today find comfort
　　　and ease.

CHAPTER SEVEN

The Four Immeasurably Great Catalysts of Being

Although growth remains an individual task which is made possible by (and starts from) inner strength and a feeling of shelteredness, regardless of whether this is induced from outside or comes directly from within, it never occurs in a vacuum or in isolation from other growth-aiding forces. Inner strength, in particular, elicits in us the capacity to reach out towards a deeper and wider dimension in human beings, which abolishes the individual's self-imposed loneliness. Inner strength makes us participate, and participation means as much to give ourselves to others as it does to receive others into ourselves. This participation occurs through four fundamental properties, which are equally agents, sensibilities, perceptibilities, and feelings: love, compassion, joyfulness, and equanimity, all of these suggesting and implying a thoughtfulness for another's welfare, well-being, success, serenity or the like, when taken in their positive connotation. Negatively, they are mere sentimental impulses inducing euphoric states in a make-believe world that is detrimental to growth.

It is in their positive aspect as honest feelings that these four aid man's growth. As such each of the four are divided into two kinds: those which have an objective reference and those which are non-referential. This distinction reveals the ambiguity in the nature of these feelings and in the use of these terms. They may be used to refer to the contents of these feelings and perceptibilities, as when 'all the sentient beings' are said to be their reference. They also may be used to mean the process of feeling or sensing, designated as 'love' or 'compassion' and so on. As 'having an objective reference' they are concerned with and overshadowed by a differentiation of content, and the integral feeling is tied and limited to the content. In this sense, as 'having an objective reference', they are 'impure' and are in need of refinement. Because of this differentiation of content and the restricted range of feeling, the danger exists that love, for instance, which is an affirmation of another's value and worth and of a loving person's concern to ensure the other's happiness by remaining aware of his value, may turn into a clinging which becomes a constant source of irritation, frustration, and blindness to the other's real value. In particular, feelings with a strong affective tone, such as love, are liable to turn into their negative counterparts. Therefore, for quite practical purposes, the cultivation of equanimity is recommended as the starting point for our growing closer to our being. Far from being a passive or disinterested state, equanimity provides the possibility of a clearer view and a sounder appreciation of what there is, be this animate persons or inanimate things that make up the world in which we live and participate with every fiber of our being.

There exists an intimate interrelationship of balancing and of effects and countereffects amongst these four feelings. Love, as has been pointed out, may turn into an inordinate clinging to the love-'object' (the notion of 'object' in the context of living beings is already a negation of the other's intrinsic value because the 'other' is seen merely 'subjectively' in terms of how to further 'my' demands), and this becomes a source of frustration which can be countered by compassion as the active force in the removal of suffering. But compassion can turn into a sentimentality and a feeling of helplessness—there is so much suffering and whatever is done about it is of no avail. This feeling can be countered by joyfulness as the affirmation of fulfillment—that which had to be done has been done and the other's development is as much a source of joy as is my own. But joyfulness may turn into a feeling of elation which with its overexcitement makes a person lose himself in unreal goals to which he becomes inordinately attached. It is equanimity that can bring the person back to solid ground, but when equanimity becomes mere apathy and passivity, love with its desire for the other's happiness and welfare acts as a potent counteragent. In a diagrammatic form this type of aiding and inhibiting may be represented as follows:

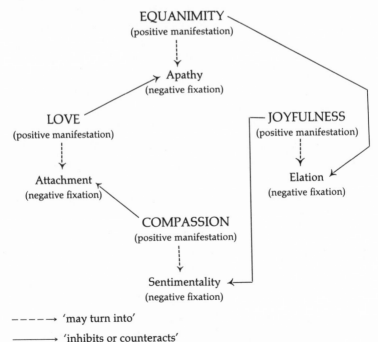

EQUANIMITY
(positive manifestation)

Apathy
(negative fixation)

LOVE
(positive manifestation)

JOYFULNESS
(positive manifestation)

Attachment
(negative fixation)

Elation
(negative fixation)

COMPASSION
(positive manifestation)

Sentimentality
(negative fixation)

- - - - → 'may turn into'

———→ 'inhibits or counteracts'

A further significant point in the distinction between these feelings as 'having an objective reference' and their being 'non-referential', is the recognition that in their referential aspect they are almost exclusively considered as to their content. As 'non-referential', however, these feelings are qualifications of an experience, as when we 'feel' distress or, speaking figuratively, our hearts melt with tenderness for someone who is unhappy or suffering. We 'feel' the urgent desire to help. Although it seems that integral states of feeling with a certain affective tone (love, compassion, and so on) can occur only on higher levels of organization (as in a human being), they are also 'primary' facets of Being. Discrimination between contents, on the other hand (e.g., seeing a person suffering and 'feeling', entering, and sharing his distress), is the result of a differentiation deriving from one's various interests. These interests may themselves lead to 'higher', less 'limited' (referential) and, hence, to 'pure' feeling experiences, technically referred to as being 'non-referential'. As 'pure feelings', love, compassion, joyfulness, and equanimity have an important role to play in the individual's development and growth.

Growth may be said to be the reconstitution of man's 'real' being from his 'fictitious' being, which, in man's ordinary way of being, is his being tainted and darkened by ego-centered emotions. His ego is itself a defense mechanism against growth, and emotions (*nyon-mongs*) are the malfunctioning of a basic and pristine cognitiveness (*ye-shes*). It is tempting to see in this reconstitution process—turning fictitious being into real or authentic being—something like a catalytic reaction. However, in view of the undeniable presence of the ego's defense mechanism against spiritual growth, the attempt to perform the 'existential reaction'

$$(1) \quad A_{\text{emotive complex}} \xrightarrow{\hspace{2cm}} P_{\text{pristine cognitiveness}}$$
$$\text{(\textit{nyon-mongs})} \qquad\qquad\qquad \text{(\textit{ye-shes})}$$

is most likely to fail or, if it should succeed, it would be a very slow process. On the other hand, if we were to discover that each of the 'four immeasurably great catalysts', in its specific operation, could aid this otherwise improbable transformation, then the following reconstitution process might occur:

$$(2) \quad C_{\substack{\text{immeasurably} \\ \text{great catalyst} \\ (tshad\text{-}med)}} \quad + \quad A_{\substack{\text{emotive} \\ \text{complex}}} \quad \longrightarrow \quad [CA]_{\substack{\text{(transitional} \\ \text{intermediate)}}}$$

$$(3) \quad [CA]_{\substack{\text{(transitional} \\ \text{intermediate)}}} \quad \longrightarrow \quad C_{\substack{\text{immeasurably} \\ \text{great catalyst} \\ (tshad\text{-}med)}} \quad + \quad P_{\substack{\text{pristine} \\ \text{cognitiveness} \\ (ye\text{-}shes)}}$$

The presence of C insures that (2) and (3) proceed at a much quicker rate than (1). C, of course, remains unaltered in the process.

To give a concrete example: let C be 'pure' love (that is, love in its non-referential aspect), and let A be 'hatred' (which is a summary term for everything we would term repugnance, distaste, dislike, detestation, abhorrence, aversion, antipathy); then, in this case, the product P turns out to be 'a mirror-like pristine cognition'. The mirror is ever ready to receive and to reveal whatever comes before it and through it there is participation in, rather than aversion to, whatever is present. The catalyst 'pure love', taking part in the reaction, remains, in the end, unaltered ('pure', 'non-referential'). The same procedure holds for the other catalysts acting with the other emotions, which are turned into pristine cognitions.

This reaction is also an impulse towards the creation of forms which are both experience and that through which experience is clarified. In terms of man's quest for being, this impulse, creative in the true sense of the word, becomes his 'founding stratum' (*sku*) which itself is a complex pattern involving different patterns. The word 'pattern', of course, is ambiguous, and can refer to both a qualitative character and a spatialized structure. Being, experienced as 'founding

stratum' (*sku*)—qualitative and structural—is never without
its 'founded cognitions' (*ye-shes*)' the one implies the other.
Although we cannot say anything about pure fact without
turning it into described fact, which only resembles or ap-
proximates pure fact, we may draw attention to pure fact by
saying that it has a large-scale homogeneity—it seems to
look the same from all points of both space and time, and is
reflected in the 'equality (sameness) pristine cognition'. And
since things (experienced as pure fact) seem to look and to be
the same at all times, there is no beginning to Being and there
can be no end to it. Being is a continuum which itself is reflected in the 'meaningfulness-continuum-pristine-cognition'. Thus, both the 'equality (sameness) pristine cognition'
and the meaningfulness-continuum-pristine-cognition' together constitute the cognitive and dynamic aspect of the
'founding stratum of pure facticity' (*ngo-bo-nyid-kyi sku*).

Inasmuch as any cognition is a dynamic process, tremendous activity is taking place in Being, crystallizing in the
'founding stratum of meaning' (*chos-kyi sku*) on which its
specific act of cognition is 'founded' as a singling out, an
individualizing of a universe of its own within the universe
of Being, and which is reflected in the 'individualizing pristine cognition'. Since this activity takes place within Being, it
interacts with the rest of Being, mirroring, as it were, Being in
its 'mirror-like pristine cognition' and thus is related to
the 'founding stratum of engagement in a world-horizon'
(*longs-sku*). Lastly, man can do nothing about the fact that he
is, but it is always *his* being which he experiences as meaningful, and it is through *his* being that he apprehends Being in
an act of sense-bestowing—'the pristine cognition cognizant
of the fact that what had to be done has been done and things
just are'. The 'founding stratum' of this pristine cognition is
the 'founding stratum of embodiments and bearers of
meaning' (*sprul-pa'i sku*). This interlocking pattern of existential experience can be shown in diagrammatic form as
follows:[1]

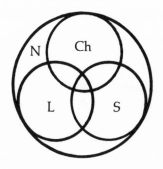

N = *ngo-bo-nyid-kyi sku*
Ch = *chos-kyi sku*
L = *long-(spyod rdzogs-pa'i) sku*
S = *sprul-pa'i sku*

As has been pointed out, the 'emotions' are a mal-functioning of 'pristine cognitions' which alone present the qualitatively authentic character of Being. Once the malfunctioning occurs, 'equality pristine cognition' shows up in unauthentic, fictitious being as 'arrogance', which is an ego-inflation, and the 'meaningfulness-continuum pristine cognition' as spiritual darkness. The catalyst for the restoration of the pristine cognition is 'equanimity'. Similarly, 'individualizing pristine cognition' turns up as a clinging to whatever has been selected, and this becomes a person's 'world'. Here 'compassion' is the catalyst. The 'mirror-like pristine cognition' takes in the character of aversion, which is to be broken down by 'love'; and the 'pristine cognition that things just are' appears as envy, the desire that things should have been otherwise, an emotion to be broken down by 'joyfulness'.

A   Thus a man who by having taken refuge has
         become the site for spiritual growth
           Will cultivate his mind for the welfare of those
         who are alive
By letting the flower of compassion blossom in the soil
         of love
And tending it with the pure water of equanimity in the
         cool shade of joyfulness.

B   As long as these four cardinal agents are not linked to
         the road to deliverance,
They are but euphoric states and remain the cause of
         fictitious being.
But if the way to inner peace has taken hold of them,
They are the four immeasurably great properties of real
         Being because they make us cross the ocean of
         fictitious being.

C   They have as their objective reference the countless
         living beings as well as the absolutely real; while
Their own observable quality is, in an all-encompassing
         way, referential or non-referential.

DI   In the former case they are related to a strictly limited
         number of living beings, and
Their (corresponding) observable mental attitudes
         being impure, they are referential and the cause of
         euphoric states.

DII   They are non-referential when they operate in the
         direction of deliverance
And they will be mastered by those who are
         compassion themselves.

Those who are unhappy or tormented by frustrations,   E
Or engrossed in their happiness and wealth, or who are
    deeply attached to or bitterly set against anyone, be
    they near or far,
Are the objects for love, compassion, joyfulness, and
    equanimity.

Their (corresponding) observable mental attitudes are   F
    the desire that there be happiness and that there be
    freedom from suffering,
That there be no separation from joyfulness, and that
    the mind may operate in calmness.

Although there is no fixed order in their practice,   GIa
The beginner should at first develop equanimity.
When he has become impassive about those near and
    far he may then develop the other three properties.

As the objective reference is all sentient beings,   GIb
You should examine your mind in this way:
To be attached to father and mother and friends
And to hate an enemy would be a bad attitude.

In the cycle of existence that has neither beginning nor   GIc
    end, even this my enemy
Has once been my father or mother and has added to
    my prosperity.
Can I harbor malice to repay his kindness?

Even this my friend here has been my enemy and has   GId
    done me harm;
And even now I am subject to the misery he has
    brought about.
How could it be reasonable to pay him back in his own
    coin?
Even neutral persons have been friends or enemies.

As there is no certainty as to prosperity or harm,
    attachment and hatred are unreasonable.

GIe   Therefore, first you have to give up being attached to
        those who are your friends,
    And you have to treat them as neutral.
    Then you have to give up being hateful of your enemies
        and have to treat them, too, as neutral, annulling the
        distinction between those near and those far away.

GIf   In order to be rid of the mental darkness (that still exists
        in dealing with others as) neutrals,
    Cultivate a mind that abolishes the emotions which will
        make you again see beings as friends or foes,
    And let it be free from fictions about the world.

GIg   Just have the sole desire, as have all others, to be happy
        and to be rid of misery.
    Otherwise, in your ignorance, you will lay the
        foundation for suffering.

GIh   Ah! Would that the emotions of beings who are worn
        out by them,
    Together with all their latent tendencies, come to rest,
        and mind calm down.
    Would that all embodied beings tormented by the
        violence of attachment and hatred
    Calm down in mind so that it no longer oscillates
        between those near and those far away, and is free
        from attachment and hatred.

GIi   Thinking in this way move on in contemplation from
        one being to two, to three,
    To one country, to one continent, to the four continents,
        and
    From one, two, three thousand worlds to all worlds.

The measure of this cultivation is to see yourself and   GIj
    others, friends and enemies, as being alike.

Afterwards you can move on to non-referential   GIk
    equanimity;
Everything is mind and this being Mind-as-such is like
    the spacious sky.
Let your mind, free from all propositions about it,
Settle in this sphere that in the ultimate sense has never
    come into existence and is utterly open.

The measure of this cultivation is the birth of a   GIl
    profound and calm understanding.

The result is that mind without the mire of nearness   GIm
    and distance
Is the spontaneous presence of ultimacy.

When thus the mind has become calm in every aspect,   GIIa
Think of all embodied beings in the same manner
As you yourself would like your mother to be happy.

The objective reference of love is all sentient beings and   GIIb
Its observable quality is a mind that intends to let them,
    temporarily, find the happiness of gods and men
And, ultimately, to realize limpid clearness and
    consummate perspicacity.
Cultivate love by moving in thought from one person to
    all beings, to the very limits of the ten directions.

The indication (of its cultivation) is a supreme,   GIIc
    all-encompassing love
Greater than the love a mother has for her only child.

Afterwards to have everything in this reach and range   GIId
    of sameness
Is the great, non-referential love.

Its indication is the unity of love and openness of Being.

GIIe   The result is, visibly, pure pleasantness and nobleness.

GIIIa   Immediately after you have engulfed living beings in
         love,
       You should develop compassion by thinking of their
         suffering
       In the same way as you are unable to bear mentally the
         suffering of your parents:

GIIIb   How wearied are my parents, having done so much
         for me,
       By various frustrations;
       They have committed evil for my sake and
       Are now tormented by heat and cold, hunger and thirst,
         and executions;
       They drown in the turbulent sea of birth, old age,
         sickness, and death.

GIIIc   How pitiable are they, drifting about in endless
         Saṃsāra,
       Desirous to be delivered from it but with no peace of
         mind,
       There being no friendly helpers to show them the right
         way.
       Could I, having seen them, possibly cast them away?

GIIId   You should think deep in your heart and marrow:
       Might all beings be delivered in a moment
       From suffering through the good (accumulated by me
         over) the three aspects of time,
       And through my bodily existence and my wealth.

GIIIe   The inability to bear the suffering of living beings is
         said to be the indication (of compassion).

The indication of having, through a non-referential   GIIIf
    compassion, entered a state of composure that
    extends into its subsequent state,
Is the unity of the openness of Being and compassion.

The result is a mind without malice and vindictiveness   GIIIg
In all its fitness and primordial purity.

Then when each living being is happy   GIVa
By being soaked with compassion, you should cultivate
    joyfulness.

The objective reference is all sentient beings   GIVb
And you should cultivate joyfulness in thinking:
Ah, there is no need for me to install
All these beings in happiness;
Each of them having found his happiness,
Might they from now onwards, until they are pervaded
    by limpid clearness and consummate perspicacity,
Never be separated from this pleasure and happiness.

The indication is the birth of joy without envy.   GIVc

Thereafter comes a joyfulness (as) in pure   GIVd
    concentration.

Body, speech, and mind are spontaneously calm and   GIVe
    happy.

The result is steadfastness and joyfulness through this   GIVf
    inner wealth.

After you have become accustomed to this you should   HI
    cultivate an order, beginning with love;
Thereby addiction to these four immeasurably great
    properties is gradually stopped.

HII   When, through the cultivation of love, you become
          attached to everyone as your friend, it is
      Through compassion that involvement in the cause and
          effect relationship of suffering is stopped.

HIII When, through an inferior compassion, you stay with
          the objective reference,
      It is through a non-referential joyfulness that weariness
          is stopped.

HIV   When, through joyfulness, the mind is agitated and
          becomes overexcited,
      You have to cultivate equanimity which is free from the
          attachment to those near and far.

HV   When equanimity is (passively) neutral and
          indeterminate,
      You have, as before, to cultivate love and the other
          immeasurably great properties.
      Thereby the cultivation (of these immeasurably great
          properties) becomes easy and steady.

HVI   A practitioner in whom this procedure has become a
          steady way
      May then cultivate the immeasurably great properties
          in their order, outside their order, in a mixed order,
          or in leaps and bounds.

HVII Thereby understanding gains freshness
      And its steadiness becomes ever more firm.

II   From among the four results of such cultivation
      Maturation is the realization of higher forms of life and
          the ultimate good.
      In the world of sensuousness you find existence as a

god or man and bring about prosperity and
happiness.

The result of compatibility with the cause is that you   I II
cannot act but in this way,
And in its experience you feel a happiness that is free
from anything which might upset it.

The dominant effect is that you are born in a pleasant,   I III
happy, and joyful country,
That people are friendly and that you are resplendent
with wealth.

The over-all effect is that the four immeasurably great   I IV
properties grow ever more and spread ever farther.
And the bitendential value of Being is spontaneously
fulfilled.

When love is present and acting on hatred, there comes   I V
in its place
A pristine cognition that is like a mirror, and the
founding stratum of meaningful engagement is
present.
This founding stratum of meaningful engagement is
adorned with the major and minor marks of
Buddhahood.

When compassion is present and acting on cupidity,   I VI
there comes in its place
A pristine cognition that is individualizing, and its
founding stratum of meaning.
This founding stratum is the distinct Buddha-qualities
such as his powers and so on.

When joyfulness is present and acting on envy, there   I VII
comes in its place

A pristine cognition that knows things to be as they
should be, and its founding stratum of embodiment
of meaning.
This founding stratum is not something fixed, but
comes in various forms:
Their spontaneous embodiments are its charismatic
activity.

I VIII   When equanimity is present and acting on arrogance
and darkness, there comes in their place
The two pristine cognitions of the equality (of all that
is) and of the meaningfulness-continuum, and the
'founding stratum of the facticity of Being'.
This founding stratum is the meaningfulness (of
experience) defying any propositions about it.

I IX   Thus the teacher of gods and men has praised love and
the other agents
As having vast qualities and being without compare.

I X   A path that does not have them is a wrong path;
Taking refuge in other teachers is an evil path;
But a path that has them is the highway
That the previous and future Buddhas through all three
aspects of time have traveled and will travel towards
spotless deliverance.

I XI   When it is claimed by the cause-dominated pursuit
that, like a seed producing its sprouts,
Appropriate action and appreciative discrimination set
up the two founding strata,[2]
While by the goal-sustained pursuit both are
acknowledged as the necessary conditions that
remove
The two obscurations[3] of the founding strata,
They are actually saying the same, since appropriate

action in itself depends upon the path delineated by
    immeasurable compassion;
Both the cause-dominated and goal-sustained pursuits
    experience alike the openness of Being as having the
    character of compassion.

Furthermore, it has been said in the Sūtras that since   I XII
    beginningless time
The absolutely positive has been there from the very
    beginning as a seed uncreated.
With this statement the Tantras agree, claiming to burn
    away the obscurations
That have, incidentally, from the very beginning veiled
    the three founding strata.
In brief, sages and saints have spoken of an outer and
    inner aspect
Of the common goal of the Sūtra and Tantra paths.[4]
Therefore, emulating the worthy Buddha-sons,
Make decisive efforts to practice the four immeasurably
    great properties.

When by this well-explained inner peace   J
The mire of mind in all living beings has cleared,
May Mind, wearied and weakened by its
Pursuits of wrong ways and its descending to low
    levels,
Today find comfort and ease.

CHAPTER EIGHT

The Ethical Impulse

ove, compassion, joyfulness, and equanimity are, apart from their capacity to counter negative trends amongst each other, of singular importance for the 'catalytic cracking' of emotions in order to obtain pristine cognitions. This cracking is done, on the one hand, in order to tap and make available the energy which will be needed for 'constructive' work, the development of the 'whole' human being. Thus, the cultivation of the four immeasurably great properties of Being as 'catalysts' is a necessary preliminary step to the 'constructive' phase in man's life. The latter starts with the 'activation of the inner potential for limpid clearness and consummate perspicacity' (*byang-chub-sems-bskyed*).[1] In its operation it is characterized as 'compassion' which does not merely mean to be made unhappy by the suffering of others, but rather to be moved to act, and thus is the motive power to live humanely in the world. It is, in other words, the ethical impulse. What we call 'the world' is not so much an array of lifeless things with some living beings thrown in for good measure, but an ongoing search for meaning which is value-structured. This constitutes a positive purpose, a purpose towards which man can drive forward, instead of being pushed from behind. This positive purpose (limpid clearness and consummate perspicacity, *byang-chub*) as the human driving force (inner potential, 'mind', *sems*) can, once it has been activated (*bskyed*), elicit an influence on events within man's life quite out of proportion to the actual 'amount' of this energy present.

Activation of the ethical impulse comprises two related phases. The one is a settled determination, having a purpose in life, which is the cracking of the emotions which have a growth-inhibiting and darkening effect. The other is the steady pursuance of one's purpose in life, which is to put to work the energy that has been set free. This manifests itself as the exercise of the six transcending functions—'transcending' because they aid us in overcoming our 'separateness' from the rest of the universe and, in establishing continuity through a return to Being, by leaving behind ('transcending') limiting and limited levels of existence.

The six transcending functions, born from the ethical impulse, are active generosity, higher self-discipline, patient endurance, strenuous and sustained effort, contemplative attention, and appreciative discrimination. They represent what we would summarize under the heading of ethical culture which, on the one hand, is the cultivation of the ethical judgment and, on the other, the cultivation and exercise of ethical actions. The ethical judgment states that life is value-structured meaningfulness as it is already implicitly present in the phase of settled determination which comprises the four immeasurably great catalytic properties of Being. To give an example of ethical judgment in this context: I love someone because I realize, maybe at first only dimly, in and through him or her a value which I cherish, but which I would lose if I tried to possess it (possession spells death for love). Ethical culture as the cultivation and exercise of ethical actions belongs to the phase of the steady pursuance of life's meaning which, in particular, is made explicit through ethical actions reinforced by ethical judgment. Hence settled determination and steady pursuance are cumulatively effective.

Neglect of ethical culture results in moral hypocrisy which in turn becomes consolidated as 'morality'. This is inevitable when subjective evaluations replace the unconditional recognition of the intrinsic value of Being because false ideals are allowed to play their fatal role. The danger of thwarting the ethical impulse and of ethical degeneration can be seen most easily in the misapplication of contemplative attention as an escape into euphoric states or indistinct feelings of infinity, entailing the abrogation of critical assessment. Euphoric states and 'oceanic' feelings of infinity may, after all the turmoil of emotionally tainted scheming and the frustrations of our 'ordinary' life, seem to provide the rest we are looking for, but in their indistinctness and transience they are the very opposite to the driving force 'compassion', the thrust towards meaning which, because it has been clearly discerned, not only is able to guide us onwards, but is also the arch-enemy of the non-purposive, the leveling, and the counterfeit. Life's meaning is not found in 'other worlds' (the realms of pure form and of formlessness). It is first glimpsed when we set out on the 'path' and is then laid bare in the moment of pure joy, which is the 'first spiritual level' within the framework of the various phases of the path and the spiritual levels that have to be traveled and scaled in the quest for life's meaning and which, at the same time, indicate man's growth. In the moment of pure joy, which is equally a pure vision, we 'have arrived there'.[2]

This 'having arrived there' is a state of composure in which our dividedness against ourselves, our separateness and isolation from the rest of Being, has been overcome or, more precisely, in which the various dichotomies and polarities have been resolved and dissolved. Inasmuch as composure is a state of having become more unified through contemplatively attending to anything that is healthy and existentially valuable and, therefore, growth-aiding as the first step in the direction of wholeness and integrated being, then to the extent that the person has become unified, he is capable of seeing more unity in the world. Dichotomies belong exclusively to partial cognitions which lack appreciative discrimination because of their being bound up in their tendencies to divide for classificatory, comparative, abstractive purposes, and because of the tendency to make subjective demands which result in less and less being perceived and appreciated. This lack of appreciative discrimination leads to a rift between values and facts which, shorn of value, are mere fictions of the mind. The capacity to see more unity in the world is the after-effect of composure. While in a state of composure the unity of Being is preserved and felt, in its after-effect the previous tendencies of seeing the world in terms of what may be useful or detrimental to my demands on it, rather than of seeing it in its own right and intrinsic value, may, and more often than not do, reassert themselves. It is only on the last three highest spiritual levels that the state of composure and its after-effect remain undisrupted.[3] On the lower levels, including the one of pure joy, the two separate, but do not become disrupted. The after-effect remains an appreciation of the ineffable richness of Being, dream-like, apparitional, a distinct value-cognition. It may be tempting to compare composure to 'closing one's eyes' and the after-effect to 'opening them again'.[4] But it must be noted that what seems to be a cutting off of the outer world is not an end in itself, but a means of permitting the inner world, man's inner potential, to come into play so that through the fusion of the within and the without, the world of Being can be enjoyed in a more integrated way and with a fresh vision. Obviously, the after-effect of a state of composure that has been merely an escape from the turmoil of our sensory perceptions and thoughts into euphoric states and other feelings of infinity, may be decidedly traumatic.

Ethical culture, in the broadest sense of the term, is community-building. However, in this process the energy of the ethical impulse is gradually drained off into a set of rules which define the morality of the community. Actually what has happened is that the ethical problem of existential 'good' has been lost sight of and the social problem of 'right' conduct substituted for it and, in the end, confused with it. 'Good' can only mean an absolute value, independent of any subjective desire, intention, or claim. 'Right', on the other hand is a subjective notion and not only contrary, but even hostile, to ethical good. Since by losing sight of ethical good a community is bound to become stagnant, it is ethical man (Bodhisattva) who keeps the ethical impulse alive and lets it inform his actions. Firmly rooted in and representative of the absolute value of Being (*rang-don*), he is able to bring out this value in others (*gzhan-don*).

Although the ethical impulse is rooted in the human individual, by its manifest form of ethical actions it links man to a wider world in which all his actions become ethically relevant. Such a world of ethical relevancy is, in miniature, the world of worship, presented as a way of exploring one's inner potential and as a framework of values, which are as determinative for man's growth as are his own capacities.

When thus you have become fully conversant   A
   with the four immeasurably great
   properties of Being
You have to cultivate the two aspects of the inner
   potential for limpid clearness and consummate
   perspicacity, the root of all meaning in life.

These rescue us from the ocean of fictitious being with   BIa
   its emotions
And burn away all evil with its fears and tribulations;
They conquer all the motivations with their karmic
   activities and frustrations,
And lead living beings from fictitious being to inner
   peace.

Even if the ethical impulse[5] is not distinctly operative,   BIb
Compassion's wholesome stream is rising ever higher.
Even in composure appropriate action and appreciative
   discrimination unite;
All you do by way of body and speech will be
   meaningful
And you become a veritable shrine in all the worlds
   with all their gods.

Other wholesome things have a diminishing return and   BIc
   become exhausted;
The wholesome that is sustained by this precious
   impulse does not become exhausted but increases:
Just like clear water falling into the ocean and
Excellent crops growing in a fertile soil.

The root or seed of all and everything is compassion.   BId

Even in this world of fictitious being it yields many
 fruits of happiness
And is the cause of sublime limpid clearness and
 consummate perspicacity, its actuality being inner
 peace.
Make every effort to activate this precious inner
 potential.

BIe It is the Wish-fulfilling Gem, the auspicious jar from
 which the splendor of good fortune comes;
It is the finest medicine from which happiness derives
 because the disease of living beings is cured.
It is the sun of pristine cognitions, the moon soothing
 afflictions.
It is, like the sky studded with the stars of spotless
 qualities,
Always bringing about prosperity and bliss.

BIf There gather the limitless clouds of intellectually
 conceivable merits;
It is as vast and wide as the reality continuum and
The most wonderful qualities of the Victorious One.

BIIa The activation of this inner potential is the desire
 to find
True Buddhahood for the sake of the limitless number
 of beings.
It is both settled determination and steady pursuance.
Moreover, intention and execution are mutually
 inclusive
As is the desire to walk and the walking.

BIIb Settled determination involves the four immeasurably
 great properties of Being,
While steady pursuance is claimed to be the practice of
 the six transcending functions.

The merits of someone who is concerned only with his   BIIc
    own good,
Venerating for many great aeons
The Buddha who extends to the very limits of the ten
    directions,
Do not equal a fraction of the merits of settled
    determination.

It is stated that a mind bent on removing just a little bit   BIId
    of the suffering of living beings, be it
Generated only for a moment, will be delivered from
    evil forms of life
And will experience immeasurable happiness among
    gods and men.

Beyond that the profitability of steady pursuance is   BIIe
    infinite,
Because it entails concrete application.
And excellent mind that is pure application for a
    moment
Is said to combine the two accumulations (of merits and
    knowledge) that (otherwise have to be gathered) for
    many aeons.

Therefore, all that has been said to require a period of   BIIf
    'three countless aeons',
Whether it be quickly completed or completed after a
    long time,
Or whether freedom is realized in a single lifetime,
    depends on the power of the intellect.
However, all that is realized through appropriate action,
    sustained effort, and supreme appreciative
    discrimination
Reflects the unsurpassable tremendous power of the
    inner potential.

BIIg   This is the solid tree of compassion
Carrying the heavy load of living beings.
Not even in the world of Brahma and the other gods has
   it been pre-existent,
Nor has anyone ever dreamt of it for himself,
Much less for others. Rejoice in the birth of this inner
   potential for limpid clearness and consummate
   perspicacity
That has never been before.

BIIIa1ai   It may come into existence through the help of spiritual
   friends
Like the rain of fulfilled desires from the Wish-fulfilling
   Gem.

BIIIa1aii   A fortunate disciple who has been made to rejoice
By a flawless teacher, replete with qualities,
Will bestow endless praise on this inner potential for
   limpid clearness and consummate perspicacity
And for all that is wholesome at the beginning, the
   middle, and the end,
Revealing the deplorable state of Saṃsāra and the
   profitableness of deliverance.

BIIIa1aiii   In a pleasant, beautiful, and clean place
You should make preparations for setting up the statue
   of the Victorious One and other sacred objects.

BIIIa1aiv   You should then imagine banks of clouds surging like
   an ocean with the Buddha-sons (on its waves)
Filling the sky in the space in front of you.

BIIIa1av   This is said to be visualized as you yourself intend it
   to be
Through the spotless power of your own mind

And through the compassion of the lord of readily
    responding sensitivity and loving-kindness.

Thereafter you should fold your hands, and with a   BIIIa1avi
    handful of flowers
Invite and ask them to be seated and offer them water,
    ornaments and dresses and so on.

With folded hands in the manner of a   BIIIa1bia
Lotus flower that is just opening
In a lovely pond, and with melodious words of praise
Let me, devotedly, greet them, (imagining myself to
    stand before them) in countless embodiments.

Such merits as accrue from this salutation are not found   BIIIa1bib
    anywhere in the three worlds
However numerous the atoms may be in this earth with
    its mountains and oceans.
Ultimately the citadel of supreme inner peace will be
    reached
After you have been a universal ruler as many times
As your prostrations equalling in number the atoms in
    Indra's world.

Materially and imaginatively   BIIIa1bii
I shall present offerings on an unsurpassable and vast
    scale.

Flowers, incense, lamps, food, water,   BIIIa1bii
Canopies, tasseled umbrellas, music,
Royal banners, yak-tails, drums and so on,
My body, my wealth, and my cherished belongings
I offer to the (Buddha-)Jewel and his spiritual sons, the
    teachers of the living beings.

I make an offering with the lovely storied palaces   BIIIa1bii

Adorned with garlands of jewels in the world of gods,
With the rain of melodious and pleasing songs
And with hundreds of ornaments.

IIa1bii1b(i)   I make an offering with jewels, mountains, groves, and
        lotus ponds
Agitated by female swans swimming in them,
With wish-fulfilling trees from which the sweet
        fragrance of healing properties drifts forth
And which bend under the burden of their flowers and
        fruits.

Ia1bii2b(ii)   I make an offering with lovely lotus flowers
Opened by the rays of sun and moon in a cloudless sky,
And with water lilies having as bracelets bees caught by
        thousands of shaking leaves.

a1bii2b(iii)   I make an offering with the fragrant, cool, and pleasant
        sandal-scented breeze
That makes the flower-buds quiver in its freshness,
With caves and rocky mountains and delightful
        meadows,
With ponds full of cool water.

biib2b(iv)   I make an offering with the white moon of an autumn
        night,
Surrounded by garlands of stars, when it has come out
        of its eclipse,
And with the sun shining in the beauty of its thousand
        rays,
The ornament of the worlds in the four continents.

biib2b(v)   Imaginatively, I make an offering to the Buddha and
        his sons,
With as many atoms as there are in the spheres and
        oceans of the ten regions,

And with all the wealth that is deposited
In the hundreds of millions of world-spheres with their
    oceans and surrounding mountains.

To the compassionate ones, the worthy shrines of   BIIIa1biib2
    worship, I make an offering
With auspicious jars, wish-fulfilling trees, the
    wish-granting cow,
The seven emblems of state,[6] the eight auspicious
    articles,[7]
And the seven adjuncts of royalty.[8]

With my mind steeped in an experience of wholeness,   BIIIa1biib
    encompassing the realm of space
I make an offering with oceans of clouds of offerings of
    the without, the within, and the mystical.[9]

I make an offering with clouds of flowers (like) a   BIIIa1biib
    pavilion resplendent in its beauty,
With cloud masses of nectar, in which incense and
    healing substances are joined,
With clouds of brightly shining lamps, tasty food, and
    sounds of music,
With clouds of oceans of melodious songs of praise.

May all the Buddhas with their spiritual sons be pleased   BIIIa1biib
With the weaving clouds of the various goddesses of
    worship
Such as sGeg-mo, Phreng-thogs, Rin-chen, Glu-gar and
    others,[10]
Representing the vastness that is the cloud of steady
    pursuance.

Let me confess all the evil I have done   BIIIa1biii
    Through karmic actions and emotions that
Since beginningless time have tended to drive me to

such actions which have become the cause of
fictitious being.

BIIIa1biv   May I always rejoice
In the vast store of merits of the living beings.

BIIIa1bv   May I continue urging that the unsurpassable Wheel of
the Quest for Life's Meaning be kept rolling
For the deliverance of all living beings without any
exception.

BIIIa1bvi   I pray that (the Buddha and his sons) stay forever and
do not pass into Nirvāṇa
Until the ocean of fictitious being has become empty.

BIIIa1bvii   May by this wholesomeness I and all beings
Without exception realize overarching Buddhahood.

BIIIa2   Just as a piece of cloth that has been washed clean
Will shine in the colors with which it has been dyed,
So mind, the very foundation of your being, will shine
sublimely when
It has been cleansed by these preliminaries.

BIIIa3   This, then, is the immeasurable result of their merits,
Encompassing the whole range of the sky as wide as the
reality continuum.

BIIIb   Thereafter you have thrice to take refuge
In the Buddha, the Dharma, and the excellent Sangha,
Praying to the Lord and his sons:
Just as in the past the Buddhas and their sons
Continued mastering the activation of the inner
potential for limpid clearness and consummate
perspicacity,
I, too, from today onwards, for the prosperity of beings

Will continue mastering the activation of the inner
  potential for limpid clearness and consummate
  perspicacity.
Let me ferry over those who have not yet crossed (the
  ocean).
Let me free those who are not yet free.
Let me have those relax who have not yet relaxed,
So that sentient beings may become established in
  Nirvāṇa.

Thus you should apply yourself to activating the two   BIIIc
  aspects[11] of the inner potential for limpid clearness
  and consummate perspicacity
Thrice during day and night.

By uttering the above words for the first time you   BIV
  determine your life's purpose,
By doing so for the second time you embark on the
  pursuance of your life's purpose, and
By doing so for the third time determination and
  pursuance of purpose are made firm and pure.

From now on I am the foundation for the spiritual life   BV
  of all beings.[12]
I have even acquired the name of a Bodhisattva and a
  Buddha-son,
Fearless in the world and acting for the sake of living
  beings;
By always being sympathetic and concerned with their
  welfare only, man's world has become meaningful.

Having planted the seedlings of the two aspects of   BVIa
  this inner potential for limpid clearness and
  consummate perspicacity

In the nourishing soil of a pure mind,
Make an effort to keep them strong, to preserve their
purity, and to increase their beneficence.

BVIb   I shall take upon myself the suffering of living beings;
And may through my actions all living beings become
happy
And never be parted from happiness until they have
realized limpid clearness and consummate
perspicacity.
I shall cultivate the four immeasurably great properties
which are the content of settled determination
Purifying in thought the medley of rejection and
acceptance,
And shall guard the mind by discarding everything that
goes against this.
I shall practice the six transcending functions, the
content of the steady pursuance of the purpose
of life
And make every effort to avoid what goes against them.

BVIc   By always being on the alert, by keeping these aspects
before my mind and by applying sustained
awareness,
I shall give up whatever is unwholesome and create an
ocean of wholesomeness.

BVII   You have to see to it that these two aspects of the inner
potential for limpid clearness and consummate
perspicacity do not crumble:
This you can do when you know what the evil is and
what comes from it
When the twenty kinds of failure have been committed:
five of royal gravity like wrong views,

Five of ministerial gravity like plundering cities, and
    eight of a plebeian nature
With two ordinary ones;[13]
And when you know what the good is that comes with
Not engaging in them so that there are no failings and
    no evil.

In brief, four black things have to be avoided   BVIIIa1
And four white things to be effected.

You will just have to avoid these four black actions: BVIIIa2a
Cheating those who are worthy of respect and feeling
    regret for what is not to be regretted,
Speaking unpleasant words to worthy people and
Practicing cunning and deceit among people.

You have to depend on these four white actions: BVIIIa2b
Relying on worthy persons and extolling their virtues,
Exhorting sentient beings to the truly wholesome,
Seeing in the Buddha-sons the teacher,
And by higher thought ensuring the welfare and
    happiness of the beings.

'The welfare of others is more important than personal   BVIIIb1
    aims'
Is the Bodhisattva's self-training.
When it is a matter of changing a situation, the seven
    unwholesome actions by body and speech
May be committed and may actually be wholesome.
The three by mind are never to be committed.

Wholesomeness insofar as it is the desire for inner   BVIIIb2b
    peace and happiness for selfish reasons
Is a failing in Bodhisattvas and Buddha-sons.

That which is otherwise unwholesome and wanton but
   profitable for others
Deserves to be studied, so the Buddha has said.

BIX   There are three kinds of Buddha-sons:
Those who, having become free themselves, desire to
   free beings,
Are king-like Bodhisattvas;
Those who want beings to become free simultaneously
   with themselves,
Are helmsman-like Bodhisattvas; and
Those who, having freed beings, desire inner peace for
   themselves,
Are shepherd-like Bodhisattvas.
According to the Sūtras they have been said
To reach freedom according to their capacities
Within thirty-three immeasurable aeons, within seven,
   and within three.

BXa   The Buddha-sons have to train themselves in every
   respect,
Primarily, however, in the six transcending functions.

BXb1a   Seeing living beings suffering from poverty

BXb1b   They make ample gifts of the necessities
Such as food, clothing, houses, chariots, oxen, and
   so on.
Higher (than this) is the gift of sons and daughters,
And still higher the gift of one's head or one's eyes and
   so on,
So worldly and spiritual prosperity is achieved.

BXb1c   Thereby all forms of avarice are conquered in you and
Others' well-being is close at hand.

Through higher inner discipline you control yourself,   BXb2a
Healthiness of mind and inner peace are found,
And through appreciative discrimination the
    bitendential value of Being in life is realized.

Self-control, living up to ethical standards, and aiding   BXb2b
    sentient beings—
In these three kinds of discipline the Buddha-sons train
    themselves constantly.

A householder decides on and pursues being a layman   BXb2c
    and observes fasts,
A person who has entered a religious order may impose
    upon himself
The rules of a Bhikṣu, a Śramaṇera, or a Bhikṣuṇi and,
    in addition,
Observe the discipline that will safeguard the two
    aspects of the inner potential for limpid clearness
    and consummate perspicacity.

You have to realize three kinds of patient endurance: BXb3a
One that does not bother about how much suffering is
    involved through the various afflictions from
    without and within,
One that is, out of compassion, concerned with the
    meaning of life,
And one that is concerned (particularly) with what
    cannot be reduced to an objective reference.

In the same way as no greater evil exists than that done   BXb3b
    out of hatred,
So no other merits exist more difficult to practice than
    patient endurance.
Try to quench the great fire of anger

In your effort to attain patient endurance in various
ways.

BXb3c   The viciousness of harmful things cannot be
enumerated;
Even if one after the other would become calm, you
would still not have overcome them all.
When mind alone is subdued, everything else is
subdued.
Try hard to preserve the vigilance in having mind
subdued.

BXb3d   The good of patient endurance comes about in the face
of harmfulness,
And such qualities as compassion and kindness grow.
Humbly and joyfully show patience to an enemy
since, like
A teacher, he has become a friendly helper in your
quest for limpid clearness and consummate
perspicacity.

BXb3e   However, without your participation it will not come
about;
Like a sound and its echo, both are related to each
other.
This mass of harm that has turned into evil
Proliferates because of my previous karmic activities
and because of my having missed the opportunity
not to engage in them,
Hence it is reasonable that this evil has come about
now.
Strive hard to subdue mind which is the only means by
which karmic power can be exhausted.

BXb3f   If something undesired happens to you, do not be sad,
If it is but a fiction, why be sad about it?

And if it is not, why bother about it since it does not
    help you.
Therefore endeavor to put up with the conditions.

If examined they are just nothing like empty space.   BXb3g
Happiness and unhappiness, love and pain, good and
    evil do not exist as such.
To hold them to be two different entities is
    meaningless.

Where there is rejoicing in the good that is just   BXb4a
    strenuous effort,
There the wholesome does not become exhausted but
    gathers like clouds
Or like bees in a cluster of fragrant lotus flowers.

Its contraries are the three kinds of laziness: BXb4b
Addiction to bad actions, self-contempt through
    slothfulness,
And failure to realize good; as the source of all evil
Through them the excellent fades and the abominable
    grows.

A strenuous person is praised by all the world;   BXb4c
A strenuous person achieves what he intends;
In a strenuous person the volume of his qualities
    increases;
A strenuous person passes beyond suffering.

Whether it is a matter of the supreme good in the world   BXb4d
Or of the path leading beyond the world,
The one collapsing any time, the other lasting,
Make strenuous efforts and stay with them.
In order to abolish what is unwholesome and to effect
    what is wholesome
Until you have attained Buddhahood,

Make efforts, never slackening in your zeal,
Since thereby your inner qualities grow larger and
    larger.

BXb5a   He who wants to cultivate contemplative attention must
    give up distractions and restlessness.
Delight in sensuous objects is like clouds in the
    autumn sky,
Unstable like lightning and very capricious.
Their enjoyment is evanescent, like a phantom palace.
They never can be trusted; give them up
And quickly resort to quiet forest groves.

BXb5b   Have few desires and be content
Because desires produce dissatisfaction.
They cause frustration building them up, preserving
    them, and finding new ones;
They create discord by saturation, craving, avarice;
They lead to evil forms of life and block the way to
    happy ones.

BXb5c   Just as bodily wounds cause untold suffering,
So also much wealth creates even greater worries.
The fewer the necessities, the greater the happiness.
Persecutions are less, and there is no fear of enemies
    and thieves;
Praised by all, you stay on the noble path.
Since duties become fewer and preoccupations
    grow less,
Always train yourself in having few desires.

BXb5d   Evil that has been done by associating with fools is
    immeasurable.
Evildoing increases and makes way for further
    unwholesomeness.
The wholesome decreases and strife and emotions grow.

Being discontented, it becomes very difficult ever to
      be glad,
And you are disturbed by many things and many duties
      and beset by restlessness;
Get out of the way of the fools who are
Like fire, snakes, and ferocious beasts of prey.[14]

Since external objects will deceive you   BXb5e
Until your mind has grown stable,
Stay happily in secluded places.

Until this body, lifted up by four persons,   BXb5f
Has turned into the crackling sound of fire,
Resort to quiet places
And free your body and mind from the enemy of
      restlessness.

Forests abound in clear water, flowers and fruits;   BXb5g
Rock-caves and stone-houses are aplenty
In solitudes adorned by the shade of trees with their
      branches hanging down,
Birds and deer aplenty are jumping about,
And at the river bank flowers are lovely with buzzing
      bees around them.

Contemplative attention increases easily in the delights   BXb5h
      of solitudes
Fragrant with the sweet smell of incense and herbs.
In your joy over the four seasons let the awareness of
      transience and disgust with the transitory grow
By witnessing the gradual change that comes over a
      lotus pond
In the hot season, summer, autumn, winter, and spring.

When you have seen how bones are scattered in the   BXb5i
      cremation ground,

The thought that my body will be like that
And become dispersed,
Will remove far away any idea of joy about
Saṃsāra, a combination of factors with nothing
   to them.
May my mind be pliable and blissful
By always being without strife and emotional
   disturbances and forever calm.

BXb5j Such groves have been praised by the Victorious Ones.
Disgruntled with fictitious being they have resorted to
   solitudes.
The merits of having made merely seven steps in their
   direction are such
That all the merits you may have acquired by having
Worshipped the Buddhas as numerous as the sand in
   the Ganges,
Do not equal a hundred-thousandth part of them.
Therefore resort to forest places of peace.

BXb6 There, having sat down with your legs crossed,
Enter, with your mind thoroughly focussed, a state of
   motionless composure,
And realize the proximate concentration engaged in by
   fools, the discerning concentration, and
The true concentration of having arrived there.[15]
Know the names of the three holistic experiences
   of those
Who have not yet entered the path and move in
The four realms of concentration on pure aesthetic
   · forms and the four realms of concentration on states
   of formlessness, of those
Who have entered the path, and of those who are
   saints.
Thereby a mind taking pleasure in sensuous objects
   will be given up

And intrinsic awareness, higher forms of knowledge,
and holistic experiences will become manifest.
Visions and supernatural cognitions will take over in
the mind.

Appreciative discrimination is of three kinds: by   BXb7a
hearing, thinking, and imagining.
By the realization of a wider perspective the welter of
emotions is overcome,
And having come to know reality as it is in its pure
experience, and as it is in reflected-on experience,[16]
You can go from the fortress of fictitious being to the
peacefulness of Nirvāṇa.

This world of appearance has from the very beginning   BXb7b
never come into existence and is like a mirror
image.
Being nothing in itself it is yet there in various (apparent)
presences.
Having seen this interrelationship as relationship and
nothing more,
You quickly reach the citadel of sublime no-fixation.

Through appropriate action sustained by appreciative   BXb7c
discrimination you become free, which is
Like putting a spell on poison.
If there is no appreciative discrimination, you are
fettered by (allegedly) appropriate action, (which is)
Like suffering from a cure that itself has become a
disease.
Therefore generate an appreciative discrimination that
understands the primordial experience of Being.

When you practice the six transcending functions,   BXc
Know them to be of the same nature as if you yourself
were a phantom.

Through the two accumulations of merits and
    knowledge in all their wholesomeness with no
    dividing concepts as to agent, action, and recipient
    of the action intruding,
The peace of the citadel of the Victorious One is
    reached.

c   Thus by the rain from the clouds of the wholesome
        and good,
A rich crop of pure minds in living beings ripens.
Wearied and weakened by having become ever more
    destitute and poor through the evil of fictitious
    being,
May Mind today find comfort and ease.

CHAPTER NINE

The Existential Approach

It is one thing to talk about the meaning of life, and another to discover it for ourselves. Yet the two are related to each other in such a way that the former may stimulate us imaginatively by addressing itself to thoughts as well as to feelings, while the latter will enrich the former and make it sound ever more convincing. Discovery is the domain of Tantra (*rgyud*), by which term both the records of the discovery and the actual process of discovering are understood. It is the latter aspect that is divided into an 'exoteric' and an 'esoteric' approach. The exoteric one is still dominated by the rationalizing capacity of the mind, dealing with surface phenomena by means of abstract categories and concepts and hence primarily concerned with externals. But since even the exoteric approach is essentially an attempt to discover the meaning of life, it cannot but gradually change from an initial outer-directedness through an inner-directedness to the ultimate unity of the within and the without. This is indicated by the gradation from Kriyā through Caryā to Yoga.

In the 'esoteric' approach, the percepts, images, and symbols with which we start are no longer instruments of mere conceptual life, but are instead means of revealing the inner structure and the very life of an experience. Since experience involves the whole man in his very Being, the 'esoteric' approach is 'existential' in the sense that Being, reverberating in and being present as and in man's existence (*rgyud*), is irreducible and indestructible. Its symbol is the diamond-scepter (*rdo-rje, vajra*) which has become the name for the existential approach, Vajrayāna (*rdo-rje theg-pa*),[1] 'the pursuit of the indestructible in man'. At the same time, this pursuit is both the restoration and preservation of the integrity of Being. Its symbol is the mantra (*gsang-sngags*), working out of the hidden depths of Being and protecting it from disintegrating into partial aspects of Being that may then be taken for Being whereby man suffers by becoming divided against himself.[2] It is the growing intensity of the experience of Being that has led to the gradation of the existential and esoteric approach into Mahā, Anu, and Ati.[3]

The meaning of life is not discovered by thinking independently of life outside meaning, but by living the very life of meaning with its images, symbols, concepts, patternings, evanescences, and resurgences. Here imagination, in its very process rather than in its finished product, is of decisive importance, because through its creation of images it reveals, lets shine forth, and, in a very specific sense, recaptures the source from which the life of meaning and the meaning of life have sprung. Once this source is glimpsed and felt, it can never be forgotten. Imagination, as the name implies, always carries with it percepts and concepts, symbols and meanings. In the ordinary usage of symbols, as in speech, the symbol is a percept and the meaning or referent (clearly distinct from the symbol) is an idea (a concept or a complex of ideas and concepts). But in imagination there is flexibility and fluidity. We can pass to and fro between percept, image, concept, meaning, and experience, so that the meanings which a while ago were images and concepts, now are again images and concepts whose meanings are further images and concepts, all of them referring to a life-experience in such a way that they are parts of a larger whole. This is what happens in what is technically known as the Developing (*bskyed-rim*) and Fulfillment Stages (*rdzogs-rim*).[4] Above all, we do not simply and coldly apprehend this shifting and fusing of 'images' and 'meanings', but we instead come to feel ever more intensely and vividly this growing richness in which Being reveals itself through our imagination.

The perceptual experience of what is designated as a deity (*lha*) may certainly evoke an idea, but also—and this may be even more important—a feeling which generally plays a considerable part in any complex system of meanings. With the experience of the deity there is given a percept which imaginatively suggests light, a brilliancy filling the whole universe, as well as a feeling of purity and translucency. The feeling and the percept coalesce into an image which is bound up with the corresponding ideas and concepts of light and purity, brilliancy and translucency, infinity and blissfulness. These concepts again become further images, and the differentiation between 'image' or 'percept', or 'symbols', on the one hand, and 'meaning' on the other, depend upon the focus of attention. The Developing and Fulfillment Stages are—taken separately—different focuses, while their unity is the experience of image and meaning in a whole.

The experience of what is termed 'deity' (*lha*) is an imaginative apprehension of the existence of the inner potential for limpid clearness and consummate perspicacity, (identified for practical reasons with 'mind'). This imaginative apprehension proceeds through its own manner of symbolization and, as such, presents (not *re*-presents) a mode of being of the person having this experience: a mode in which 'mind' lives and is its possibility of actualizing itself, and even is the actuality of this possibility and potential. Thus the 'deity' is the actualized 'expression' of the existence of the inner potential which, in turn, is 'expressed' *in* and *as* the 'deity'.[5] The relationship between 'expression' and 'expressed' is not that of a sign (the signifier) to a thing (the signified). For instance, this table (the signified) is not itself 'in' the phrase 'this table' (the signifier); it is only indicated by it. In the case of 'deity' and 'mind', however, 'deity' is not a sign at all, but a presence which does not symbolize something else (the 'mind')—but precisely is 'mind' as 'deity'.

However, in whichever sense we may understand 'mind', it always comes embodied by and in a specific individual 'body' which, in the narrower sense, is my animate organism. This 'body' can only be understood by my own experience of this organism, because the body investigated by the various sciences is not 'my' body, but 'a' body as a physiological, bio-chemical, or other system. My animate organism is and expresses me: it is the self-embodiment and self-expression of my psychic life. Beyond that, it provides the basis for a decisive moment in the origin of the objective world by responding to situations of a certain type which become poles of actions or their 'meanings'. All this implies being both perceptive of a world and being prepared to act on it, which further implies being 'at home' in it, because the world as lived by me in my embodiment is already there.

My animate organism is thus a potency that co-originates with a certain milieu of existence. This animate organism further manifests a certain style of actions. In walking, sitting, talking and so on, there is manifested a particular style of bodily attitudes, behavior, intonation of voice and the like, all of which characterize this animate organism as mine and not somebody else's. This typical style is, as it were, 'transferred onto things', so that the environment of my animate organism has a certain physiognomical style, founded on the style of my animate organism, by which it (my house, my belongings, and so on) reveals me. The same occurs on higher levels. Thus, the objects of my environment are meanings

—what is called 'the' world is a texture and co-texture of meanings, and the primordial unity and 'ground' of all our projects and perceptions is the 'home' of 'mind'.

These considerations will help to understand the complexity and the symbolism of the maṇḍala, which is said to be my 'body', inhabited and animated by my 'mind', and is on another level the 'palace' in which the 'deity' resides.

In simplest terms, a maṇḍala is said to be 'anything that is enhanced by its environment',[6] and, more specifically, it is a field having a charge, the charge being the primary and truly fundamental factor, and the nature of the field depending upon the quality of the charge. As such the maṇḍala is a potential for and thrust towards a climax along a path that is grounded in a self-existent pristine cognition which, though pre-predicative and pre-positional, is nevertheless cognitively aware and the central 'charge'. The cognitive capacity operating in it shows that the maṇḍala is an 'intentional structure'. Furthermore, as 'ground' the maṇḍala comes as a spontaneous presence which is a structure predelineating what is to become man's concrete structure as body, speech, and mind which are, as it were, the tangible contents of his existentiality, his communion and communication with his world of Being, and his pre-disruptive cognitiveness and spirituality. The spontaneous presence elicits a responding, that is, the presence is not so much a static something being there, but a dynamic appeal to respond, touching the very depths of man's Being by means of what, for want of a better term, may be said to be an act of self-restoration, of self-discovery, or of self-recovery. This act is man's 'path' to his Being or actuality, and is also an art and an experience in which symbolical activity occurs in very special ways.

In this sense as a path, the maṇḍala is perceived imaginatively and actively in many ways by a mind-and-body. In ordinary sense-perception, we perceive the gates of a palace 'out there', but in our imagination, in our aesthetic experience, we perceive their meaning of 'access' as pervading, as inherent in the whole texture and patterns of the palace, and we discover this access to be any one of the four immeasurably great catalysts of Being. Thus what is on one level a 'gate', is on another an 'access', and on, maybe, still another 'love', 'compassion', 'joy', or 'equanimity'. But this is not to say that the gate evokes in me a feeling which leads me to call it 'love'. Love (or compassion or any other of the great catalysts) is an integral quality of the access to my Being. This formula can be applied to all the other 'architectural' elements of the palace, which are thus the facets of the 'path' as responding to an appeal. With reference to the Developing and Fulfillment Stages this implies that man discovers meaning in the work he is doing, in his creating his life out of his Being (Developing Stage), and does not know it until he has made and discovered it (Fulfillment Stage).

As 'climax', the maṇḍala is man's actuality which has the transparent character of man as a being who, in his being, is a presence-to-the-world precisely because he is a presence-to-himself. Thus, in whichever sense we may understand the term 'maṇḍala', be it as ground, as path, or as climax, it points to something of greatest significance in man's quest for himself. As 'pictured' Being, it begins and ends with Being and everything takes place in the framework of Being.

The world in which man is 'at home' is one which is fundamentally actualized by ways of acting. It is a 'construction', a palace, whose inner content is 'meaning'. However, these ways of acting, which carry meaning as an integral component, seem to be like 'programs'—just as an acorn is a program for an oak tree, a gate is a program as 'mode of access to something', and love is a program which enhances positive approaches and inhibits negative facets of life. In all three examples, the inner 'content' of the program exhibits a specific modality of meaning: the inner 'content' of an acorn carries a genetic meaning; that of a gate is 'meaning-as-access-to'; and that of love is meaning as 'positive-enhancer-*cum*-negative-inhibitor'. But any program presupposes a programming which can only be effected by higher levels than the one on which the program operates. This higher level is the excitatory charge surrounded by its field of lucencies or the 'ground' maṇḍala. At the same time, the ways of acting point to an agency whose expression they are. This agent is 'mind', which is not so much an isolated entity but a whole system and as such a 'program' itself. This program is constituted in a complex manner, each of its operations revealing itself as a further complex. On the one hand, every perceptual content is present as being functionally correlated with certain operational patterns of the if/then type which again are of a complex nature. Thus, *if* I open my eyes, which constitute a potency correlated to the event of my opening my eyes, *then* a perceptual act will occur by which certain visual contents will be actualized: I see a colored patch which, in turn, is correlated with the meaning 'dancing girl', for instance. On the other hand, precisely because of this functional correlation, the mind (in this case, visual consciousness) is itself co-experienced simultaneously with the content. This formula applies to any other 'mental' operation. It is these intra-psychic processes that on the level of their experience are 'gods' (heroes) and 'goddesses' (heroines)—the male-female symbolism emphasizing the felt intimacy of this functional correlation.

Whether in this realm of the maṇḍala we direct our attention to the 'world', the 'palace' of the maṇḍala, or to the 'deities' who are 'at home' in this world, the fact remains that in each case an intense awareness is involved. This awareness and the apprehension occurring in the appreciation of this maṇḍala-world, apprehended synoptically as a single complex whole, causes a further heightening of awareness and an enhancement of mental vitality, which is the reason that its experience is so highly valued. Value is both objective and subjective: it is objectively embodied in the object, while subjectively it is how we feel about the object. The 'object' includes ourselves, for man is the strange being who is both subject-and-object and in so being is also a task that needs attention. If a task is to be successfully completed it needs all our attention and anything that reinforces our attention to it. This reinforcement comes by the 'empowerments' which have two aspects—the removal of what prevents us from recognizing value, and the increase of our capacity to attend to our task. The recognition of value, on the other hand, involves the endeavor to preserve it. This attempt is aided by the 'commitments' which range over the whole of man's behavior as they manifest themselves in his actions by body, speech, and mind. In this respect, 'commitment' has, like 'empowerment', a double connotation. By firmly guarding the recognition of the value of man's Being, whatever is detrimental to this value is burnt away, while by slipping from the value that is man's existentiality, his communication with the depths of his Being, and his spirituality, he is consumed by the fire of hell.[7] He is fallen low and has lost his dignity.

*W*hen you thus have activated the inner
potential for limpid clearness and   AI
consummate perspicacity
You can concern yourself with the meaning of the
Developing and Fulfillment Stages which are the
exoteric and esoteric aspects of the Mantrayāna
discipline.

Moreover, since Mantrayāna offers many techniques,   AII
involves no hardship
And, although the ultimate value sought is the same (in
all spiritual pursuits), is not in a maze about the
manner in which to realize it,
And addresses itself to those of highest acumen,
The four approaches—Kriyā, Caryā, Yoga, and
Anuttara—have been expounded.

There is a corresponding gradation as to time, social   AIII
status, and intelligence:
The Kṛtayuga, the Tretayuga, the Dvāparayuga, and
this Kaliyuga age of strife;
Brahmins, overlords, rulers, and tribal people or
commoners;
The dull, the mediocre, the bright, and the very bright.
(Accordingly)
The Kriyātantras teach ablutions and purificatory rites
as being of primary importance;
The Caryātantras teach the equal importance of actions
by body and speech and contemplations by mind;
The Yogatantras teach contemplation as being of
primary importance and actions by body and
speech as mere adjuncts.

The Anuttarayoga relegates purificatory rites to a
 minimum
And considers as of supreme importance the attention
 to and cultivation of sheer lucency in which lies the
 real meaning of mind,
Without being involved in preoccupations with actions
 by body, speech, and (ordinary) mind, and without
 resorting to a subject-object division.[8]

AIV   Further, Kriyā, Upa(ya),[9] and Yoga are the names
For Buddha-(proclaimed) 'existential' pursuits[10]
 (involving) duties, moral behavior, and
 contemplative harnessing (respectively).

AV   They are the exoteric aspect of the Mantra discipline. In
 the symbolism of the deities,
Their followers are unable to cultivate contemplatively
 the union of polarities
And refrain from the use of the five kinds of meat and
 the five kinds of nectar[11] and so on.
They remain preoccupied with rites of purification.

AVI   The Anuttarayogatantras also are of three varieties,
And as 'Father', 'Mother', and 'supreme Non-dual'
 Tantras
Teach the Developing Stage, the Fulfillment Stage, and
 their Non-duality as of primary importance
 (respectively). Hence
They are termed Mahā, Anu, and Ati.[12]
In the symbolism of the deities their followers make use
 of embraces, copulations; and as to specific
 consecrated ingredients,
They do not maintain a duality between clean and
 unclean, but see everything as having one and the
 same value
In being the creative play of a single maṇḍala (as the
 self-manifestation of Being).

In the Kriyā a person debases himself and extols a   AVII
    deity;
Through a master-servant relationship he receives his
    reward.
In the Caryā a person sees himself and the deity as
    being equal,
He receives his reward through a relationship in which
He considers himself as a committed person and the
    knowing deity before him as his friend.
In the Yoga a person receives his reward in the manner
    of water being poured into water,
But while there is no duality in the basic pattern (of the
    person conceiving himself as the deity),
In the actual contemplative process and its conclusion
    he introduces a duality by inviting and dismissing
    the deity.

In the Mahā the technique of the Developing Stage and   AVIII
    (attention to) the moving forces (in the elemental
    forces) is of primary importance;
In the Anu the appreciative discrimination in the
    Fulfillment Stage and (attention to the feeling of
    pleasure in the person's) total make-up is of
    primary importance.
In the Ati a pristine cognition in which everything is
    present in the non-duality (of subject and object) is
    of primary importance.
In all three, however, experience comes in the manner
    of knowing
That everything has been from its very beginning in a
    state of sameness.

Since I and all the other beings have been since the very   AIX
    beginning in a state of Buddhahood,
Let me cultivate the two stages through which

My psychophysical constituents, my total
   physico-spiritual make-up, and my sensory creation
   of my world is luminously transfigured into a single
   maṇḍala.[13]

BIa1   There are four ways of creative imagination according
            to the four kinds of birth.
         Transmutation of the tendencies leading to birth from
            an egg:
         After the two accumulations of merits and knowledge
            have been effected,
         The former by taking refuge, by activating the inner
            potential and by briefly (envisaging yourself as a
            deity) through the Developing Stage,
         The latter by contemplatively understanding at the end
            of having imaginatively created a divine realm and
            performed your worship, that all this is nothing in
            itself,
         The creative imagination of the Developing and
            Fulfillment Stages in their elaborate phases at
            this time
         Is like there being an egg from which a bird is hatched.
         You may creatively imagine the Developing and
            Fulfillment Stages within their condensed or
            elaborate phases.

BIa2   Transmutation of the tendencies leading to birth from a
            womb:
         The creative imagination in its elaborate phase involves
         Taking refuge, activating the inner potential, and
            (visualizing the emergence of) the divine seed out of
            the open dimension of Being, as
         Well as (the emergence of) existential values and
            radiating light intensities out of the symbols (of the
            deity).

The (creative imagination of the) Developing and
    Fulfillment Stages, not preceded by the condensed
    phase as in the previous one,
Is like the growth of the embryo from its conception
Through the interaction of motility, psychic factors, and
    vitalizing energies,
Until it is born as a complete organism.

Transmutation of the tendencies leading to birth from   BIa3
    heat and moisture:
The creative imagination of the Developing and
    Fulfillment Stages involves
Taking refuge, activating the inner potential, and the
    emergence of the deity in a brilliant light out of the
    open dimension of Being
By the mere utterance of its name.
Just as out of the combination of heat and moisture
A bodily organism is easily set up and born,
There is here no need for a divine seed and for
    symbols.

Transmutation of the tendencies leading to   BIa4
    spontaneous birth:
The creative imagination of the Developing and
    Fulfillment Stages takes place in a moment and in a
    flash.
Just as spontaneous birth comes in a moment
There is no need to imagine the Developing and
    Fulfillment Stages taking form gradually from the
    name (of the deity).

While there are thus four ways of creative imagination,   BIa5
You should deal with all of them in order to transmute
    the tendencies

While primarily, in each case, you deal with the
    condensed form.
Particularly a beginner should start with 'birth from
    an egg',
And when he has some familiarity with it, may imagine
    'birth from a womb';
And when he is quite familiar with it, he may imagine
    'birth from heat and moisture',
And when he is thoroughly familiar with it, he may
    contemplate 'spontaneous birth'.

BIb1   The Fulfillment Stage is either one in which there is still
    a 'presence' or one in which there is no 'presence'.
When the Developing Stage contracts into itself and is
    made to fade into the realm that is unobjectifiable,
Like clouds dispersing in the sky, there is the one in
    which there is no 'presence'.
When you know the Developing Stage to be the
    Fulfillment,
And cultivate it in your imagination, imperturbably
    leaving it in its state of
Defying any proposition about it—as has been the case
    ever since it has been there as a presence—
There is the one in which there is a 'presence'.
The beginner will have to overcome his inclination to
    take the Developing Stage (as a concrete reality);
Being a 'presence' counteracts this desire to take it as a
    concrete reality.
Those who are familiar (with these techniques) will
    have to overcome their desire to take the Fulfillment
    Stage (as a concrete reality).
Being an 'utter openness' counteracts this desire to take
    it as something qualified.

BIb2   Later on whatever is a presence is the Developing Stage
    (which, in turn) is 'appropriate action';

And any cognition into which no subjective demands
enter, is the Fulfillment Stage (which, in turn) is
'appreciative discrimination'.
At all times they will arise in such a manner that they
cannot be subtracted from or added to each other.

The Developing Stage is the cessation of the desire to   BIb3
take this world of appearance as an absolute reality;
The Fulfillment Stage abolishes the idea that it is an
apparition.
When there is appearance-nothingness with no desire
to take it as a concrete reality,
There is the naturally pure reality in which the
Developing and Fulfillment Stages do not exist as a
duality.

This is Vajrayāna having reached its end.   BIb4
By it an intelligent person becomes a real Buddha in his
lifetime.
Thereafter the various Buddha-activities are performed
spontaneously
Wherever there is a world with beings to be taught.
This is the deeply profound and hidden short-cut
(taken by)
Countless (persons who realized the status of)
rDo-rje-'chang.[14]
Fortunate people who want deliverance in their lifetime
should use it.

You will realize full limpid clearness and consummate   BIIa1
perspicacity by following the arrangement of the
Tantra which you favor.
First, you have to think about the spiritual precepts as
detailed in each tradition comprising
Initiation, permission, empowerment, and so on,
As thereby your mind will fully mature.

BIIa2   In particular, this path of the highest mystic approach
Has four maturing empowerments and the (two)
    liberating Developing and Fulfillment Stages.
The 'jar' empowerment purifies the body,
The 'mystic' empowerment, speech,
The 'pristine cognitions through appreciative
    discrimination' empowerment, thinking (in
    subjective terms),
And the 'metaphor' empowerment purifies latent
    tendencies, and confers the due rewards.
While through the first three empowerments the
    accumulation of merits is completed,
Through the fourth empowerment the accumulation of
    knowledge is completed, and
Both emotional and intellectual obscurations are all
    removed.
Therefore, through obtaining the four maturing
    empowerments
You have to cultivate the liberating Developing and
    Fulfillment Stages.

BIIa3   Here, he who wants to delve into the meaning of the
    non-dual Ati,
Having received all empowerments and observing his
    commitments,

BIIb1a   Should sit down crosslegged on a comfortable seat,
Take refuge and rouse his inner potential for limpid
    clearness and consummate perspicacity.[15]
(Then he should imaginatively visualize) how out of
    the Hūm
That has evolved from the reach and range where
    everything is an openness, having no ontological
    status, and defying any propositions about it as
    such,[16]
There develops a vast and huge protective circle[17]

Extending above, below, and in all directions,
Its ten spikes mounted by the ten awesome deities.[18]
In the center of its blazing fire, raging within and
    without,

There is the great maṇḍala of Samantabhadra.   BIIb1b
It has four gates, four corners, four pediments,
Five-layered walls, pedestals,
Tiles, lattice-work, balustrades, railings,
Eaves with flowers of jewels.
In the center of the maṇḍala, surrounded by eight
    cremation grounds,
On thrones formed by a lotus flower, sun and moon,
And supported by lions, elephants, horses, peacocks,
    and *shang-shang*,[19]

The five world-horizons of meaning[20] as male-female   BIIb1c
    formulations of energy (attended by) eight 'heroes'
And eight 'heroines', eight guardians, four male, four
    female,
And the six 'puissants',[21] have taken their seats.
From their bodies, perfect in color, emblems, and
    ornaments,
Infinite rays of light spread to the ends of the ten
    directions.

Then you should imagine Samantabhadra-as-ground,   BIIb1d
    residing in the heart of the principal deity (of the
    maṇḍala),
In intimate embrace with his consort, his body bearing
    all the major and minor marks,
Spotless like the sky, of a deep blue color, in
    crosslegged posture,
As a blazing ball of light about an inch's size.
The rays that issue from it purify all the worlds and the
    beings in them.
Everything, transparently pure, is the realm of gods and
    goddesses.

BIIb1e
> The recitation of three syllables and of the creative
> nucleus of the five world-horizons of meaning
> Becomes the unoriginated sound-nothingness, just like
> an echo.
> Compose yourself in the genuineness of reality.

BIIb2a
> Since your mind has been since the very beginning
> a deity,
> Its body is a maṇḍala and speech a mantra[22]—
> A reach and range of pristine cognitions in which
> everything is spontaneously perfect.
> There is no aspect of it which is, on the one hand, a
> person committed, and on the other, a being
> acknowledging the commitment;
> Since there is neither an inviting nor a coming,
> There is no need to ask for a departing; neither is there
> good nor evil, neither acceptance nor rejection.
> Except that there takes place a glowing with light of what
> From the very beginning has been a maṇḍala, through
> knowing it to be so,
> There does not occur a 'creation' of what has not been
> there.

BIIb2b
> Afterwards, if there is some desire for it, let it gradually
> contract and
> Leave it where it cannot be objectified and no
> propositions about it prevail;
> If there is no desire, dedicate all that is positive to the
> welfare of sentient beings
> In a feeling that all is but an apparition, like the moon
> reflected in water.

BIIb2c
> Let all your ways of acting be of the nature of an
> apparition, nothing as such and yet lucent,
> And know at every moment, imperturbably,
> That all appearance and all sounds are deities and
> mantras,
> That all thinking and intending are pristine cognitions.

Keep your commitments pure, the basic ones as well as   BIIc1
    the subsidiary ones,
Which in groups of five must be known, not broken,
    acted upon, readily accepted, and fulfilled.
These twenty-five ways distribute over body, speech,
    and mind.
Above all, keep your mind in purity.

You should endeavor to perform your devotion, ritual,   BIIc2
    and worship
On the fifteenth of each month, at new-moon,
The eighth and twenty-ninth, and the tenth in each half
    of the month.

You should make efforts to penetrate to the   BIIc3
    quintessence
Of what is meant by motility, mentation, structure, and
    creativity;[23]
By cultivating the paths of the unity of bliss, lucency,
    and non-dividedness by concepts,
You become a scepter-bearer[24] and in this your life a
    perfect Buddha.

Wearied and weakened in the fictitious world of karmic   C
    actions and emotions indulged in by all sentient
    beings,
Yet living so close to the citadel of Heruka-śrī,
May thus, by this most mystic, unsurpassable thrust
    towards Being,
Mind today find comfort and ease.

CHAPTER TEN

The Perception of Being

One of the objectives of engaging in the practice of the Developing and Fulfillment Stages is to free our vision from the drab blur of triteness and 'familiarity', and to enable us to see our 'familiar' world anew, aglow, afresh, and alive. This is achieved by a shift in perspective which supersedes our ordinary way of perceiving. As a rule, we look at the world and perceive things (including ourselves) in terms of 'projects' or 'tasks-at-hand' (*gzung*), or as 'objects' to whose solicitation for attention and for doing something about we respond selectively, by choosing what to grasp and what not to grasp (*'dzin*), and by identifying this operation with ourselves as 'subjects'.

'Perception', however, can never be divorced from the concrete situation of the individual whose perception it is. To see the traffic-light when I am driving a car and to see 'objectively the same' traffic-light at another time (when, maybe, I merely watch the traffic moving along the highway from the window of my office) are not at all the same perception, but reflect distinct variations in the perceptive potential. In one case, I am 'caught up' in what is a distinct traffic situation; in another, I am more 'detached' from it. What these two have in common is that they are perceptual situations.

Further, perceptions always occur as 'typical' ways of doing something about a 'typical' kind of object. These typical ways of doing become sedimented (*bag-chags*) since they are simultaneously a synthesis of identification of objects and a synthesis of differentiation of perceptions of them. It is within the framework of this complexity that my 'perceptions' of my 'world' occur. However, what I am going to perceive depends upon the situation in which the perception is going to take place. Not only is there no certainty about what at any given moment is going to solicit for and elicit a response, even my response to what may be 'objectively the same' depends upon my needs and interests. In any case, my response is a bestowing of meaning on what presents itself to me as my doing something about the 'there'. To bestow meaning is a tacit evaluation. This introduces the distinction between the 'really' real and the 'seemingly' real, leading to the endless strife among philosophers about which is which, or to the equally boring discussions about first and second intentions.

Although much that occurs in the experience of the practice of the Developing and Fulfillment Stages is similar to what happens in aesthetic experience, where perception, too, is given a wider scope, and where feeling and imagination are freed from the narrowness of specific 'practical' pursuits, it would be a mistake to claim (or dismiss) them as identical. The primary aim of aesthetic experience is to elaborate and intensify intrinsic perception and to see things as intrinsically valuable and fine. The primary aim of the experience in the Developing and Fulfillment Stages is to pave the way for insight into Being as it comes as 'thereness'. This Being is not something and, by implication, also not nothing, hence also it is nowhere else than in its 'thereness'. We may note that the word 'in' here does not mean that its 'Being' is in something other than itself, like water in a jug, which would turn Being into some*thing*. The inadequacy of every language is most conspicuous in this case.

The most innocuous way to point to Being is to speak of it as an 'open dimension' or 'openness' (*stong-pa*). That something 'is there' (*snang-ba*) cannot be said to be its fault for ever having come into existence. 'Thereness' has never come into existence but just is, and as such is a 'no comment' fact. The indivisibility of 'openness' and 'thereness' lies in their fact of Being, not in the seemingly being-so-and-so of the one or the other. What is there as 'this or that' certainly has come or is coming into existence in functional correlation, and also goes out of existence, and very much can be said about this. But while things, in their relativity to each other in their being so-and-so and this-or-that, are transitory and relative to each other, their Being is not affected by this their 'being so-and-so' and 'being this-or-that'. Hence, the fact that all that is is relative to each other, is not itself relative to the fact or absoluteness of their Being—relativity and absoluteness mean the same.

There has always been the tendency to 'absolutize' Being (as if its 'absoluteness', its very facticity, needed some 'proof' or rationalization). This tendency has always, and inevitably, resulted in the 'relativization' of Being as being something 'beyond' or 'behind' the phenomena which then are 'explained' as deriving from it, like gastric juice from the stomach. Absolutization, as well as its relativization effect, belong to speculative thought that postulates an 'absolute', be this a self, or *the* Self, God, Spirit or any other invention.

The absoluteness of Being (not its absolutization as something) is identical with the thereness of Being (not of some 'sort' of being that is either so-and-so or this-and-that), and in this its 'thereness' it exposes itself to possible judgments (comments, propositions) about itself. Strictly speaking, this self-exposure (thereness) is both self-objectification and self-encounter. The latter is possible only through the former, but 'object' is not the same as 'subject'. How can it be possible for Being to encounter itself, in view of the fact that there is no other 'Being' that it might encounter, and in view of the fact that encounter is always with some 'other'? In other words, 'direct' self-encounter is impossible, there can only be an 'indirect' self-encounter, and this at once poses the question of what kind is this 'other' or 'object' that it can serve as the vehicle of Being's encounter with itself? The image of the mirror comes in handy. Thereness is the mirror in which Being 'mirrors' itself, and this means—and cannot mean anything else—that the 'mirror' is not something alien to Being but is, so to say, of its own making so as to serve as a means of presenting itself to itself and, in so doing, 'judging' (commenting upon, making propositions about) itself.

Any judgment presupposes 'cognitiveness', which is not something added to Being, but already implied by it. Being, which *as* Being is said to be utterly open, is, as cognitiveness, termed 'Mind-as-such' (*sems-nyid*). Its 'judging' is termed 'mind' (*sems*) which, as should be clear from all that has been said, is not so much an entity but an intentional operation. In this judging process, thereness (*snang-ba*) is turned into an 'object' (*snang-ba'i yul*), an apprehendable something (*gzung*) to whose solicitation a response (*'dzin*) in the form of a subjective demand comes forth, first selectively, then discursively. This procedure marks our customary subject-object division, which is a way of acting that, because of its subject-object character, is necessarily an ego-activity. Subject and object are merely poles in a coherent structure, not independent elements or entities that have to be related to each other by devious means.

In one sense, this intentional operation which is termed 'mind' (*sems*) is a 'going astray', a 'getting progressively lost' in the maze of the fictions of its own making (*'khrul-pa*). In another sense, it is a loss of or decline (*ma-rig-pa*) in the lucidity and lucency of the pure cognitiveness (*rig-pa*) that is 'Mind-as-such' (*sems-nyid*). Thus, Mind-as-such is 'cognitive' in an undimmed light, and operates as 'pristine cognition' (*ye-shes*) that deals with thereness (*snang-ba*) as 'pure' thereness (*dag-snang*). But 'mind' is a loss of this lucency and, quite literally, a 'groping in the dark' (*gti-mug*), fancying 'what is there' to be something that it is not—an 'object' with which it as 'subject' has to cope—thereby turning 'pure' thereness into 'impure' thereness (*ma-dag-pa'i snang-ba*).

If we understand 'cognitiveness' as the operationality of Being—an operationality which is in no way different from the 'openness' of Being—we can understand the loss and decline in the lucency of cognitiveness as a malfunctioning of the operation of cognitiveness as pristine cognition. Taking the Tibetan terms as notations we arrive at the following diagram:

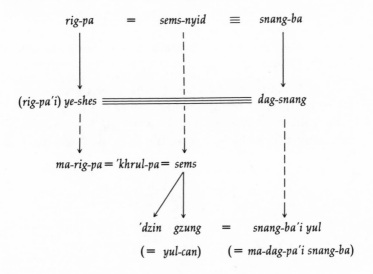

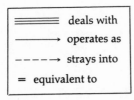

Certain consequences follow from this analysis. There is only one constant or 'invariant' in terms of cognition, Mind-as-such, which may operate at certain times as the 'radiancy' of pristine cognition, and at others as its malfunctioning as the 'dullness' of mind. This enables us to say that:

1. Mind-as-such is (Mind-as-such = Being = Experience).
2. Before there was the radiancy of pristine cognition, Mind-as-such is.
3. Before there was the dullness of mind, Mind-as-such is.
4. Within Mind-as-such there are both radiancy and dullness, but they are the same for Mind-as-such.
5. Outside Mind-as-such there is neither radiancy nor dullness.
6. Mind-as-such as Being remains Being (invariant, same).

With this analysis the question about man's real nature is answered: man is a being who in his 'dullness' judges himself to be a mind, a soul, a body, or anything that catches his fancy, but who in his Being is able to know ('perceive') his Being.

A He who thus experiences within himself
   the unity of the Developing and
   Fulfillment Stages
Enters into the openness of Being, the unoriginatedness
   of all that is.

BI Moreover, all that is, thereness and fictitiousness,
      Saṃsāra and Nirvāṇa,
   Has never been something in its own right and has
      remained inaccessible to propositions about it.
   It is through your subjective demands in the wake of
      the loss of intrinsic awareness that you are drifting
      in this world of fictitious being:
   Although there is present this variety of Saṃsāra and
      Nirvāṇa, of happiness and frustration,
   Its thereness remains the openness of Being.
   Know it feelingly to be like an apparition, a dream.

BII Thus, all the concrete things that are there ('appear') as
      external objects
   Appear in a mind but are not the mind,
   Nor are they found anywhere else than in mind.
   Although through the power of inveterate tendencies
      there seems to be there a duality of subject and
      object,
   There has never been such a duality in this thereness.
   It is like a face and its reflection in a mirror.

BIII Although the face appears there (in the mirror)
         it is not there,
   Nor has there been a transmission of an observable
      quality other than the face.

In the same way as there is distinctly present the duality
(of subject and object), without it existing as such,
All the various things you should know to behave in the
same way.

As long as they are not critically investigated they are a   BIV
source of joy, but if they are critically investigated
they are thoroughly elusive,
And if they are even more critically investigated they
remain utterly beyond any attempt to express them
in words.
Their being or non-being is not observed, nor is there
anything of limitlessness or non-limitlessness.

Even if they seem to come into existence in the manner   BV
of an apparition,
There has been no coming into existence ever since
they have been there;
They are like water in a mirage or the reflection of the
moon in a well.

In particular, this thereness as the six kinds of sentient   C
beings, which is an impure (presence),
Is a presence of what is not, deceptive shapes due to
inveterate tendencies.
Just as a person suffering from cataract sees hairs in
front of his eyes, and
Must undergo treatment for phlegm if he wants to get
rid of his affliction,
So also a person wishing this deceptive thereness to
clear, must remove the film of lack of intrinsic
awareness.

You have to indict the inveterate tendencies leading to   DI
Saṃsāra as being an openness,

By a pristine cognition that stems from the cognitive
   intrinsicality[1] (of Being), in order to counter them,
And be convinced of their openness being (this)
   thereness;
Then you will know what is meant by 'two truths'[2]
   which are the non-duality of thereness and
   openness.
Having arrived at the centrality (of Being) which does
   away with staying in either of the extremes,
You do not abide in their fictitious world nor in tranquil
   quiescence, but are free in the sphere (of Being
   which is as vast as) the sky.
This is the absolutely certain and truly real,
The actual and full completeness of the presence (of
   Being).

DII   Thereness itself has nothing to do with benefit or harm;
Since you are fettered into fictitious being by your
   proclivity to believe in it (as being something that it
   is not),
You need not investigate discursively the various
   manifestations of this thereness,
But should eradicate tendentious demanding mind.

DIII   Mind, indeed, is there, but there is nothing to it.
You will not find it by searching for it; you will not see
   it by looking for it.
It has neither color nor form; it cannot be grasped
   as a fact;
It has no without nor a within; throughout time it does
   not come into existence, nor does it cease to exist;
It has neither parts nor sections; it has no concrete basis
   or root;
This mind which passes beyond any thought object and
   which cannot be pointed out as 'this is it',

Is not observed in its past nor is it in the future;   DIV
It also does not reside in the present; it remains the
        same as what it is.
Without looking for mind by means of mind,
        just let be.

The moment of attentiveness and cognitiveness with its   DV
        affirmation and negation is the object before your
        subjective mind.
Merely a flash of presence it is neither outside nor
        inside.
What is sought is the seeker himself, deceived in his
        seeking.
That which is sought is never found by itself.

This genuinely real that has never come into existence   DVI
Is Mind-as-such, abiding nowhere, never ceasing,
An open dimension since throughout time it has no
        foundation or root.
In its unceasing thereness as the ground for the
        emergence of a variety (of things),
It is not something eternally existing, because it has
        neither substance nor quality,
Nor is it something eternally non-existing, because its
        self-presentation never ceases.
It is ineffable because it is neither these two nor their
        negation.
It cannot be grasped concretely because it cannot be
        established as 'this is it'.
Know its being to have been pure from the very
        beginning.

In the same way as it is not when investigated, so also it   DVII
        is not when not investigated.
Since in its primordial facticity which in itself is not a
        duality,

Neither good nor evil, neither acceptance nor rejection,
    neither expectations nor fears, have any validity,
What is the point of dealing with it selectively and
    discursively?
Throughout time just do not stir up your mind's frenzy
    of searching.

EI   While there is no understanding when the mind
        agitated by the chaff of the rationalist's
        propositions[3]
Is disturbed and moves like the wind,
There is the vision of reality as it is
When the potential for limpid clearness and
    consummate perspicacity,—
That is unconcerned with negating and affirming,
    coming and going—and
This very fact of untainted pristine cognitions,
    all-creative,[4] is left to itself.

EII   What is here the use of various philosophical systems,
Of thought, words, and notions?
The absolutely certain has nothing to do with proofs
    and non-proofs;
It has neither a periphery nor a center, nor do the
    divisions into spiritual pursuits apply;
Pure like the sky, it is not disrupted nor biased.
Since it is distorted when investigated by the intellect
    with its categories of existence and non-existence,
How can that which cannot be expressed in words, be
    explained in words?
One only wears oneself out with what is meaningless.[5]

EIII   It is like quarreling about what agrees or does not agree
With the qualities someone imagines to exist in
A park with many flowers, fruits, and waterfalls
In the middle of the sky.

The pure Mind-as-such, stainless in every respect,   EIV
Is never seen by the stains of the fictions (about it).
What is the point of practicing the Developing and
    Fulfillment Stages (supposedly) concerned with it?
That which is itself lucid concentration is merely
    vitiated by cultivating it.

Since in Mind-as-such, pure in itself since the very   FI
    beginning,
There is nothing of rejection and what aids rejection,
    nothing from which it is freed and nothing that can
    be reached, quit your preoccupation with it.
Since there is no without nor within, nothing
    apprehendable nor any apprehending, give up your
    intentions about it.
Since it cannot be grasped as 'this is it', put an end to
    your desire for it.
Since there is no obtaining nor non-obtaining, dismiss
    any speculations and fears.

In whatever observable quality something may present   FII
    itself, due to various conditions
In the intrinsic cognitiveness of Being that does not step
    out of, nor turn into, something other than itself,
This presentation is free in its very presenting itself.
Like water and its waves, it is the one overarching
    reality in its experience as founding stratum of
    meaning.

When it is seen somewhere, the seer leaves his place   FIII
But does not find it by searching for it. It is not in any
    place or any direction.
The seeker himself is not observed and is inaccessible
    to any proposition.
There being no creator, there is nothing to create
    for him.

FIV Having come to this primordial sphere, spotless like
the sky,
There is no place for you to go back to, and where will
you go to now?
You have reached a point at which everything is over;
there is no further arriving.
Where am I that I am not seen by anyone?

G If you know this, you are no longer in need of anything
else,
And those who have become free have, like me, cut
through deceptiveness.
I have no questions now; the ground and root of mind
is gone.
There is no prop, no grasping, no certitude, no 'this
is it'.
There is continuousness, uninterruptedness, wideness,
overarchingness.
Having understood it thus, now I sing:
I, Dri-med 'od-zer ('the sun's spotless rays'), have
pointed out (this) with my coming (rising) and have
gone.[6]

HIa Friends! look at the objects in their thereness.
All of them are alike in never having come into
existence and in being an open dimension.
However varied the images may be that appear in a
mirror,
They are the same in being the brightness of the
mirror's surface.

HIb Look hither at the mind that introduces the distinctions.
Mind is like the sky,[7] independent of all affirmation
and negation;
Clouds may appear and disappear in the sky,

But the sky's magic remains not-two and pure.
  So also it is
With primordial Buddhahood, spotless in itself;
It is uncreated, spontaneously present meaningfulness.

In what is pure from the beginning, where object and   HIc
    mind do not exist as two,
Rejection and acceptance do not obtain as two, nor is
    there affirmation nor negation concerning partial
    aspects.
Whatever is there has no independent reality, and what
    presents itself is the open dimension of Being;
The fact that everything is the same (in its Being) means
    that it is independent of any support.

In the same way as thereness is varied, there being no   HId
    certainty as to (what is to be) object,
So also the intellect is without specific contents and has
    no limits.
Know this to be absolute completeness.

Thus as to the whole of thereness and fictitiousness,   HIe
    Saṃsāra and Nirvāṇa,
Things of the past are the sameness (of Being) in their
    no longer being seen;
Things of the future are the sameness (of Being) in their
    not yet having come into existence;
Things of the present are the sameness (of Being) in
    their not staying on.
The three aspects of time as well as no-time are the
    sameness (of Being) in their having no foundation
    or root.
Everything is the reach (of Being) complete from the
    very beginning.

Thereness and fictitiousness, Saṃsāra and Nirvāṇa, are   HIf
    images of the mind;

This mind itself is the continuum of experience as vast
    as the sky;
This sky itself, throughout time, does not step out of
    itself or turn into something other than itself;
This unchangingness itself is primordial Nirvāṇa;
As Being it has remained limpid clearness and
    consummate perspicacity—Samantabhadra.

HIIa   This primordial range, in which thereness and openness
    are indivisible,
Is not objectifiable as one or many; it is independent of
    the propositions about it.
This self-sameness and equality of all that is, having no
    fragmentation nor segmentation in it,
Remains the same as thereness, the same as openness,
    the same as truth, the same as falsehood,
The same as existence, the same as non-existence, the
    same in transcending every limitation.
It is the one continuum, the reach and range that has
    remained pure from the very beginning.

HIIb   All that is postulated by the intellect is devoid of any
    substance;
Names are incidental; essences are imputations.
Truth and falsehood do not exist as two; objects and
    mind have no relationship.
The one does not shroud the other—there is no
    apprehendable (object) nor apprehending (subject).

HIIc   Just as in a mirror an image will appear,
So in sensory cognition an object's observable
    quality will arise;
By apprehending it (as something) you go astray into a
    fictitious world of attachment and aversion.
If you look closely you will find that the mind has not
    gone out to the object

And the object's observable quality has not arisen in
    the mind.
Because neither has anything to it, they cannot be
    established as two.

All the objects are one and the same in not having an   HIId
    essence, and
All the intellects are one and the same in not being
    apprehendable in the concrete;
Thereness and mind do not exist as two: they are one
    and the same in being pure from their very
    beginning.
There is no need to select and go discursively over the
    one or the other.
They are one and the same in their freedom that has
    been their ground.

Saṃsāra and Nirvāṇa do not exist as two, they are one   HIIe
    and the same in the realm of mind:
The various rivers are one and the same in the vastness
    of the ocean.
Everything is alike in its value, one and the same in its
    togetherness with experience.
The change and transformation of the elemental forces
    are one and the same as to space.
Mind's affirmations and negations are one and the same
    in the openness of Being.
What presents itself and what is free in itself are not
    existing as two; they are one and the same in their
    purity.
The dance of the waves is one and the same as the
    expanse of water.
If a person understands it thus, he is a sage.

All the entities of reality which cannot be grasped   HIIIa
    concretely in their variety

Are images that do not exist as a duality.
Let this play, where neither good nor evil, neither
    acceptance nor rejection apply,
Happily go on where the intellect does not introduce a
    duality.

HIIIb This ultimate roaming of pure awareness with no
    subjective demands entering into it
Over thereness with no specific object in it and nothing
    to stop it,
Is the manner in which absolute completeness is
    present.

I   When by the equality of all that is,
The reach and range, free from the intellect's working,
    has been judged to have nothing to do with
    subjective demands,
Wearied and weakened through its unlimited pure
    awareness having been fettered into serfdom,
May Mind today find comfort and ease.

CHAPTER ELEVEN

Being and Creative Imagination

*H*owever important the perception or vision of Being may be, as the ultimate meaning of life, it is but a humble beginning which merely gives the individual the impetus and the goal towards which to strive. To actualize this experience and make it live on in the individual's concrete existence, to establish meaningful being in the now, not the tomorrow, or the never—this is the task of creative imagination. It is the capacity of conceiving images, grasping their implications, controlling their expression into articulate presentations, as well as achieving a unified multiplicity of content beyond what is merely sensed and intuited. Creative imagination is a higher form of art inasmuch as it exhibits the characteristics of pure presentation, unmarred by presuppositions. Therefore also it cannot be deduced from conceptual schemes whose expression requires and returns to the dualities of 'within-without', 'subject-object', and, above all, 'means-end'.

Creative imagination resolves duality into unity and spontaneity, and in its renewal of spontaneity it is freedom itself, always new because ever the same, and always the same because ever new and different. It may have a dream-like quality, but it is not dreaming and it has nothing to do with delusions and mental disorders. It never abrogates the critical faculty, rather it uses it to its utmost capacity. Without it, it would no longer be imagination, let alone creative. Creative imagination is founded on the recognition of fact and develops from its acceptance and appreciation, not from attempting to subordinate it to one's illusions. The moment it becomes separated from the critical faculty it is turned to evil use and deludes the mind from which it has sprung.

Creative imagination, as understood here, is an original, sincere actualization of man's being. It is original because it emerges from and presents a world whose being is prior to any judgments and propositions, and is sincere because it is not tied to any purpose that attempts to reach for something outside or beyond itself. It is never 'grasping', which presupposes something 'to be grasped' and, by implication, its misuse for selfish purposes, which ultimately leads to frustration. Inasmuch as creative imagination resolves the self-induced fragmentation caused by 'grasping', it is—by symbols and images that are more convincing than any sensuous reality—creative in the true sense of the word, mind being at work and watching itself work. As such, it carries with it an element of seriousness which is religious in the deepest sense of the word because, as long as it is at work, it keeps alive the sense of omnipotence that is Being itself.

However, our capacity to look upon life through creative imagination is the same as our capacity to live out life as being wholly our own, in the sense that it is the free possibility of being which is self-*and*-world-forming. In this process, we catch ourselves as being at-one with the power of Being. It is a cognitive feeling which illumines its object by allowing it to shine in its own light which is none other than the lucency of its being inseparable from Being, and at the same time this light reinforces and gives new appreciative discrimination and pristineness to the cognition. Careful observation reveals that what happens is like a returning home from an alien world, and the intimacy can hardly be better expressed than by the phrase 'mother and child huddling together'. In this act all the worries are over and there prevails a feeling of tenderness that is an all-encompassing, intentless 'compassion', the capacity and ability to 'feel *with*'. This feeling moves us and opens our minds to be receptive, serving to increase insight and attention and, at the same time, detachment from subjective concerns which are always distracting, preventing man from finding himself and separating him from Being. The gradation of the emergence of lucency in four phases is based upon experience and also implies the extension of the experience by imagination.

Creative imagination is something that most of us achieve only at rare intervals. Still fewer are those who live very much of their lives on the level of creative imagination. Because of this concrete, empirical, psychological fact, a classification into three types of persons has been set up. There is the person of genius who has a certain natural predisposition which renders him fit. He differs from others in the same way as a crystal from ordinary glass, and as diamond from graphite. He has the capacity of capturing the rays of light which shine forth from the lucency of Being and of illumining the world around him with its light. Then there are the vast majority of people who have to strive hard in order to break down the barriers that separate them from their being. For them, the various stages of concentration have been pointed out. Concentration involves both thinking and feeling, and its ultimate aim is to set the mind free, not to lead it into a fixation. This is not contradicted by the reference to the necessary prerequisite of having the mind well-focussed. As a matter of fact, speaking figuratively, only when the light has been gathered can it be beamed onto its source.

A   **W**hen thus you have seen what it means
         that all that is, is alike,
         It becomes imperative that you also settle in the
    reach and range of primordial experience.[1]

BIa   This will be pointed out by means of the gradation in
         intellectual capacity:
    A person of highest intellectual acumen is free through
         his (direct) understanding of the primordial
         experience.
    When he has seen that in it neither a subject engaging
         in its cultivation nor an object to be cultivated exists,
    Mind-as-such, free from what is any basis for thereness
         and fictitiousness, need not be searched for; and as
    Pure awareness, divorced from any bias, it flows like
         the current of a river.

BIb   Since this Samantabhadra field, where everything is
         free in itself,[2]
    Which cannot be temporalized and which cannot be
         grasped as 'this is it',
    Which has no characteristics and measurements, but is
         a self-existent vast ground,
    Remains in its reach and range as it is and as it has been
         since beginningless time,
    There is in it no straying nor a place into which to
         stray,[3] nor is there any exertion necessary, nor is
         any vested interest involved.
    Once (this person of highest intellectual acumen) has
         decided that there is neither attainment nor
         non-attainment,

He is this very moment now a perfect Buddha, without
    having to long for this state.
Such a state reached through exercise is (as) vast and
    encompassing (as) the sky.

Those of mediocre and low intelligence must make   BIc
    efforts to become attuned to this state.
They have to cultivate various contemplative methods
Until the belief in a self has completely subsided.

In particular, it is through evil notions that they are led   BId
    into fictitious being.
In order to be freed from this, concentration is taught as
    a method.
Afterwards there will rise an appreciative
    discrimination that is free from (clinging to)
    extremes[4] and is vast in scope.

While by inner calm the emotions are crushed,   BIe
By wider perspective they become eradicated.[5]

Therefore, for a person of highest intellectual acumen   BIf
    evil notions dissolve in the founding stratum of
    meaning;
If there is neither good nor evil, there is no necessity to
    cultivate what will counter (evil).[6]
When for a person of mediocre intelligence, through
    his cultivating a union with the brightness of Being,
Good and evil notions have completely subsided,
His direct understanding of unity will expand
    like the sky.[7]
A person of low intelligence will first have to attain
    steadiness of mind in the face of anything before it
Through his search for inner calm;
Afterwards, by cultivating an individual insight that
    comes with a wider perspective,

The without and the within, thereness and mind will be
   experienced as absolute freedom.[8]
For these reasons, it is imperative to know the gradation
   in intellectual capacity.

BII1a   Now the creative imagination by one of mediocre
            intelligence will be shown:
         Just as in billowing and turbulent water
         A bright image will be unclear and shaky,
         So also when the subjective mind, restive, fickle and
            giving in to all sorts of notions,
         Sticks to its various propositions,
         Mind-as-such, which is sheer lucency and transparent
            pristine cognitions,
         As well as higher visions and supernatural cognitions
            (which are like) the stars (in the sky), will not rise,
            hence
         It is imperative to be unwaveringly composed in this
            singleness of experience.

BII1b   When on the body, assuming a posture that has seven
            characteristics[9] and being like the world mountain;
         The senses, divested of their limitations, receive their
            objects as a well reflects the sparkling stars,[10]
         Let Mind-as-such, open and lucent, like the bright
            sky,[11]
         Remain in a state where neither elation nor depression
            enter and which is divorced from all propositions
            about it.

BII1c   At that time, there is actual oneness, the primordial
            reach and range,
         The founding stratum of meaning antedating the
            concretization into subject and object.
         As stainless sheer lucency, the energizing power
            of the sun

Rises in bliss, lucency, conceptual undividedness,
    having no periphery nor center.

Thereness and openness, all (fuse) in overarching   BII1d
    oneness;[12]
Beyond the confines of existence and non-existence
There is no division into fictitiousness and
    quiescence, and
The knowing and the knowable become one fact—
This is seeing meaningfulness which has neither
    sameness nor not-sameness (as qualifying attribute).

This is the cause-factor in pristine cognition seeing the   BII1e
    'noble truths';
Since afterwards the most excellent founding stratum of
    meaning (exemplified by) the Victorious One
Is intuited by the mind's eye seeing this reality as it is,
Fortunate people should forever remain composed.

In Mind-as-such, unborn, a pure vastness like the sky,   BII2a
Mental events should not be objectified but be allowed
    to disperse like clouds.
By a cognitive process that is unagitated and divorced
    from propositions about it,
Become composed in this reach and range as it is and as
    it has been since beginningless time.

Let it be, lustrous and smooth like the ocean,   BII2b
Without waves, free from the slime of subject
    and object.

Let it be, open and bright like the sky,   BII2c
Without taking sides, with no clouds of concepts.

Let it be, firm and unshaking like a mountain,   BII2d
Without expectations and fears, without affirmation and
    negation.

BII2e   Let it be, clear and bright like a mirror,
With the images of the objects of thereness appearing
    unceasingly in it.

BII2f   Let it be, like the rainbow staying in its place freely
    since its beginning,[13]
Clear and bright with neither elation nor depression
    upsetting it.

BII1g   Let it be, like an archer undistracted,
In its natural pristine cognitiveness, neither rallying
    forth nor retreating into itself.

BII2h   Let it be, like one who has finished his work and knows
    so for certain,
Spontaneously present, without expectations or fears.

BII2i   This is a holistic experience, pure in itself;
In it inner calm and wider perspective are united.
By staying in the range that is unborn, there is inner
    calm;
By being free from propositions (about its) lucency and
    openness, there is wider perspective.[14]
Their indivisibility is their unity by virtue of their being
    one fact.

BII3a   Since at this time, mind profound, calm, not harboring
    any propositions,
Sees the meaning (of Being) defying all attempts at
    verbalization,
This dawning of pristine cognition, is utterly without
    dividing concepts,
Is sheer lucency, termed the transcending function of
    appreciative discrimination.

BII3b   By seeing this very lucency mind becomes very calm,
And the desire to affirm or to negate the without or the
    within grows less.

Out of this open range an impartial compassion arises,
And the person is urged onto and engages in what is
    wholesome both for himself and others.
He delights in solitudes and cares little for excitement
    and haste.
Even in his dreams he engages in what is wholesome.
Thereby he has taken hold of the way to deliverance.

When afterwards he becomes more and more deeply   BII3c
    involved with this,
His mind becomes clearer and pristine cognitions[16]
    range farther than before.
He thoroughly understands thereness to be like a
    dream or an apparition.
When he sees all that is as having neither come nor not
    come into existence,
Since in the reach and range where no duality obtains
    everything has but one flavor,
His widening pristine cognitions become utterly
    without dividing concepts,
And a stage of concentration adorned with pure joy is
    reached.

At that time body and mind become purer than they   BII3d
    have been before,
And an understanding arises in which appropriate
    action and appreciative discrimination are spotlessly
    united.
With his supernatural perceptions, he has, through
    compassion, the well-being of others assured,
And through his disgust with the world his mind
    extricates itself from it,
And even in his dream there is this understanding that
    all things are like this.
Inside and outside his body there are no lice nor nits
    nor worms,

Free from elation and depression, day and night,
    holistic experiences are assured.
Such a person will quickly see the saintly path.

BII3e   When afterwards he becomes ever more deeply
    involved and his experience gains in intensity,
A holistic experience, the sun of understanding, as
    never before arises.
Since after having seen what it means that all that is is
    alike in its oneness,
He commands unshrouded visions and supernatural
    perceptions,
He sees Buddha realms by the hundreds, thousands,
    billions and more.
At that time there is present an unfailing noble pristine
    cognition[17]
Which is the immediate cognition of 'it has been
    reached'.

BII3f   By letting this experience grow ever stronger and
    deeper
The holistic experience in understanding (Being) gains
    countless qualities;
From meaningfulness that remains alike in the presence
    or absence of concepts
Pristine cognitions, (like) clouds of spiritual sustenance,
    expand immaculately;
Forever in a state of composure where composure and
    non-composure are no longer two,
(Such a person) displays inconceivably vast
    manifestations of meaning,
And he enters immeasurable Buddha realms and
    pristine visions.[18]

BII3g   When the structuring schemata of embodiment have
    become transparent, and when psychic life moving
    along these schemata with all its richest qualities

Has become very wide-spread and immaculate,
There begin to operate the pristine cognitions called
    'bringing the person close to the ultimate goal',[19]
Whereby, after the completion of the noble path,
    limpid clearness and consummate perspicacity are
    quickly realized.
This is the spiritual pursuit in which sheer lucency is
    the driving force;
Through it fortunate people realize in their lifetime
    their goal of freedom.

The stages in creative imagination for a person of low   BIII1
    intelligence
Are first of all a training in inner calm and wider
    perspective separately,
And then, when each has become a firm experience, the
    cultivation of their individual unity.
This has to be learned by countless techniques.

First, the procedure in searching for inner calm is   BIII2ai
To sit down in a secluded spot and
Remain there for days on end, taming the conceptual
    flow
By breathing techniques involving attention to colors
    and counts.

Afterwards he will have to gain composure,   BIII2aii
    undistractedly focussing attention
On any suitable wholesome object
Such as a painting, a sacred book and so on,
And practice the four virtues such as love and the rest,
    the two arousals of his inner potential, and the
    Developing and Fulfillment Stages.

When in this way composure has been achieved, the   BIII2aiii
    mind will become pliable,

Not straying elsewhere but holding fast to its chosen
object,
And it will stay composed for as long as it is settled.
When body, speech, and mind are suffused with
pure joy,
An inner calm that is well-focussed and does not
swerve, is assured.

BIII2bi   Afterwards he has to learn what is involved by wider
perspective:
The things of the external world (in their) thereness of
appearance and the fictions (about them), Saṃsāra
and Nirvāṇa,
In their multifarious thereness, are like a dream, an
apparition,
An image, a miracle, a cloud castle,
A mirage, a flicker, with nothing to them.
Nothing and yet there, they remain the openness of
Being.

BIII2bii Since everything is like the sky and has no essence,
Let it be in this state that has no origination and stays
divested of all propositions about it.
Thereby comes the understanding that the things of the
external world have no essence,
And that the apprehendable object and the
apprehending subject do not exist as such.

BIII3ai   Thereafter he has to examine mind within as follows:
Mind has various notions but no factuality;
It goes out towards objects such as negation,
affirmation, truth, falsehood, happiness, sorrow,
indifference,
But it cannot be grasped as such.
First, from where have you come, where are you now,
Finally, where are you going, what is your shape,
your color?

When it is investigated in such a way, it will be seen in
    this way:

First, mind is devoid of any cause responsible for its   BIII3aii
    origination,
Second, for its staying here, and lastly, for its cessation.
It has no color and no shape, it cannot be grasped as
    something.
Past—it has ceased; future—it has not yet come into
    existence;
Present—it does not linger. It is neither within nor
    without nor anywhere.
Know it to be like the sky and immune to propositions
    about it.

At that time, without your giving a thought about mind,   BIII3aiii
Let it be at ease and relaxed like someone who has
    recovered from his ordeal.
Do not think of anything and dismiss your ruminations.
Let it be in the sphere where everything remains the
    same in its non-duality.

Thereby it will be understood that the individual who   BIII3aiv
    believes in an ego has no essence,
And that the mind entertaining such a belief does not
    exist in itself.

Afterwards comes a genuine pristine cognition in which   BIII3av
    inner calm and wider perspective form a unity,
Of thereness and mind not being two but like water and
    the moon reflected in it.

By apprehending a duality (where there is none) you go   BIII3avi
    astray into fictitious being,

While by knowing that there is no duality you go to the
    peace of Nirvāṇa.
Therefore try to understand non-duality in the
    following way:
All that is has never come into existence (and is one
    with) the pure fact of mind.
Mind's actuality is pure and without stains;
Let it be in its state that is without stains, open, lucent
    and divorced from the propositions about it.

BIII3avii   Thereby the muddy turbulence of the emotions
    becomes very calm
And absolute pristine cognitions with no dividing
    concepts are present;
Pure awareness, supernatural perceptions, holistic
    experiences are assured
And there is the understanding of centrality where
    neither subject nor object nor any limitations
    obtain.

BIII3aviii   At that time while mind is like the sky,
No object is postulated and no propositions are
    entertained.
Since in this state of meaningfulness where there is
    nothing to be cultivated and no one to cultivate
    something,
There is nothing to be created and no one creating
    something; this primordial reach and range
Is the immaculate and naturally pure state of
    Buddhahood.

BIII3aix   No apprehendable object is found, rather what is there
    is like the reflection of the moon in water or a
    mirage;

No apprehending subject is found, rather what is there
    is steadiness and no taking sides.
This reach and range where (duality) has been
    transcended and mind and its apparent (object)
    do not exist,
Is profound, calm, immune to propositions, lucent,
    uncontrived;
Imbibe this nectar-like meaningfulness.

If you have crossed the ocean of the three worlds of   BIII3ax
    your fictions
By this boat of a holistic experience that is so vast in the
    absence of a demanding subject,
You have come to the sphere that is complete in and by
    itself
And where the bliss of reasoning mind mingles
    uninterruptedly with the bliss that is Being.

Out of inner calm which, because of its being there, is   BIII3axi
    the openness of the founding stratum of meaning,
    there comes
Wider perspective which, because of its shining forth, is
    the presentational thereness of the founding strata
    of apprehendable meanings.
This means that appropriate action and appreciative
    discrimination, the two accumulations,[20] and the
    Developing and Fulfillment Stages are all there.

When wider perspective has brought about an   BIII3axii
    appreciative discrimination that understands (Being)
It is through inner calm that you stay on in this state.

When the reasoning mind is no longer occupied with   BIIIaxiii
Ideas of subject and object, substance and
    non-substance,

Then, in the non-duality of the continuum of Being and
    its pristine cognition,
Mind and its mental events no longer objectifiable have
    subsided.

BIII3bi   When in Mind-as-such, pure from the very beginning,
The incidental concepts, for the time being, have
    become pure,
The nine altered states of consciousness,[21] multiple
    personality experiences as well as supernatural
    perception, come into operation;
Countless holistic experiences and clouds of spiritual
    sustenance are spontaneously present.

BIII3bii   When a mind belonging to the world of desire, in which
    as human beings we find ourselves, is well-focussed,
There develops a holistic experience in which selective
    and discursive thought processes are operative, and
    which
Is accompanied by feelings of joy and happiness. This
    is the first concentrative stage.
From this state there develops a holistic experience in
    which selective processes no longer operate, but
    only discursive ones.
Here the mind is essentially lucent, joyful and happy.
    This is the second concentrative stage.
From this stage there develops a holistic experience in
    which neither selective nor discursive thought
    processes are operative,
Rather, the mind is saturated with joy and happiness.
    This is the third concentrative stage.
From this stage there develops a holistic experience
    which is pure joy.
This is the fourth concentrative stage accompanied by
    what is beneficial and valuable.

From this well-concentrated mind there develops a state
    of mind that is clear and translucent like the sky;
This is the attainment of the expanding state of sky-like
    infinitude.
From this state there comes the expanding state of
    consciousness infinitude
In which all that is (is understood to be) Mind-as-such
    with no proposition distracting it.
From this state there comes the expanding state of
    nothing whatsoever existing,
In which neither something apparent nor a mind is
    found and which is divorced from all propositions.
From this state comes the expanding state of
    non-predication
In which the mind has become divested of all
    propositions about existence and non-existence.
From this stage there comes the attainment of a state of
    utter calm
In which mind (usually) engaged in its various
    emotionally toned responses, has ceased to be
    operative in this way.

When a person practices these nine altered states of
    consciousness as they follow one from the other,
Either in their ascending or descending order or in leaps
    and bounds,
He will come to know his and others' actions in
    previous and later forms of existence,
And in what activities mind will become engaged—
And also see death, transmigration, birth, and even
    what lies behind the screen.
He can turn into one or many forms and display their
    features;
Without the emotions interfering he knows things as
    they are and as they are related to each other;
He sees the Buddha realms filled with Buddha sons.

BIII3bv   When you fully understand that thereness is but an
               apparition
           There comes the holistic experience of everything being
               like an apparition;
           And because the afflictions of the mind have
               disappeared and the muddy turbulence (of the
               emotions) calmed down,
           There is the holistic experience of immaculateness like
               the moon;
           And since all that is is no longer found (in its
               separateness) but is one (in) the vastness of
               sameness,
           There is the holistic experience of unshroudedness like
               the sky.
           Hundreds and thousands, nay, countless such
               experiences are assured.

BIII3bvi   Through wider perspective things (and life's meaning)
               are properly understood,
           And through inner calm this wider perspective is kept
               in focus;
           Hence (the one as) spiritual sustenance and (the other
               as) holistic experience should be spontaneous in
               union.

CIa   By traveling the five stages of the Path in their
               respective order you become free:
           On the low level stage of preparation you must
               cultivate
           The four inspections relating to the physical world, the
               world of feeling, the world of the mind, and the
               world of concepts and meanings.

CIb   On the medium level you must give up the four
               attachments to good and evil
           By willingness, eagerness, resoluteness, and
               perseverance.

On the high level you must cultivate the four footholds   CIc
    for higher forms of cognitions
By willingness, intentionality, discursiveness, and
    attentiveness.

On the stage of linking (your preparatory exercises with   CII
    the decisive moment of seeing) you have to cultivate
The five controlling powers of confidence,
    perseverance, attentiveness, holisticness, and
    appreciative discrimination, belonging to the two
    early phases in this stage, marked by a feeling of
    warmth and its rise to its peak value;
And then the same five powers as inner strength,
    belonging to the two later phases in this stage,
    marked by acceptance and what is termed the
    supreme moment.

On the stage of seeing, the level of pure joy,   CIII
You have to cultivate properly the seven accessories to
    limpid clearness and consummate perspicacity:
Confidence, perseverance, attentiveness, appreciative
    discrimination, holisticness, joy, and refinement.

The stage of creative imagination has a low, medium,   CIV
    and high level, and each level
Has the same triple gradation, so that
There are nine spiritual levels in all:
The Stainless One, the Illumining One, the Flaming
    One,
The One Difficult to Conquer, The One Immediately
    Present, The One Going Far, The Unshakeable One,
The One Having Good Understanding, and the Cloud
    of Meaningfulness.
On them the eightfold noble path is traveled from
Proper view, proper concepts, proper speech, proper
    actions,

Proper way of living, proper resolutions, proper
    attentiveness, to proper holisticness.

CV   When you have come to the end of the cultivation of
    these four stages of learning comprising
The thirty-seven topics leading to limpid clearness and
    consummate perspicacity,
You pass into Nirvāṇa that is nowhere and yet is the
    level where nothing has to be learned anymore.

CVI   There has never been anyone who has become a
    Buddha
Without having traveled these paths and scaled these
    levels.
All those who throughout the aeons, generations, and
    lifetimes have become free
Have followed this path, and hence
Those who have embarked on a spiritual pursuit, be it
    the one in which the cause or the one in which the
    goal is emphasized,
Must travel in the knowledge of these paths and levels.

D   When thus through the driving force of the lucency of
    Being, profound and calm,
The muddy turbulence of the mind in all sentient
    beings has thoroughly subsided,
May Mind, wearied and weakened by its preoccupation
    with the propositions about this fictitious world for
    such a long time,
Today find comfort and ease.

CHAPTER TWELVE

The Constituents
in Experienced Being

N either the perception of Being, which is more like a self-mirroring of the nature of the being of the perceiver than a registering of an impingement of the without on the within, nor creative imagination, which is the attempt to resolve the secret of the structural patterns presented to and present in perception, and which in this attempt discovers new relationships and fresh meanings, is sufficient to itself. Rather, all this serves as a guide to action occurring contextually by involving an agent and his intentions. Thus, both perception and imagination are like vectors, pervasive connections, which occasion actions that reach toward 'meaningfulness' and become intentive modes of behavior, rather than being their granular or atomistic foundation.

It is significant that the discussion of the dynamics of perception and imagination has preceded the discussion of the agent or perceiver or experiencer who is already implicated in, if not determined by, the various modes of intentionality as their existential center. However, this center is

neither a Pure Ego nor a Transcendental Self, neither an isolated entity nor an external essence. These latter are but
anaemic, lifeless and, more often than not, deadening abstractions from the wider context of lived experience. Rather,
this center is a developing and operational base with vectorial radiations such as perceiving and valuing 'things', imaginatively elaborating their 'meanings' and enacting these
meanings as 'life-styles'. From this it follows that the 'center',
the concrete living and experiencing person, is already disposed ('programmed') toward finding meaning in life and
'seeing things whole' and thus is inextricably embedded
in the configuration of experience–experiencing–Being. In
this organic unity, the experience and the act of experiencing
(which may involve 'bodily' events such as 'observable'
postures, but is commonly associated with 'mental' events
'lived through'), as well as the dynamic field of Being (the
background, which in its experience becomes the foreground), can be selected as the focus of attention. This focus,
in turn, serves as a basis for further perspectives.

Inasmuch as an individual is disposed towards striving
for optimal value, for finding life's meaning, which is Being
itself and is experienced as lucidity and satisfaction, the
method of finding this optimal value gains special importance. This method involves two related processes, 'inner
calm' and 'wider perspective'. In a certain sense, both are
self-manifestations of Being on the individual's level as the
optimizing program that has to be worked out.

> Within the ongoing process of Being (*gzhi*) the existential
> mode of the actuality of this operational cognitiveness (*sems*),
> which has not come from somewhere, does not go some-
> where, and does not stay (as some entity), exists as an over-
> arching homogeneity throughout time. From its unfolding
> lucency and limpidness there comes wider perspective, and
> from its presence and thereness, inner calm. Since these are
> not two (unrelated entities) they are termed vectorial. As to
> the existence (of this operational cognitiveness) it always

exists in all sentient beings, but its inherently stable lucency
is easily encountered in moments of relaxation and ease.[1]

'Inner calm' derives from both representational, objectifying thinking and non-objectifying, non-representational thinking, the former leading to the latter without being
temporally prior to it. Rather, in non-objectifying, non-representational thinking, the configurative context is as yet
undisturbed by objectifying and differentiating perceptions.
Such objectifying perceptions move freely in representational thinking, occasioning attentive focussing or possible appearances of 'things' as 'standing-over-against' a subject,
regardless of whether these 'things' are claimed to be objects 'external' to or events happening 'within' the observer.
While the 'external' is predominantly tied up with cognitive
meanings, the 'within' represents felt meanings—both 'external' and the 'within' belonging to the context of observed
and observable objects and events which tend to harden into
relatively inflexible patterns.

Non-objectifying, non-representational thinking does
not deal with denotable facts or objects, but rather opens a
path to understanding. In such non-objectifying thinking,
the subject-object structure of representational thinking is in
abeyance, hence this is a thinking which is neither subjectivistic nor an utter blankness. On the one hand, it is the
foundation for the specification of that which is to be subjective and that which is to be objective in representational
thinking, but a foundation that is in constant interplay with
objectifying thought (which has become merely latent in
non-objectifying thought). On the other hand, non-objectifying, non-referential thinking is the path towards Being by
releasing thought from its compelling object-against-subject
configuration, and hence goes the way of understanding
lived experiences.

It is 'wider perspective' that is concerned with the interpretive meanings of that which is immediately presented in
and as experience without the interventions of mediating

concepts. Hence it does not move in the direction of cognitive-informative meanings, but rather grasps and 'sees' its contents, not as objects or entirely isolated and distinct items, but as ingredients in a lived-through situation. To be sure, the reference to apparitions, dreams, mirages and so on, does not provide us with information about apparitions or dreams and mirages and the like. Nor does it provide information about a subject or an object, but rather discloses a possible way of being. But in this disclosure the experience is already an experience reflected on and an explication of what is found in the experience, although we must be careful not to confuse the 'what' in the experience with the 'what' of representational objectifying thought. The 'what' in the experience comes more like a 'how'. As experience reflected on, it is distinct from the experience qua experience, the process of experiencing. But this is a 'distinction' without separation from the creativity of Being or from the exercise by Being of this creativity in and through the experiencer, who thus is an open finitude, the 'is' being his way of being.

'Inner calm' and 'wider perspective' can be separated for purposes of practice, but they mix and mingle with each other, and ultimately remain inseparable in the upsurge of lived experience:

> By exercising inner calm and wider perspective as a unity there rises a sheer lucency in which inner calm, like the ocean in which the waves have subsided, has taken over; the mind remains in lucency and limpidness without grasping from a subjective point anything that it encounters and without being harmed by the flow of concepts; their surging is simultaneous with their freedom. When the sheer lucency of wider perspective, which is like the sky in which the clouds have dispersed, has taken over, this is the time of seeing the naked facticity, open and lucent, of Mind-as-such, not stepping out of itself nor turning into something other than itself, divested of all artificiality and deceptiveness. Should the mind be present it remains in the reach and range of experience qua experience and has regained its assurance that from the very

beginning it has been innocent of such predications as being this or that or not being this or that; and, should it move away, its moving comes as the playfulness of experience qua experience, whereby whatever appears is known as the creativity of pristine cognitiveness, and this is the time when whatever appears under certain conditions does so in utter freedom in and as self-existing cognitiveness.[2]

A   Thus you have to study the three constituents
of unwavering wholeness
Which has its cause in a concentration on unity.

BI   They are the constituent of agent—he who will achieve
realization;
The constituent of method—how realization is effected;
And the constituent of the (underlying) facticity of
Being—the realization of non-duality.

BIIai   The individual who will achieve realization must be one
who is motivated to extricate himself from his
fictitious world:
Staying physically far away from places ringing with
the bustle of worldly affairs
And mentally being removed for long from the crowd
of propositions,
He will quickly realize this wholeness.

BIIaii   When he has confidence, self-respect, and decorum,
Is conscientious, of pure character, delights in what is
wholesome,
Is learned, has few desires and knows contentment,
He will quickly realize this wholeness.

BIIaiii   When he is controlled in body and mind, enjoys
staying in solitudes,
Has given up drowsiness, idleness, and delight in
mere talk,
Is neither indolent nor regretful and has few
associations with others,
He will quickly realize this wholeness.[3]

When he is averse to the bustle of the people in cities   BIIaiv
    and towns,
Lives in lonely places and avoids many contacts,
Has no interest in the various values of the world and
    their procurement,
He will quickly realize this wholeness.

When he does not bother about the pleasures in this   BIIav
    life and those in the next
And about peace for selfish ends, but, for the sake of
    living beings,
Desires deliverance from fictitious being, extricates
    himself from it and feels disgust with the world,
He will quickly realize this wholeness.

As to the constituent of method, how realization is   BIIb1ai
    effected:
He has done away with the five
    obscurations—drowsiness, sluggishness, elation,
    depression, and doubt—
And he properly effects the union of inner calm with
    wider perspective.
Drowsiness and sluggishness utterly obscure inner
    calm;
Elation and self-reproach upset wider perspective;
And doubt harms both and is not conducive to them.

These five are summed up as depression and elation.   BIIb1aii
If there is depression, think of something revitalizing,[4]
    and if there is elation, try to focus the mind.[5]

A wider perspective without inner calm is carried away   BIIb1aiii
    by contentions;
Inner calm without wider perspective becomes
    monotony.

Their union is the supreme path, counteracting the
　　obscurations.

BIIb1bia　Inner calm sets in when body, speech, and mind have
　　become quiet.
That is, the utter suspension of the intentionality of
　　representational thinking (with its subject-object
　　correlation) in
The reach and range where all that is is alike, is the
　　primary feature;
To hold the mind onto a single instant of this
　　intentionality, is the attendant feature (aiding the
　　procurement of the former).

BIIb1ib　There are here two aspects, one which involves an
　　apparent object, one which does not.
Since there also is an external and internal aspect, there
　　are four aspects in all through which the mind can
　　be taken hold of.
The one which involves an apparent object refers to the
　　objects of the five senses, color-form and so on;
The one which does not, refers to having the mind
　　settled in the reach and range where no dividing
　　concepts intrude and where it remains focussed.
The external one are stones, trees, statues and so on;
The internal one is the vibration of the heart-lotus and
　　so on.

BIIb1bic　To settle the mind by having it focussed on a single
　　terminal object of its intentional operation
Is the constituent of the method whereby inner calm is
　　effected.

BIIb1bid　When thereby a well-focussed inner calm is born,
In order to make it spread and become stable, it has to

be sustained by pristine cognitions in wider
  perspective.
To derive full benefit from this calm it is imperative to
  have it reverberate in all modes of behavior.
Once you have come across this calm you have to attend
  as before to the springiness of body and mind.
Thereby inner calm will quickly set in.

When it comes to wider perspective, to experience   BIIb1biia
  everything and anything
From within, the reach and range of lucent and limpid
  mind is the primary feature;
To have the mind in a state of composure where no
  dividing concepts enter, is the attendant feature.

The primary feature has two facets: the experience   BIIb1biib
  interpreted and the experience as experience.
The experience interpreted means to look at it by way
  of eight analogies beginning with that of an
  apparition;
The experience as experience means to exercise the
  creativity of the open dimension of Being
  comparable to the sky.
By letting the experience be as it is in its own reach and
  range, pristine cognitions rise.

Once you have come across this wider perspective,   BIIb1biic
  different things have to be exercised
So that their apparitional character and their openness
  as not being two, are seen to be transparent to
  Being.
When there is a stirring away, the mind has to be
  composed in the reach and range of inner calm.
At that time a sheer lucency which is like the sky
Becomes the seeing of the pure fact of the openness and
  lucency (of Being), divested of the propositions
  about it,

Thereby freedom from the clouds of the two kinds of
  obscurations is realized.
At other times there rises a sheer lucency which is like
  the ocean;
Its limpid reach and range with its surging in freedom is
  without dividing concepts and is spontaneously
  present.
To derive full benefit from it, have it reverberate in all
  modes of behavior.
Thereby wider perspective will quickly establish itself.

BIIb1biid Their unity is the reach and range which remains the
  same whether the cognitive capacity stirs or stays.
In both cases pristine cognitiveness with no concepts
  intruding is the primary feature.
Divestedness of the propositions about existence and
  non-existence is the attendant feature.

BIIb1biie By letting the concepts be as they come and stay in this
  reach and range,
They are free in their coming and they are alike in their
  being present.
Inner calm and wider perspective as vectors rise as
  bliss, lucency, and conceptlessness:
Thereness and openness, appropriate action and
  appreciative discrimination, Developing Stage and
  Fulfillment Stage come spontaneously.

BIIb1biif Once you have come across this unity, inner calm and
  wider perspective can be exercised separately,
And when depression and elation set in, wider
  perspective and inner calm have to be attended to
  respectively in order to repel these defects.

BIIb1biig The benefit that derives from this is that there arises a
  cognitive capacity open and lucent, divested of all
  propositions about it.

(As happens) by looking at the sky when one has turned
    one's back to the sun
At a time when the sky is bright and cloudless,

Outwardly, the clear sky serves as an example;   BIIb1biih
Inwardly, there is experience as experience, the real
    sky, larger than the former;
Mystically, there is the sky of the motive force (of Being
    which is) sheer lucency;
Know experienced Being to be structured as three skies.

The constituent of the facticity of Being, the realization   BIIc1
    of non-duality:
In the reach and range of absolute completeness where
    everything is the same by virtue of its being,
Do not reject and do not accept; dispel the desire to
    objectify;
Every desire to grasp it subjectively is a motivating
    force in the direction of fictitious being;
If there is no objectifying, there is neither bondage nor
    freedom, like the sky (unlimited and unrestrained).

Just like the various images and the surface of a mirror—   BIIc2
So are the various things and the openness of Being.

Just like the various clouds and the expanse of the sky—   BIIc3
So are the various affirmations and negations and
    Mind-as-such.

Just like the various rivers and the vastness of the ocean—   BIIc4
So are the various cognitive feelings and creative
    imagination.

Just like the various apparitions and the range of magic—   BIIc5
So are the various assertions of Saṃsāra and Nirvāṇa
    and the reach and range of experience qua
    experience.

BIIc6   Just like the sky in the ten regions and the spaciousness
            that has no ground beside itself—
        So are the things, free since all beginning, and the scope
            of their vision.
        Just like water poured into water is an expanse where
            no duality obtains—
        So is the reach and range in which mind and
            Mind-as-such are indivisible.

BIIb7   Just like the varied dreams and the span of sleep—
        So is the reach and range of one's actions in which the
            duality of acceptance and rejection does not obtain.
        Just like the ocean and its waves are the expanse of
            water—
        So is the reach and range in which the rising of concepts
            and the state of conceptlessness are the same.

BIIc8   Just like a successfully concluded business is the extent
            of pleasure—
        So, when hope and fear no longer obtain, there is
            the goal.
        Know the reach and range of completeness, the one
            overarching reality,
        To be experience qua experience, an all-encompassing
            continuum.

   c   Thus through the one-flavoredness of variety in unity
        All beings are set free from the notions of self and
            other, subject and object, and so
        May Mind, wearied and weakened in this world of
            fictitious being, deceived by its looking for the
            'this is it',
        Today find comfort and ease.

CHAPTER THIRTEEN

Meaningful Existence
and Existential Disclosure

*T*he quest for life's meaning reaches its completion in the realization and enactment of meaningful exist-ence (*sku*) which implies, as inseparable from it, a sensitivity to and discovery of meanings in lived-through experience (*ye-shes*). However, behind this short and man-ageable term 'meaningful existence' lies a complex struc-ture which can be circumscribed by the rather clumsy and yet more precise phrase of 'existence-as-a-thrust-towards-meaning-orientated-concreteness-in-lived-through-experi-ence'. The hyphens serve to indicate the close bond that holds in an interlacing manner between 'existence' and 'meaning' and 'experience', and also make it possible to grasp these configurative constituents more specifically without sacrific-ing the contextual frame.

'Existence', as used here, is neither a designation of that-ness nor a designation of finite existents in general. Rather it points to an open texture and dimension which in its very openness is already pregnant with possible meaning. 'Meaning' also is not something fixed once for all, but is an emerging, developing, and projective movement of the open dimension of existence, and acquires its full scope in lived-through experience. Since meaning is always meaning for someone, who yet never stands outside the configuration of lived experience, this circumstance points to the human being (or existent) who, in the search for 'meaningful existence'—for the meaning of (his) existence—cannot but start from the 'experience' of existence as the being he himself is. Such a starting point precludes any attempt to resort to such notions as 'substance' (which means different things to different persons, be they philosophers or lesser mortals), or 'particular existent', which is always meant to be a particular 'this' in contrast with some other particular 'that', and about which propositions are entertained as to the 'what' this particular existent is, be this 'what' then declared to be a substance or an essence.

The configuration 'existence-meaning-experience' is therefore not a category in the traditional sense. Its presentational and, at the same time, developing character directs attention to the 'how' rather than to the 'what', and it is this 'how' that introduces the dynamic character into what otherwise might be conceived as something static and lifeless. Moreover, this 'how' is presented in immediacy and is present as a kind of invitation to a response. The response is never mechanical, but always interpretive by virtue of lived-through experience. Presentational immediacy is already a situation open to interpretation. In its openness it is bound to the open texture of Being, and in its dynamic unfolding it is self-presenting, self-projective, and linked to interpretation which can take two different directions: the one, preserving cohesion, leads to 'meaningful existence'; the other, losing its anchorage, leads to 'fictitious being'. However, the important point to note is that 'existence-meaning-experience' is both configuration and process, and as such the constituents are throughout dialectically interpenetrating ontological features at work in every lived-through experience.

This configuration-process character of Being—an idea

characteristic of rDzogs-chen thought and a distinct contribution to Buddhist philosophy—is in terms of facticity described as 'unchanging' and 'indestructible', for which latter
term the symbol of the diamond (*vajra*) is used. In terms of
presentational presence it is described as a 'thrust towards
and invitation by limpid clearness and consummate perspicacity'; and in terms of experience, as 'calmness', which is
meaning-orientatedness and meaning-saturatedness in the
experiencer's concrete existence. Each of these three 'layers'
acts as a 'founding stratum' and they all are related to each
other by 'mutual foundedness'.

The first set of terms is used to make it clear that
throughout experience an element of facticity is already in
force which, negatively stated, implies that existence as existence can do nothing about its 'existing' and hence can
neither be subject to change (qualitatively) nor destroyed
(substantially). As facticity the open texture and open dimension of Being is in no way prejudged, contradicted, or
restricted. 'Thrust towards and invitation by limpid clearness
and consummate perspicacity' points to the projective character which is inseparable from open texture in facticity, and
in its presentational immediacy it preserves elements of this
open dimension and facticity and solicits a response to its
presence. 'Calmness' illustrates the response to the presentational immediacy of existence in experience which gives it
its specific 'meaning', that is 'calmness'. In the same way as
the projective feature of existence retains its open-dimensional character, so also 'meaning' is not merely a passive
resultant of the stimulus-response interaction. It, too, retains
the projective texture by opening up ways towards understanding. It is therefore obvious that this configuration-process complex, first of all, is not an object alongside other
objects (which in order to gain meaning would necessitate a
subject). Objectification is made possible by virtue of the
projective character of this configuration-process complex.

Secondly, it follows that this configuration-process complex also is not a subject in the manner of transcendental ego, be this of the Kantian or Husserlian variety, the one synthesizing the operation of perception, imagination, and conception, the other functioning as the ultimate source of intentional consciousness. The constitution of a subject emerges late and in conjunction with the process of objectification. Moreover, the subject-object structure which belongs to and underlies all forms of representational thinking as one possible direction, but certainly not the only possible one, into which interpretation can move, simply does not apply here.

When this configuration-process complex is stated to be a realm, a citadel, a reach and range for Victorious Ones, that is 'Buddhas' who in their multiplicity do not perceive each other, this is to reaffirm that the subject-object structure does not apply, and that the objectifiable figures—realm, citadel, Victorious Ones—are not isolated items within a representational scheme which is supposed to provide information about objects and subjects standing over and against each other in well-defined regions at determinable moments of time. Consequently, 'Buddha' cannot and must not be equated with an 'object' or a 'subject'. Rather as this configuration-process complex, 'Buddha' points to experience which makes the emergence and constitution of a subject-object determined world-horizon possible. In this primary sense 'Buddha' is a term that sums up what we would call the ontology and ontogenesis of experience, which from the outset is configurative, open-dimensional, dynamical, meaning-orientated and meaning-saturated, and includes the experiencer in whom it is concretely present and who in this phase is 'Buddha'. When in the interpretive analysis of experience the latter's existentially significant, embodying and embodied character is singled out and referred to as 'founding stratum of meaning' (*chos-sku*), where founding stratum is understood as the absoluteness of Being concretely experienced, knowing as a process of disclosure (*ye-shes*) is already at work.

It is from the dynamic and projective feature that there emerges the disclosure of a world which is not a totality of isolated entities, but an experienced life-world presented in and as a variety of life-styles. It is here that the configurative character of experience becomes ever more evident. Five constituents are distinguished which are indicated by the designations of place, time, teacher, message, and entourage. Again these must not be understood as isolated items—each constituent is vectorially joined to the other. The distinct mentioning of time and place (space) in connection with the dynamic aspect of Being abolishes a mechanistic conception of space and time as pre-existent entities, and shows that it is experience that occasions space (where representational thinking 'locates' its abstractions) and time (which representational thinking dissects into events 'located in' what is said to be time). Therefore, the experienced life-world constitutes its own space (which is not somewhere 'out there' nor somewhere 'in here') and its own time (which is not a succession of nows or a flow of postulated entities succeeding each other in an orderly fashion of coming to be and passing away). Further, the experienced life-world involves a being-with-others. This is to say that the self and the other are already co-present. Vairocana (subject, self) is with his entourage (object, other) and this being-with-others involves a transactional structure: action passes from the speaker (Vairocana or any other 'self' in this life-world) to the hearer (the 'other' in this life-world), and in the unfolding dialogue the hearer becomes speaker and the speaker becomes hearer and 'meanings' are exchanged. These meanings do not come from the outside to experience, but are embedded in and pervade this experience presenting itself as experienced life-world ('Og-min [Akaniṣṭha] or whichever other life-world emerges). The experienced life-world is thus a founding stratum (*sku*) that provides a world-horizon of such a kind that subject and object can appear and 'engage' in a 'dialogue' (*long-spyod*). But although in this configuration we may speak of the 'self' as the center of its circle formed by 'others' in a 'world' and, in the narrower sense, see in this center the 'founding stratum', this configuration is itself not yet determined by objectification and subjectification as they come into play by representational thinking. Rather this 'founding stratum of full engagement' (*longs-spyod rdzogs-pa'i sku*) provides the foundation for a specification of what is going to be subjective and what objective, present already in latent form, and for the 'how' of this engagement 'pictured' in peaceful and wrathful manifestations of the participants.

This points to a very important feature of experience. It has within itself both a prereflective and a reflective movement, each of which displays an organizational pattern of its own. The reflective movement remains part of the experience and occurs strictly within it. This, however, does not mean that reflection is a movement that turns back on itself. Rather, it is directed towards the configurative constituents of the experience and thus it considers what it finds in experience. In the experience of being engaged in a world-horizon, which may be considered as the prereflective level of the experience (although the reference to the 'teacher' and center already points to the contribution of reflected-on experience to the prereflective level), the configurative complex of the experience is as yet undisturbed by reflective discrimination. But the presence of the reflective movement initiates and occasions a semi-concretization of the configuration and its meaning, so that there then comes into existence a phase aptly termed 'a founding stratum of meaning taking concrete shape within the experiencer's world-horizon constituted by the dynamic stratum of Being' (*rang-bzhin sprul-pa'i sku*).

From here it is not far to the customary realm of representational thinking with its reification of the configurative constituents of lived-through experience into the concrete entities sharply demarcated from each other by the subject-object dichotomy, the subject an 'in here' and the object an 'out there'. Nevertheless, representational thinking retains some connection with non-representational thinking, and with the latter's concern for 'felt' meanings rather than 'abstracted' meanings. As two movements, representational and non-representational thinking feed on each other. Only from this interweaving of representational and non-representational, prereflective and reflective movements can we understand the 'founding strata of concrete embodiments and bearers of meaning' (*sprul-sku*) which are to be found in both the animate and inanimate worlds, constructs of representational thought. In the animate sector we can and do find persons who, being bearers of meaning themselves, can and do arouse us from our passivity and make us set out to find meaning, simply because 'meaning' radiates from them. Meeting someone—indeed, anyone—means something more important to our living in the world than the abstract statement that this someone is but a complex homeostatic biosystem. And the same applies to any 'object' in our environment, be it a natural or cultural one! The fire of a diamond means something more adequate to our perception than the scientific explanation of the diamond as a mineral in the native-element family that is composed of pure carbon, having a very high refractive power which gives it its extraordinary brilliance. The fragrance of a lotus flower or the flavor of an apple mean something more significant to our sense than their botanical and physiochemical explanations, and a home or a garden mean something more important to us than its definition in terms of architecture or ornamental design. Such analytical and reductive explanations have their validity in their restricted areas, where what is under discussion is merely represented by objectifying thought but not apprehended in its presential immediacy. Where man as a living being, not as a lifeless abstraction, is concerned, this immediacy is of primary importance because of its being and remaining relevant to his lived existence.

The diagram shows the interrelationship between the 'founding strata':[1]

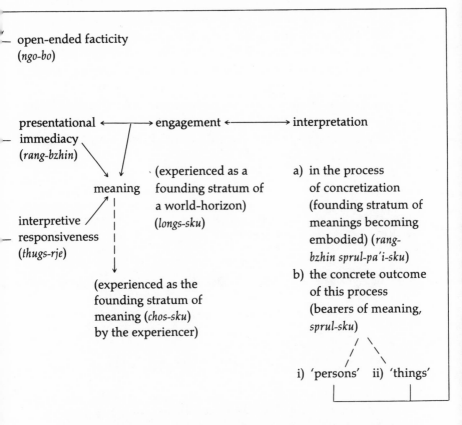

This very idea of ' "founding" strata of meanings(s)' (*sku*) involves the idea of ' "founded" cognitions of meaning(s)' (*ye-shes*), which is to say that active cognitions do not create their contents (or 'meanings'), but receive them ready-made from the 'founding' strata. Hence, the quest for life's meaning (*chos*) is possible because meaningfulness (*chos-nyid*) is already operative; but while the former needs the latter, the latter is independent of the former. The pervasive vectorial connections of the 'founding strata' in experience are also present in the 'founded cognitions'. Thus, the 'founded cognition' pertaining to the 'founding stratum of meaning' (*chos-sku*), because of its openness and purity, defies any attempt at verbalization or representation, while the 'founded cognitions' pertaining to the 'founding stratum of an engagement in world-horizons' (*long-sku*) carry with them the meanings of these horizons in their specific 'colorings'. Lastly, the 'founded cognitions' pertaining to the 'founding stratum of embodiments of meaning' (*sprul-sku*) exhibit the prereflective-nonthematic aspect and the reflective-thematic (configurative) aspect of lived-through experience. The 'foundedness' of pristine cognitions' can be shown diagrammatically as follows:[2]

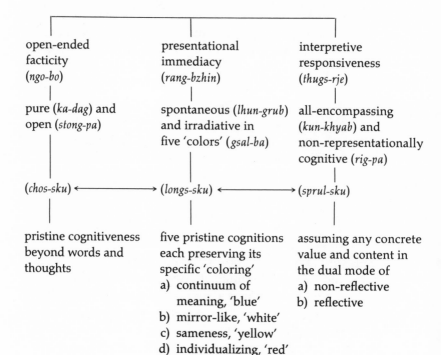

open-ended facticity (*ngo-bo*)	presentational immediacy (*rang-bzhin*)	interpretive responsiveness (*thugs-rje*)
pure (*ka-dag*) and open (*stong-pa*)	spontaneous (*lhun-grub*) and irradiative in five 'colors' (*gsal-ba*)	all-encompassing (*kun-khyab*) and non-representationally cognitive (*rig-pa*)
(*chos-sku*) ⟶	(*longs-sku*) ⟵	(*sprul-sku*)
pristine cognitiveness beyond words and thoughts	five pristine cognitions each preserving its specific 'coloring' a) continuum of meaning, 'blue' b) mirror-like, 'white' c) sameness, 'yellow' d) individualizing, 'red' e) accomplished, 'green'	assuming any concrete value and content in the dual mode of a) non-reflective b) reflective

A   W hen thus appropriate action and
     appreciative discrimination have reached
     their ultimate limits
The charismatic activity of meaningful existence and
     pristine cognitiveness spontaneously commences.

BI   When the mind and the mental events together with the
     ground of all and everything enter the continuum
     of pure experience and there completely come to
     rest, and
The continuum and its pristine cognitiveness are not
     two but have turned into one flavor,
Then there is the presence of the two purities[3] in which
     all propositions have come to rest.

BII   The reach and range of this thrust by sheer lucency that
     has no origin whatsoever
Is like the moon having set at the end of the month in
     the sky.
Its subtle pristine cognitiveness has become furled in its
     space-like continuum.
When there are no dividing concepts anywhere and
     calm has been obtained,

BIII1   To this aspect which since its very beginning has been
     pure and which is
Prereflectively experienced meaning, as yet
     unobjectified, not stepping out of itself or changing
     into something other than itself throughout time,
The name 'founding stratum of unchangeability and
     indestructibility'[4] is given.
It is the ultimate in prereflectively experienced meaning
     in which the 'ground-continuum' is all that is.

If you are requited with the transcending function of
    efficacy and so on,
Because you have gone to the ultimate limits of the
    capabilities of abandonment and of intrinsic
    understanding
Whereby the actuality of Being has been divested of its
    incidental obscurations
And the ocean of omniscience has been reached,
This aspect is labeled 'founding stratum of a thrust
    towards and solicitation by limpid clearness and
    consummate perspicacity'.[5]
This is the ultimate source from which the distinct
    Buddha qualities arise.

BIII2

Although in the presence of a cognizable object the
    intellect does not become involved with it and
Although in the cognizing intellect subjectively
    appropriating activity is not observed,
There persists this supreme, yet subtle pristine
    cognitiveness which like an inner lucency, not
    blotted out while having become latent, is
Like the moon having set in the sky; and it does
    so in the manner of being the factual source (of
    everything) because of its sensitivity to anything.
Since from it qualified sensitivities as founding strata of
    apprehendable meaning spread out, and
Since it is a treasure of qualities that are made to appear
    to others,
It is called 'founding stratum of meaning (present as)
    calmness'[6]
In view of its most subtle pristine cognitiveness being
    utterly calm.

BIII3a

These strata do not become objects of the external
    world and
Yet they are not non-existence; rather, because of their
    very subtleness

BIII3b

They are beyond the confines of the four alternatives
  offered by eternalism *a parte ante* and *a parte post.*
This reach and range of what lies beyond the above
  confines and about which words fail, even if one
  intended to speak of it,
Is an openness in which all objectifying tendencies have
  come to rest;
It is no realm for those who are not Victorious Ones.

BIII3c Although in the citadel of the continuum of pure
  experience that has never come into existence
  (as an entity)
The Buddhas of the three times are forever present,
The one does not see the other because each is
  prereflectively experienced meaning;
This is called 'to reside in natural profoundness and
  calmness'.
In this reach and range the Victorious Ones have one
  significance
In the same way as space is space regardless of whether
  it has once been occupied or is going to be occupied
  by a jar.

BIII3d This is the prereflectively experienced meaning,
  an open dimension in which appreciative
  discrimination and the accumulation of pristine
  cognitions and the Fulfillment Stage have reached
  their limits.

BIII4a Out of its reach and range there comes a
  self-manifested founding stratum of engagement in
  world-horizons
With the excellences of place, time, teacher, message,
  and entourage.

BIII4b1a The place is sheer lucency, the Ghanavyūha realm,
Sublime in its five-colored light, lucent and brilliant,

Just like a translucent and luminous rainbow filling the
  whole sky,
Extending over the whole range of the sky and into all
  directions,
This beautiful palace has four gates with pediments,
Five-layered walls and tiles and lattice work
And parapets and balustrades and eaves and
  waterspouts.[7]

Jeweled curtains, baldachins, yak-tails, garlands of   BIII4bib
  bells,
Canopies, banners and so on, filling the sky;
Clouds of goddesses, offering their adoration with what
  is desired,
Move forward and, surrounded by rays of light, cover
  the within and without.
In the center and at the four sides, decorations
  corresponding
In color, as well as other color schemes, have been
  arranged.
Their size is not determined but manifests itself as you
  look at them.
Their number is countless and they cover the whole
  space;
It is as if the shell of sesame seed has been broken
  open.

Within this palace there is (a throne supported by)   BIII4b1c
  lions, elephants, horses,
Peacocks, *shang-shang*, and (consisting of) sun and
  moon and lotus flower.[8]

The time is not a determinate event, but the ground   BIII4b2
  (Being-as-such) being complete and not altering
  (position) or changing.

Samantabhadra time, in which the three aspects of time
    are timeless,
The overruling prereflectively experienced meaning in
    which everything is complete and alike,
Is a reach and range pure in itself from the very
    beginning.

BIII4b3   The teacher aflame in his major and minor marks
Is (either) Vairocana (or) Akṣobhya (or) Ratnasambhava
    (or) Amitābha
(Or) Amoghasiddhi, each of these five surrounded by
    the other four.
With them is Ākāśadhātvīśvarī, Vajramāmakī,
Buddhalocanā, Pāṇḍaravāsinī, Samayatārā,
In close embrace, complete with all their ornaments.
Rays of blue, white, yellow, red, and green shoot forth:
Below, the peaceful aspects; high up, the angry ones.[9]
Buddha, Vajra, Ratna, Padmakara, Heruka-śrī—
Five in clusters of five—
With five Krodheśvarīs in union;
Words fail to describe them in detail.

BIII4b4   The message is the reach and range of absolute
    completeness,
An expanding center, about which words fail even if
    one intended to speak of it.

BIII4b5i   The entourage is the self-manifestation of none other
    than (the teacher) himself—
The eight 'heroes' and the eight 'heroines',
The four gate-keepers and the four gate-keeperesses.[10]
From among the forty-two peaceful aspects of oneness,
Six, because they manifest themselves to others,
    become founding strata of concrete embodiment
    and bearers of meaning,[11]

Two, because they stay in the continuum of pure
  experience, remain the founding stratum of
  meaning;[12]
Peaceful in their self-manifestation, the (remaining)
  thirty-four are the founding stratum of engagement
  in a world-horizon,[13] and
The specific entourage is twenty-four.[14]

The angry entourage are the eight wrathful females, BIII4b5ii
  Kaurima and Semha and the rest,
The four guardians of the gates, and the twenty-eight
  lords.
From among the fifty-eight angry forms[15]
Forty-eight make up the specific entourage,
Wearing flaming emblems, showing their terrifying
  teeth,
And performing their dances, utterly unendurable.

There are as many self-manifesting founding strata of BIII4b6
  engagement
As there are body-patterned maṇḍalas,
But all the peaceful and angry forms that are visible
  to others
Are founding strata of concrete embodiment and
  bearers of meaning;
They are not the self-manifesting founding stratum of
  engagement.

Since all these five excellences BIII4b7
Are self-manifesting, they are neither good nor evil.
From all of them rays in brilliance and abundance shine
  forth—
Shimmering, glimmering, glittering.[16]
They are the realms of the leaders (of mankind) where
The one looking at the other extols the other's fame.

BIII4b8   These beautiful realms that are everywhere set up,
Cannot be seen even by the most refined beings.

BIII4b9   As unimaginable as is self-manifesting openness as
formedness,
So is the self-manifestation of the Victorious Ones of
the three aspects of time.

BIII4c1   Out of this reach and range there come into the world
of those who are to be trained
Teachers who will train them, in this order:
The teacher as the founding stratum of meaning taking
concrete shape, the training teacher, and the
variegated world as teacher.
In these three forms (Being) acts (as teacher) on behalf
of living beings.

BIII4c2i   The teacher as the founding stratum of meaning taking
concrete shape
Is any of the five exemplars such as Vairocana,
Akṣobhya and so on,
In the five realms of 'Og-min, mNgon-dga', dPal-ldan,
Padma-brtsegs, and Las-rab grub-pa.[17]
In arising in countless peaceful and angry forms
Through flaming rays that are their major and minor
marks,
Such teachers act spontaneously for the bitendential
value of Being[18] applying to living beings.

BIII4c2iia   Moreover, (each form of the teacher) has five kinds of
pristine cognitions:
A cognition that remains in and as the continuum of
pure experience;
A cognition that is (receptive) like a mirror;
A cognition that (is cognizant of) sameness;

A cognition that is individual experiencing;
And a cognition that is (self-)accomplished.
Four form the entourage of each one, and
They are the reach and range in which everything has
    one flavor in its alikeness.

The cognition that remains in and as the continuum of   BIII4c2iib1
    pure experience is absolutely unshakeable—
It is beyond all limitations by propositions
    engendered by the subject-object framework
    (of representational thought).

The mirror-like cognition, lucent and open, is like a   BIII4c2iib2
    source—
It is the birthplace of all other forms of cognition.

The sameness cognition is the reach and range in which   BIII4c2iib3
    all that is remains alike in its being—
It is the absolute completeness of the alikeness of
    Saṃsāra and Nirvāṇa as not being two separate and
    contesting entities.

The individualizing cognition knows everything in its   BIII4c2iib4
    distinctness—
It is seeing things as they are and as they are related to
    each other.

The cognition that knows what is to be as it should be   BIII4c2iib5
    is most excellent charismatic activity—
(It never is stuck with all that can be known).[19]

The entourage consisting of those to be trained, are   BIII4c2iii
    those of the ten spiritual levels;
The message is a holistic experience saturated with
    light rays.
Then mind cleansed of the (respective) obscurations of
    these levels is born,

Jealousy and the other obscurations are given up, and
    the Victorious Ones are seen.
The obscurations are removed when you see your own
    specific obscuration (in contrast with)
The purity of these teachers,
And you are established on the level of 'Light
    Everywhere'.
It is a (charismatic activity) like a beautiful figure before
    a mirror.

BIII4c2iv   The time does not stop until the living beings are free,
    and
In the realms pertaining to the founding stratum of
    engagement in world-horizons it is perpetually
    presenting itself.

BIII4c2va   Although every being certainly belongs to one of the
    five life-style patterns,
It is only when the thick darkness engulfing the trainees
    is removed
That the realm 'Og-min, the teacher Vairocana,
And the message, the cognitiveness in and as the
    continuum of pure experience, are disclosed.

BIII4c2vb   In the same way, by removal of hatred there is
    Akṣobhya's realm,
Of arrogance, Ratnasambhava's, of cupidity,
    Amitābha's,
Of envy, Amoghasiddhi's.

BIII4c2via   Since in the realm pertaining to the teacher as the
    founding stratum of engagement in world-horizons
His entourage and the other constituents are other than
    the teacher,
Not everything is engagement in a world-horizon and
    therefore
A semi-concrete movement becomes the founding

stratum of concrete embodiments and bearers of
meaning;
Since this does not take place for others who are not on
the (above) spiritual levels,
(This movement) is termed a semi-apparent founding
stratum of embodiments and bearers of meaning.

These realms (where they occur) are alike in their   BIII4c2v
layout as a beautiful palace,
Built of seven jewels with light rays shining in the ten
directions;
With countless Buddha-sons born from lotus flowers;
A rain of all the things that one desires, falling;
In the four times the peal of the clear presentation of
the message resounding;
And beautified by oceans of wish-fulfilling trees and
gems—
These are the founding strata of semi-concrete
embodiments and bearers of meaning in peaceful
forms.

In the same way there are infinite maṇḍalas of wrathful   BIII4c2vi
forms (which are)
The home of the aerial spirits from which clouds of
Ḍākas and Ḍākinīs emanate.
These realms of the five exemplars (beginning with)
Heruka-śrī,
Clearly appear to those who are mystics.
This today is said to be 'traveling over the expanse
of bliss',
Praised by sages and saints.

Out of this reach and range there come the founding   BIII4c3i
strata of concrete embodiments and bearers of
meaning to train the beings
And appear in the six kinds of life-forms as their
respective teachers:

Indra, Avarala, Śākyamuni, Senge-ge-brtan,
Jvālamukha-deva, Ava-glang-mgo-se.
These six 'puissants'[20] individually purify
The existential make-up of the six kinds of beings.

BIII4c3ii These six primary bearers of meaning
Have further inconceivable bearers of meaning;
Even in the realms of the gods, in each of their
    locations, from
The Brahma and Śiva abodes up to the Akaniṣṭha
    realm,
They appear as teachers to each of them respectively.

BIII4c3iii In the human world wherever there is someone to be
    trained, there they appear;
In manifesting themselves as Śrāvakas,
    Pratyekabuddhas, Bodhisattvas,
Kings and so on, they train human beings;
Also in the realm of the demigods they do so;
Among the animals they appear as birds to the birds,
And among the deer as lions and so on.
Training each, the teachers are inconceivable.
So also among the spirits and in the world of the
    denizens of hell
They act in a shape appropriate to them.

BIII4c3via These trainers of living beings have two kinds of
    pristine cognition,
The one that is sensitive to what there is in its is-ness
    and the one that is sensitive to interrelationships.
Not mixing prereflectively experienced meaning and
    the reflected-on meaning, but
Being aware of them in their distinctness, they deal with
    the bitendential value of Being applying to[21] those
    to be trained.

BIII4c3ivb The cognition that is sensitive to the what-there-is in its

is-ness is sensitive to the open dimension (of Being
and experience),
And teaches beings the meaning of coming to rest;
The cognition that is sensitive to interrelationships is
sensitive to the working of the mind and the
intellectual capacities,
And, being aware of their difference, it teaches infinite
methods.

This is (the teacher) appearing before unpurified beings.   BIII4c3v
His realm is the world of the six forms of beings;
The teacher is his appearance according to their ideas;
The message is to various spiritual careers which are
indeterminate (as to which is for whom);
And the time is the one similar to a kalpa of these
beings.

Thus these six worlds of the six kinds of beings   BIII4c3vi
Are the variety of karmic actions and the tendencies
towards them, with good and evil as cause and effect
bringing about their
Happiness and sorrow, heights and depths.
The six teachers also are but appearances before the
minds of living beings.
Just as in a dream there may be Buddhas and ordinary
beings,
Pure as to facticity but impure as to observable quality,
These various appearances have come as the play of
compassionate response.

This is the magic of limitless compassion; and   BIII4c3vii
As long as the world lasts, its charismatic activity is not
stopped.

From this reach and range there come various other   BIII4c4i
embodiments and bearers of meaning
Appearing in the form of inanimate material things;

Paintings, relief-pictures, natural monuments,
Scriptures and places of worship,
Lotus flowers, fruit trees, parks,
Elegant houses and pleasure groves,
Caravanseries, ships, and bridges,
Lamps, jewels, food, clothes, carriages and so on.
In these material forms that help people in many ways
    (the teacher) is present.

BIII4c4ii   Having, for the time being, created pleasing and
    pleasurable places,
In the end, by setting them on the road to peace
Through these various bearers of meaning, the welfare
    of beings is spontaneously assured.

C   If there is none to be trained the trainer disappears,
The self-manifesting founding stratum of engagement
    in world-horizons submerges in the founding
    stratum of meaning.
If there is no vessel the reflection of the moon in its
    water disappears in the sky.
It is through the power of its phases that the moon
    disappears,
Just as when at the end of the (lunar) month the moon is
    neither waxing nor waning.
If there is someone to be trained, the manifestations
    come about as before.
This is the goal spontaneously present.

D   Thus through this sublime inner peace
May all living beings encounter the continuum of
    Mind, sheer lucency,
And wearied and weakened by the pollution of the evil
    that is the belief in fictitious being and passive
    quietude as ultimates,
May Mind today find comfort and ease.

By this copious rain of inner peace and bliss
From the clouds of merits which are this
    dissertation,
May prosperity of the beings in the three regions grow
And thus the Buddha's richness be spontaneously
    available.

Nowadays people whose intellectual eyesight is
    dimmed
Hold the paths followed by the Tantras and the Sūtras
To contradict each other, and do not know how to
    combine them;
Therefore, they have but a partial view.

In O-rgyan-rdzong in Gangs-ri thod-dkar,
I, Dri-med 'od-zer, have composed
This manual for study, in which I have combined
The excellent and profound meanings of both the
    cause-orientated and the goal-sustained spiritual
    pursuits.

Through this good work may all sentient beings in the
    world
Without exception reach the glorious citadel of inner
    peace,
And may the unity of meaningful existence and pristine
    cognitiveness
In all directions and for all times spread its blessings.

Appendices

APPENDIX

The Thirty-seven
Facets of Self-growth

These thirty-seven facets of self-growth are divided according to the Five Paths, which follow a developmental progression from I to V.

I. The Preparatory Stage (*tshogs-lam*)
   A. Low level:
      The four applications of attentiveness (*dran-pa nyer-bzhag bzhi*) to:
      1. the physical world (*lus*)
      2. the world of feeling (*tshor-ba*)
      3. the world of the mind (*sems*)
      4. the world of concepts and meanings (*chos*)
   B. Intermediate level:
      The four renunciations (*yang-dag-par spong-ba bzhi*):
      5. to prevent that which is unwholesome from coming to power
      6. to leave behind all that is unwholesome
      7. to let all that is wholesome come to power

8. to increase all that is wholesome
   Each facet involves:
   - a) willingness to do so (*'dun-pa*)
   - b) eagerness to do so (*'bad-pa*)
   - c) perseverance in doing so
     (*brtson-'grus*)
   - d) keeping the mind in check
     (*sems rab-tu 'dzin-pa*)
   - e) having the mind firmly settled
     (*sems rab-tu 'jog-pa*)

C. High level: ˙

The four footholds for higher forms of cognition
(*rdzu-'phrul rkang-pa bzhi*):

9. holistic experience (*ting-nge-'dzin*) through willingness
   (*'dun-pa*)
10. holistic experience (*ting-nge-'dzin*) through perseverance
    (*brtson-pa*)
11. holistic experience (*ting-nge-'dzin*) through intentiveness
    (*sems-pa*)
12. holistic experience (*ting-nge-'dzin*) through discursiveness
    (*dpyod-pa*)

Each holistic experience may be:

Hampered by:	Countered by:
a) laziness (*le-lo*)	i) willingness to counter it (*'dun-pa*)
	ii) confidence (*dad-pa*)
	iii) sustained effort (*brtson-'grus*)
	iv) refinement (*shin-tu sbyang-ba*)
b) forgetfulness (*brjed-byang*)	v) attentiveness (*dran-pa*)
c) elation-depression (*bying-rgod*)	vi) cognitive alertness (*shes-bzhin*)
d) lack of motivation (*'du mi byed-pa*)	vii) intentiveness (*sems-pa*)
e) over-motivatedness (*'du-byed-pa*)	viii) equanimity (*btang-snyoms*)

II. The Link-up Stage (*sbyor-lam*)

    A. The tentative phase:

        i) warmth ("warming up")   }   13. confidence (*dad-pa*)

        ii) its maximum level   14. sustained effort
                                        (*brtson-'grus*)

                                  15. attentive inspection
                                          (*dran-pa*)

                                  16. holistic experience(s)
                                          (*ting-nge-'dzin*)

                                  17. appreciative
                                          discrimination
                                          (*shes-rab*)
                                          (As 'powers', these
                                          five initiate processes
                                          of refinement.)

    B. The decisive phase:

        iii) acceptance   }

        iv) supreme moment   18–22

                                  (The same five
                                  as above, but
                                  as 'strengths' which
                                  overcome all that
                                  impedes the link-up
                                  with the Stage of
                                  Seeing.)

III. The Stage of Seeing (*mthong-lam*)

    Corresponding to the first spiritual level of Pure Joy.

    The seven adjuncts to limpid clearness and consummate
    perspicacity:

        23. attentive inspection (*dran-pa*)

        24. investigation of meanings and values
            (*chos rab-rnam-'byed*)

        25. sustained effort (*brtson-'grus*)

        26. joy (*dga'-ba*)

        27. refinement and serenity (*shin-tu sbyang-ba*)

        28. holistic experience(s) (*ting-nge-'dzin*)

        29. equanimity (*btang-snyoms*)

IV. The Stage of Cultivation (*sgom-lam*)

Extending from the second to the tenth spiritual level reflecting a low level (2, 3, 4), intermediate level (5, 6, 7), and high level of refinement (8, 9, 10).

The noble eightfold Path:

30. right view (*yang-dag-pa'i lta-ba*)

31. right conception (*yang-dag-pa'i rtogs-pa*)

32. right speech (*yang-dag-pa'i ngag*)

33. right action (*yang-dag-pa'i las-kyi mtha'*)

34. right living (*yang-dag-pa'i 'tsho-ba*)

35. right exertion (*yang-dag-pa'i rtsol-ba*)

36. right attentiveness (*yang-dag-pa'i dran-pa*)

37. right kind of holistic experience
     (*yang-dag-pa'i ting-nge-'dzin*)

V. The Stage of No-more Learning (*mi-slob-lam*)

The eleventh spiritual level, 'Light Everywhere', or the level of Buddhahood.

Notes

NOTES TO INTRODUCTION

1) In his *Zab-mo yang-tig*, part Wam, p. 201, Klong-chen rab-'byams-pa explicitly states that his teacher Kumaradza is a manifestation of Vimalamitra.

2) Klong-chen rab-'byams-pa himself gives this date at the end of his *Bum-thang lha'i sbas-yul-gyi bkod-pa-la bsngags-pa me-tog skyed-tshal*, a poem about the beauty of Bum-thang.

3) He seems to have been a contemporary and disciple of Klong-chen rab-'byams-pa. His work bears the title: *Kun-mkhyen Dri-med 'od-zer-gyi rnam-thar mthong-ba don-ldan*.

4) According to the names he uses at the end of his works, three major phases can be distinguished: his youthful writings under the name Tshul-khrims blo-gros; his subsequent writings under the names sNa-tshogs rang-grol Klong-chen rab-'byams-pa or bSam-yas-pa Ngag-gi dbang-po or sNa-tshogs rang-grol; and his mature writings under the name Dri-med 'od-zer.

5) *Kun-mkhyen Klong-chen rab-'byams-pa'i gsung-rab mdzod-bdun-la blta-bar bskul-ba*, p. 154.

6) These are the most widespread theoretical and practical aspects of Tibetan Buddhism. Mādhyamika epistemology and Pāramitā ethics developed in India, so did the Mahāmudrā mysticism among the Mahāsiddhas. Both the gCod-yul and the Zhi-byed go back to Indian teachers, but these forms were more distinctly developed by the Tibetans themselves. The gCod-yul is related to Dam-pa sangs-rgyas, alias Pha-dam-pa, a man from South India, who visited Tibet several times beginning in 1092 and who died in 1117. The most prominent representative of this form of Buddhism was the remarkable woman, Ma-gcig Labs sgron-ma (1055–1149). The Zhi-byed form also derives from Dam-pa sangs-rgyas. George N. Roerich, *The Blue Annals*, vol. 2, pp. 867 ff.

7) The following order is given according to rDza dPal-sprul O-rgyan 'Jigs-med chos-kyi dbang-po in his eulogy of these works.

8) *Padma dkar-po*, p. 41.

9) Klong-chen rab-'byams-pa wrote a guide to contemplation on this work, the *Yid-bzhin-mdzod-kyi don-khrid zab-don rdo-rje snying-po*. A condensed presentation of the philosophical systems that developed among the Buddhists, on the basis of the *Yid-bzhin-mdzod* and its commentary, was prepared by Mi-pham 'Jam-dbyang rnam-rgyal rgya-mtsho (1846–1912) under the title *Yid-bzhin-mdzod-kyi grub-mtha' bsdus-pa* (translated into English by H. V. Guenther, *Buddhist Philosophy in Theory and Practice*, Penguin Books, 1971). Mi-pham also prepared a structural analysis of the basic work, the *Yid-bzhin-mdzod-kyi sa-bcad bsdus-sdom Kumuda'i phreng-ba*, and a kind of commentary on problems in the presentation of the traditional Buddhist systems, the *Yid-bzhin rin-po-che'i mdzod-kyi dka'-gnad ci-rigs gsal-bar byed-pa*.

10) These works are essentially of a contemplative nature and complement the *Ngal-gso skor-gsum*. Their titles are:

rDzogs-pa chen-po Sems-nyid rang-grol,
rDzogs-pa chen-po Chos-nyid rang-grol,
rDzogs-pa chen-po mNyam-nyid rang-grol.

Each work has a commentary, the *'Od-kyi 'khor-lo,* the *'Od-kyi snye-ma,* and the *'Od-kyi dra-ba,* as well as a guidance summary, the *Chos-sku rang-shar,* the *Chos-sku rang-babs,* and the *Chos-sku lhun-grub,* respectively. All these works seem to have been lost. Only the guidance to the general meaning of the three works, the *rDzogs-pa chen-po Sems-nyid rang-grol-gyi lam-rim snying-po'i don-khrid* together with its litany, the *Sems-nyid rang-grol gsol-'debs,* the *rDzogs-pa chen-po chos-nyid rang-grol-gyi don-khrid Yid-bzhin snying-po,* and the *rDzogs-pa chen-po mnyam-nyid rang-grol-gyi don-khrid Rin-chen snying-po* are still available. The first work in the trilogy, *rDzogs-pa chen-po Sems-nyid rang-grol,* has been translated into English as "The Natural Freedom of Mind" (H. V. Guenther, *Crystal Mirror,* 1975, 4, 113–46).

11) rDza dPal-sprul O-rgyan 'Jigs-med chos-kyi dbang-po has utilized and expanded this work by inserting the beginning of the respective verses. This summary bears the title: *Sems-nyid ngal-bso'i* (sic!) *bsdus-don Pad-ma dkar-po'i zil-mngar.*

12) P. 93.

13) Ibid., p. 102.

14) Ibid., p. 103.

15) This is the *Chos thams-cad rdzogs-pa chen-po byang-chub-kyi sems kun-byed rgyal-po* (in *rNying-ma rgyud-'bum,* vol. 1, pp. 1 ff), one of the earliest Tantras translated by Vairocana, the foremost Tibetan representative of the *sems-sde* (mentalistic) interpretation of the rDzogs-chen teaching. Klong-chen rab-'byams-pa, following Vairocana's interpretation of the translation, wrote a guide to its meaning, the *Byang-chub-kyi sems kun-byed rgyal-po'i don-khrid rin-chen gru-bo.* It bears the signature Klong-chen rab-'byams-pa and thus belongs to his earlier writings. The quotation given here is more of a summary than the exact passage which, on p. 25, reads:

There is nothing that is not complete here.

> One—complete; two—complete, (and) since all is
>   complete,
> Acts are bliss in their excellence.
> One—complete: complete in mind as limpid clearness and
>   consummate perspicacity;
> Two—complete: complete in being made by mind;
> All—complete: complete in excellence.

This exact passage is quoted by Klong-chen rab-'byams-pa
in his *sDe-gsum snying-po'i don-'grel gnas-lugs-rin-po-che'i mdzod*,
p. 37, but in his *Grub-pa'i mtha' rin-po-che'i mdzod*, p. 331 f, he
gives the following version:

> One—complete: two—complete: in mind complete;
> One—complete: complete in being made by mind;
> Two—complete: complete in excellence;
> All—complete: complete in mind in limpid clearness and
>   consummate perspicacity,

and he offers the following explication:

> Here, 'made by mind' means: all that is subsumed under
> the headings of the psychophysical constituents, the ele-
> mental actional fields, and the spread of the sensory activ-
> ities, all of which comes as the world as a 'container' and
> the living beings as the 'essence' in it, together with all their
> manifestations and possibilities (the fictions about them) as
> Saṃsāra, (felt and judged as) 'impure', as well as vision,
> attention to the vision, enactment of the vision, claimed to
> be the starting-point, the path, and the goal of the spiritual
> pursuits—all are deceptive creations by the experientially
> initiated potentialities of experience ingrained in the mind
> (*sems*). That is to say, they are incidental artifacts made by
> the mind as a craftsman. Since they do not exist as such,
> although they seem to be quite real because they are pres-
> ent as a deceptive presence to an (equally) deceptive agent
> (trying to) grasp them, they are complete because they have
> never moved out of the reach and range that is a self-exis-
> tent pristine cognitiveness (*ye-shes*).
>   'Complete in excellence' means: the facticity of the
> self-existent pristine cognitiveness, a sheer lucency, in be-
> ing an utter openness, is the founding stratum of meaning;

its actuality, in being radiance, is the founding stratum of an engagement in a world-horizon of meaning; and its responsiveness, in its being pure awareness, is the founding stratum of embodied meanings. Since the three founding strata have been complete in their own right from a beginning without a beginning, there is completeness in the fact that they have not to be sought for and set up elsewhere.

'Complete in mind as limpid clearness and consummate perspicacity' means: all that makes its presence felt, be it the 'pure' or 'impure', in its presentation and in the fictions about it, is gathered within the reach and range of self-existent pristine cognitiveness, its root, and arises from it, and stays in it. It does so in the same way as a person's sleep and the various dream images are contained within the reach and range of his psychic life, arise from it, and are founded on it. Hence there is completeness in Mind-as-such (*sems-nyid*)—the mind is limpid clearness and consummate perspicacity (*byang-chub-kyi sems*). Moreover, since the mind (*sems*) as conceptuality, has come from a stratum of all sorts in eight perceptual patterns, it is a pollution that has to be cleaned up. What is termed 'mind in limpid clearness and consummate perspicacity', 'mind-as-such', 'sheer lucency', 'mind's excellence', 'conceptless pristine cognition', 'continuum of experience', 'founding stratum of meaning', 'ultimate reality', 'just this', 'absolute completeness', must be taken as pure fact in the ultimate sense of the word—and it is what one has to concern oneself with as the thrust towards limpid clearness and consummate perspicacity which is the very self-existent pristine cognitiveness (of Being).

There are other interpretations of 'absolute completeness' within rDzogs-chen thought, but within the framework of the *Sems-nyid ngal-gso* this one serves the context.

16) Saraha, *Dohākośa*. This is one of the most frequently quoted aphoristic verses of Saraha.

17) Calvin O. Schrag, *Experience and Being*, p. 47.

18) *Ngal-gso skor-gsum-gyi spyi-don legs-bshad rgya-mtsho*, pp. 94 ff. In

this passage the quotation from other works in support of his interpretation have been left out as they do not add substantially to Klong-chen rab-'byams-pa's argument.

NOTES TO CHAPTER ONE

1) *dpal kun-tu bzang-po.* In his *Ngal-gso skor-gsum-gyi spyi-don legs-bshad rgya-mtsho*, p. 104, Klong-chen rab-'byams-pa explains this term to mean in the context of the present work: "*dpal*—a pristine cognition into which no duality enters; *kun-tu bzang-po*—from which the good for others spreads forth because of its being everywhere adorned with infinite capabilities that are profound and vast."

2) *gdod-ma'i mgon-po.* Despite the anthropomorphic diction, in rDzogs-chen thought this term refers to the unity of structure and function. When, therefore, in his *Shing-rta chen-po*, p. 117, Klong-chen rab-'byams-pa equates this 'Lord rediscovering his limpid clearness and consummate perspicacity in the absoluteness of Being' with the Exalted Teacher (Buddha), he indicates that Buddha, even when seen as a living organism, is the expression of an orderly functioning process, though, on the other hand, this process is sustained by underlying structures and organizing patterns. The presence of these structures and patternings in each living being, variously termed *gdod-ma'i sangs-rgyas* 'beginningless primordial Buddha', or *gdod-ma'i mgon-po* 'beginningless primordial Lord', and qualified as *'od mi-'gyur-ba* 'unchanging lucency', is discussed by Klong-chen rab-'byams-pa in his *mKha'-'gro yang-tig*, part 2 (Ah), pp. 194 ff. Inasmuch as the *gdod-ma'i mgon-po* is 'in' us, he comes essentially as a presentation of a 'felt experience' in all its intimacy and immediacy and he has no separate ontological status. Neither is 'he' imposed on us as passive receptors, nor is 'he' the arbitrary product of our fancies; rather, 'he' is the outcome of man's persistent attempt to give meaning to his experience.

3) *yon-tan.* According to *Zab-mo yang-tig*, part Wam, pp. 221 ff, these are 'creativity' (*rtsal*), 'adornment' (*rgyan*), and 'playfulness' (*rol-pa*).

4) *mkhyen-pa*. This is the capacity for knowing immediately through seeing or perceiving unrestrictedly, particularly in the sense of a sensitivity to perceptual experience, so as to understand the meaningfulness of whatever there is. See also the following note.

5) *brtse-ba*. This is the capacity for expressing one's softer emotions with delicacy and gentleness. While *mkhyen* is 'cognitive', *brtse* is 'affective'. The former has to do with 'topics' (*shes-bya*), the latter with 'living beings' (*sems-can*). See Klong-chen rab-'byams-pa's *Padma-dkar-po*, p. 5.

6) *'od-gsal*. The vibrant source of experience, ever present in the experience and preceding the objectifying tendency of empiricism and the subjectifying tendency of idealism in philosophy. It is more or less identical with *sems-nyid*. See *Shing-rta rnam-par dag-pa*, pp. 38 f; *Ngal-gso skor-gsum-gyi spyi-don legs-bshad rgya-mtsho*, p. 103.

7) *chos-sku*. To attempt anything resembling a full interpretation of this term, would necessitate the space of an encyclopedia. Underlying the formulation of this term is the experience of the 'meaning of Being' (*chos*) as inseparable, and aesthetically indistinguishable, from the perception of its 'stratum' (*sku*), where 'stratum' is not an object of the physical sciences but that which is known and felt in perception, and where 'meaning' is something emerging *by virtue of* experience and discovered *in* experience. In his *Lung-gi gter-mdzod*, p. 132a, Klong-chen rab-'byams-pa defines *chos* as 'facticity' and *sku* as 'support for it' and quotes from the *sGra thal-'gyur-ba*, (in *rNying-ma rgyud-'bum*, vol. 10, p. 473), which says that *chos* is 'the proper path' and *sku* 'that which comes from its pursuance'. But then, in the same work, p. 197a, he explains *chos* as the openness, lucency, and absoluteness of Being for which one ultimately strives and *sku* as the continuum of Being or the 'stratum' which serves as the foundation for all existential and cognitive experiences. In his *rNam-mkhyen shing-rta*, p. 657, 'Jigs-med gling-pa combines both definitions given by Klong-chen rab-'byams-pa.

Still another interpretation is given by Klong-chen rab-'byams-pa in his *Tshig-don rin-po-che'i mdzod*, p. 455: "*chos* is the openness-lucency (of Being) having the two kinds of purity and being beyond determinate qualities; *sku* means that (Being) does not step out of itself or turn into anything other than itself." The two kinds of purity are detailed by Klong-chen rab-'byams-pa in his *Bla-ma yang-tig*, part E, p. 503: "Since the actuality of this continuum of Being in experience has never been felt to have had any contamination in it since its beginningless beginning, it is 'pure as to its actuality'; and since it remains pure from the contamination by the tendencies leading towards Saṃsāra, together with the eight perception-patterns in the wake of the (emergence of the) ground of all and everything, all being but incidental contaminations, when, in addition, its actuality is knowingly experienced, it is 'pure as to the incidental (contaminations)'." In other words, Being-Experience remains, or is, unaffected by any forms or contents it may assume or hold.

As a 'founding stratum', *sku* is intimately related to the 'founded' (*ye-shes*; on this term as used in rDzogs-chen thought, see note 18). This relationship between a 'founding stratum' (*rten* or, more specifically, *sku*) and the 'founded' (*brten* or *ye-shes*), so significant for rDzogs-chen thought and elaborated by Klong-chen rab-'byams-pa in his many works (notably his *Theg-pa'i mchog rin-po-che'i mdzod*, vol. 2, pp. 23 ff; *Grub-pa'i mtha' rin-po-che'i mdzod*, pp. 228 ff) is suggestive of the same problem in modern phenomenology. For a lucid discussion of this problem, first noticed in Western philosophy by E. Husserl, see Richard M. Zaner, *The Way of Phenomenology: Criticism as a Philosophical Discipline*, pp. 169 ff.

8) *rgyal-ba'i khams.* In his *rNam-mkhyen shing-rta*, p. 801, 'Jigs-med gling-pa defines this term more specifically as "a pristine cognition sensitive to the facticity of Being in view of the fact that Being as a continuum (i.e., a dynamic field of experience, *dbyings*) exists as inner lucency, ever present to be experienced individually". Inasmuch as the facticity of Being (*ngo-bo*) is nowhere else than in its own presential and presentational form (*rnam-pa*), this pristine cognition is also sensitive to the endless forms of Being, that is, to all the observable qualities of all that is. In its former aspect it is called *ji-lta-ba mkhyen-pa'i*

ye-shes and in its latter *ji-snyed mkhyen-pa'i ye-shes*. A detailed analysis of these terms is found in Klong-chen rab-'byams-pa's *Tshig-don rin-po-che'i mdzod*, pp. 476 ff.

9) *ma-rig-pa*. In rDzogs-chen thought it refers to the loss of the optimum level of excitation and a simultaneous dimming of the lucency of *rig-pa*—'pure awareness' in terms of epistemology, 'energetic charge' in terms of the dynamics of a living organism.

10) *srid-pa*. It exists only as that which makes itself felt in a state of having gone astray through taking something to be the case when it is not. In his *bDen-gnyis gsal-byed zla-ba'i sgron-me*, p. 45, Yon-tan rgya-mtsho says: "*srid-pa*, because it exists merely as a presence where there has occurred a straying away from Being." In *Bi-ma snying-thig*, vol. I, p. 110, *srid-pa* is explained as the belief in an I and mine. Its fictitiousness, because it derives from what has no foundation, is elaborated by Klong-chen rab-'byams-pa in his *Theg-pa'i mchog rin-po-che'i mdzod*, vol. I, p. 443.

11) According to *Shing-rta chen-po*, pp. 120 ff:

Where there is a small amount of unwholesomeness involved and actions are characterized by dullness, birth among beasts takes place; where there is a medium amount of unwholesomeness involved and actions are characterized by desirousness, birth among spirits takes place; where there is a large amount of unwholesomeness involved and actions are characterized by hatred, birth among denizens of hell takes place. Where wholesomeness and meritoriousness tempered by arrogance is involved, birth among gods and men takes place, and where wholesomeness and meritoriousness is tempered by envy, birth among demigods takes place. There each being is engrossed in his respective life-form with its pleasures, sorrows, indifference, healthy and unhealthy actions; drifts about helplessly in this desert of fictitious being, so difficult to cross, having neither a beginning nor an end; and the belief in what is meaningless and unreal as an I or a self is like the presence of a dream. Although when properly investigated it is not something existing in itself, still as long as this state of having gone astray persists it seems to be quite real and well-established.

12) *sems-nyid*, translated here as Mind (with capital letter), is cognitive absoluteness, not what is ordinarily termed *a* or *the* mind, which is termed *sems*. *Bla-ma yang-tig*, part Wam, p. 13; *Theg-pa'i mchog rin-po-che'i mdzod*, vol. I, pp. 437 f, 625 f. Nevertheless, as Klong-chen rab-'byams-pa points out in his *Ngal-gso skor-gsum-gyi legs-bshad rgya-mtsho*, p. 103, this cognitive absoluteness is nowhere else taken hold of than in *sems*, the noetic-noematic structure of representational thought, and in its specific operations, *sems-byung*. See also note 17.

13) In his *bDen-gnyis gsal-byed zla-ba'i sgron-me*, p. 32, Yon-tan rgya-mtsho quotes from the *Nam-mkha' rin-po-che'i mdo*: "Exalted One, how do we have to view a unique occasion (*dal*) and the right juncture (*'byor*)? The Exalted One answered: If the mind is divided by concepts, it is agitated and this means to be engaged in all sorts of projects-at-hand. When the agitation of mind by concepts has subsided and it is in a state of what it has been, this is called 'a unique occasion'. 'The right juncture' means to know mind in the state of what it has always been. It is called so also because it engages the intellectual capacity in that which is truly meaningful."

14) According to *Shing-rta chen-po*, pp. 125 f, the first three belong to the body, the fourth to speech, and the last four to mind. In his *Padma dkar-po*, Klong-chen rab-'byams-pa lists twenty-four unfavorable conditions. The first eight are identical with the ones given here, except that the state of a dumb person is mentioned last:

> The difficulty of thinking about (a unique occasion and
> the right juncture) for those being in unfavorable
> conditions, is
> That these eight states of being as denizens of hell, a spirit,
> an animal, a long-living god,
> A savage, a person holding wrong views, a person living in
> an age where there is no Buddha,

And a dumb person, are such as not being a vessel for
  (holding) life's meaning (p. 687).

The second set of eight unfavorable conditions applies to men
beset by aggravating circumstances:

These are the eight unfavorable conditions aggravating the
  situation:
Maddened by the poison of the five (emotions), stupid
  and deceived (by evil friends), led astray by evil
  powers,
Lazy, immersed in an ocean of evil deeds,
Held in bondage, haunted (by terror) and prompted (to act
  in self-preservation), hypocritical—
They are no vessel for holding life's meaning and the way
  to deliverance, but pervert (a unique occasion and the
  right juncture) (p. 688).

Lastly, there are the eight unfavorable conditions that bar the
mind from ever realizing Being:

Tightly fettered (by material goods, children, wealth,
  relatives, and friends), fallen into very bad habits,
Undaunted by (the evils of) Saṃsāra, having no trust
  whatsoever,
Doing everything that is unwholesome and evil, having no
  inclination to set out on the quest for life's meaning,
Having forsaken one's duties and broken one's
  commitments—
These eight unfavorable conditions that bar the mind
  from realizing Being
Have turned (a man) far away from life's meaning, and the
  lamp on the path to deliverance has burnt out (p. 689).

These verses are also quoted by Yon-tan rgya-mtsho in
his *bDen-gnyis gsal-byed zla-ba'i sgron-me*, p. 31, with slight
variations.

15) In his *Padma-dkar-po*, pp. 692 f, Klong-chen rab-'byams-pa
makes it quite clear that these events are the outcome of one's
actions done previously. This is to say that the past lives on in
the present which extends into the future; in other words, the
historical past is not an isolated unit, a previous and atomistic

'now' cut off from the present 'now', and the future is not some 'now' falling into reality at some later time, but an anticipatory goal of human existence. For the implication of 'lived time' as contrasted with 'calculated time' in the context of Western philosophy, see Calvin O. Schrag, *Experience and Being*, pp. 57 ff.

16) The logical connection of those five events is discussed in *Padma dkar-po*, pp. 494 f.

17) *sems* and *sems-(las) byung-(ba)*. As Klong-chen rab-'byams-pa points out in his *Shing-rta chen-po*, pp. 131 f, *sems* 'mind' is here understood as a pre-predicative intentionality turning into and becoming determined by the objectification of representational thought, while *sems-byung* 'mental event(s)' fills in the details such as the color, the form, the texture, and other features and 'qualities' of the selected topic. The operation of 'mind' and 'mental events' range over the three spheres of the world and, since they are representational, objectifying, isolating *'objects'* (which exist for a *'subject'*, and thus introduce a rift in the unitary character of experience), they belong, properly speaking, to the level of *ma-rig-pa*, 'loss of pure awareness', and are its turbid, muddy, murky operations. In this state they are automatically caught in the web of emotional reactions. Once this objectifying and subjectifying character of 'mind' (*sems*) has lost its hold over us there is the status of a 'Buddha' (*sangs-rgyas*). The Tibetan term means that conceptual schemes and calculating procedures have gone (*sangs*) and that Being, not susceptible to measurement and predication, has been opened up and can unfold itself (*rgyas*). The state of *sangs-rgyas* is free from the urge to control, dominate, demand. As an appreciative perceiving and thinking (*rig-pa*), it is pristine cognitiveness (*ye-shes*). The distinction in rDzogs-chen thought between *sems* and *rig-pa* or *ye-shes* is similar to the distinction in phenomenological thought between 'representational thinking' and 'hermeneutical thinking'. See Calvin O. Schrag, *Experience and Being*, pp. 111 f.

The contrast between *sems* and *ye-shes* (*rig-pa*) marks the divergent ways experience can go. This contrast is a recurring theme in rDzogs-chen thought; see, for instance, Klong-chen rab-'byams-pa's *Tshig-don rin-po-che'i mdzod*, pp. 111 ff; *Bla-ma yang-tig*, part E, pp. 442 f; *Theg-pa'i mchog rin-po-che'i mdzod*, vol. I, pp. 608 ff; 'Jigs-med gling-pa's *rNam-mkhyen shing-rta*, pp. 645 f, 659 f; Yon-tan rgya-mtsho's *Zab-don snang-byed nyi-ma'i 'od-zer*, pp. 432 ff; Rig-'dzin rGod-kyi ldem-'phru-can's *rDzogs-pa chen-po dgongs pa zang-thal*, vol. 2, pp. 491 ff, 589 ff.

18) *ye-shes*. In rDzogs-chen thought it is a cognition which has been since the beginningless beginning of Being and is, as it were, its dynamic component. Its definition always empha- sizes its pristineness (*ye*) and cognitive operation (*shes*) before there is anything like a mind (*sems*), which is a loss of pristine and pure awareness. *Theg-pa'i mchog rin-po-che'i mdzod*, vol. 1, pp. 608, 629 ff; vol. 2, pp. 44 f; *Bla-ma yang-tig*, part E, pp. 184 f; *Lung-gi gter-mdzod*, p. 132b; *Tshig-don rin-po-che'i mdzod* pp. 122 f, 464 f. Its connection with the 'founding stratum' (*sku*) is such that *ye-shes* is the higher level component or the 'founded' and thus gives the whole complex its vitality. Although for analyt- ical purposes a distinction between 'founding' and 'founded' can be made, they are a single 'fact'. The character of *ye-shes* as the 'founded' varies with the character of its 'founding stra- tum'. This is the topic of the last chapter in this work.

19) *Shing-rta chen-po*, p. 130: "When the mire of mind and mental events has cleared, Mind, pristine cognitiveness in sheer lucency, rises from the depth (of Being); by becoming accus- tomed to it one speaks of 'the way of limpid clearness and consummate perspicacity', and day and night, without letting anything interfere with one's endeavor to experience this, one should remain in a state in which drowsiness and indolence have been given up."

'Limpid clearness and consummate perspicacity' attempts to render what in rDzogs-chen thought is understood by *byang-chub(-sems)*. To say that this term corresponds to Sanskrit *bodhi(citta)* and, then, to go on using the Sanskrit term or its English rendering 'enlightenment', which is taken from the Sanskrit, is of no value for understanding Tibetan thinking. In his *Chos-dbying rin-po-che'i mdzod*, p. 23, Klong-chen rab- 'byams-pa defines *byang-chub-sems* as follows:

> The vast (experiential) ground and range (of) self-existent
>   pristine cognitiveness
> (Is) limpid clearness (*byang*) (because) being immaculate

from its beginningless beginning it has not been defiled
by Saṃsāra; (and)

Consummate perspicacity (*chub*) because, (its) capabilities
(being) spontaneously present, it is beyond cause and
effect; (and it is one's)

Mind (*sems*) because (its) vitalizing power (as) pure
awareness in itself is transparent sheer lucency.

In *byang-chub-sems* everything gathers (and) is pure in every
respect.

In his *Lung-gi gter-mdzod*, p. 173, Klong-chen rab-'byams-pa
comments on the above verse:

> The term *byang* is used because Saṃsāra has never been
> experienced as something existent in view of the fact that
> the facticity of pure awareness has never been tainted. The
> term *chub* is used because in this vitalizing power capabil-
> ities are spontaneously present, and this is because (its
> actuality) exists as the possibility of rising as anything. The
> term *sems* is used because of the fact that responsiveness (to
> the solicitation of actuality) is present in an all-encom-
> passing way so that by its lucency both Saṃsāra and
> Nirvāṇa are encompassed, and because it comes as an in-
> dividual experience. Since the ordinary mind and its mental
> events with their host of dividing thoughts make their ap-
> pearance out of the creativity of playful energy in impure
> forms, they are not *byang-chub-sems*, and since they contra-
> dict the latter because they are samsaric mind, there is a
> great difference between creativity as such and what ap-
> pears as playfulness deriving from creativity.

He then goes on to quote from the *Chos-thams-cad rdzogs-
pa chen-po byang-chub-kyi sems kun-byed rgyal-po* (in *rNying-ma
rgyud-'bum*, vol. 1, pp. 13 f) in support of his definition. The fact
that *byang-chub* is a compound (*byang* and *chub*) has never been
lost sight of in rDzogs-chen thought.

20) *chos*. This word is as rich in connotations as is the Latin word
res. In his *bDen-gnyis gsal-byed zla-ba'i sgron-me*, pp. 12 f, Yon-tan
rgya-mtsho explains this word as follows:

> The substance of *chos* is the elimination of any obscurations,
> be they of an emotional or cognitive nature, or the means of

their elimination. Its definition is to medicate our emotionally infected state of being in the same way as we would use medicine in a case of illness. Its division is the contents of the texts and their understanding or the validity of the path leading to the cessation of suffering. Its etymology is derived from the word *dharma* which is 'to hold', that is, not to slip into the way leading to Saṃsāra and evil forms of life, but 'to hold to the straight path'.

In his *Pad-ma dkar-po*, pp. 348 f, Klong-chen rab-'byams-pa explains the word *chos* as "what is the basis of intellectual knowledge, what one becomes involved in by acceptance and rejection after having come to know, and what one acquires as one's desired object after having become involved in it."

Notes to Chapter Two

1) They are those above, on, and below the earth.

2) In *Shing-rta chen-po*, p. 161, the east wall is said to consist of crystal, the south wall of beryl, the west wall of ruby, and the north wall of gold. But in *Pad-ma dkar-po*, p. 46, the east wall is said to be of either silver or crystal, the west wall of either ruby or red crystal. The space of the four regions is colored, accordingly, white, blue, red, and yellow.

3) These qualifications, according to *Shing-rta chen-po*, p. 169, refer to 'body', 'speech', and 'mind' respectively.

4) A plantain tree has a false trunk and its fruit no seed.

5) *'byung-ba*. As 'forces' they comprise both 'radiation' and 'materialization', as detailed in *Zab-mo yang-tig*, part Wam, pp. 154 ff.

Notes to Chapter Three

1) The following is based on Klong-chen rab-'byams-pa's explication of the cognitive process, in his *Shing-rta chen-po*, pp. 205–208.

2) In his *Theg-pa'i mchog rin-po-che'i mdzod*, vol. 1, p. 599, Klong-chen rab-'byams-pa is quite outspoken against those who consider *gnas-'gyur* to imply a change *into* something or other. If there is any 'change', it is to be understood figuratively. When we say of a person that 'he has changed', we certainly do not mean that his person has all of a sudden turned in-to, say, a horse. That *gnas-'gyur* does not mean 'change into' is clearly elaborated in such works as the *rDzogs-pa chen-po lta-ba'i yang-snying sangs-rgyas thams-cad-kyi dgongs-pa nam-mkha' klong-yangs-kyi rgyud* (in *rNying-ma rgyud-'bum*, vol. 7, p. 151; *Vairocana rgyud-'bum*, vol. 8, p. 34); the *rDzogs-pa chen-po 'khor rtsad-nas gcod-pa chos-sku skye-med rig-pa'i rgyud* (in *rNying-ma rgyud-'bum*, vol. 7, p. 396); the *rDzogs-pa chen-po Nges-don thams-cad 'dus-pa ye-shes nam-mkha' mnyam-pa'i rgyud* (in *rNying-ma rgyud-'bum*, vol. 8, p. 287).

3) For these terms see also notes 12, 17, and 18 to Chapter One.

4) *khams gsum*. These are the realms of sensuous desires and ordinary projects-at-hand, of aesthetic forms, and of form-lessness where nothing has to be but where the possibility exists that man can make himself in his own absence.

5) According to *Shing-rta chen-po*, p. 192, deer are attracted by the sound of the flute and then killed by the hunter; bees become trapped in flowers; fish are baited; buffaloes and elephants may drown in the cool water of lakes.

6) *bsam-gtan*. In his *Lung-gi gter-mdzod*, p. 21ab, Klong-chen rab-'byams-pa distinguishes between a meditation in which the ego-centered mind focusses upon an object of its interest and a meditation which is spontaneous and in which the subject-object structure of representational thought does not obtain. The former merely intensifies the tendency to isolate its ob-jects for a subject that is to control or to manipulate them. On pp. 105a ff, he specifies rDzogs-chen meditation which is based on the distinction between 'mind' (*sems*), the noetic-noematic complex with its objectifying tendency, and 'pure awareness' (*rig-pa*) in which thought has been released from the compulsion for control and is left to itself and concerned with meaning. On p. 106a he sums up this distinction as follows:

In brief, while the cultivation (*sgom-pa*) of the mind involving an objectifying process, is the peg and rope by which the subject-object structure is held up, a meditation (*bsam-gtan*) in which pure awareness is being left to itself, is the vital wheel of meaningfulness, self-rotating. Hence there is a great difference between raising the mind to higher realms which, after all, are but the cause for worldliness and Saṃsāra, and to stay in one's real place, the intentionality of Buddhahood (*dgongs-pa*) which is to be directly involved in liberation and Nirvāṇa.

The higher realms are those of aesthetic forms and of formlessness, as referred to in note 4.

The distinction Klong-chen rab-'byams-pa draws here between *sgom-pa*, *bsam-gtan*, and *dgongs-pa*, is based on the *Rig-pa rang-shar chen-po'i rgyud* (in *rNying-ma rgyud-'bum*, vol. 10, pp. 14 and 17 f). The two first terms can also be, and are used, in a general sense of the formulation of a concept in detail and its enjoyment as envisioned. It is in this general sense that *bsam-gtan* is used in this instance.

7) They are the jewels of the wheel, elephant, horse, gem, woman, treasure, and counselor.

8) *kun-gzhi'i rnam-par shes-pa*. In his *Shing-rta chen-po*, p. 209, Klong-chen rab-'byams-pa quotes the *'Jam-dpal ye-shes rgyan-gyi mdo*: " 'Mind' (*sems*, perceptual readiness) is the perceptivity of the ground for all (differentiation), the belief in an ego is (conceptual and emotional) elaboration (*yid*)."

In strict rDzogs-chen thought the term *kun-gzhi'i rnam-par shes-pa* refers to a kind of radiation proceeding from a stratum (*kun-gzhi*) that is otherwise indeterminate. This radiation then spreads to and constitutes the perceptivity of the senses which contribute to the 'ego-acts' and their emotionally toned performances. See *mKha'-'gro yang-tig*, part 3, p. 120. According to the same work, p. 202: "From the perceptivity of the ground for all differentiations as the source for all cognitive processes, (resting on or residing) in an otherwise indeterminate stratum which is the primordial loss of pure awareness, there come, outward-directedly, the five sensory perceptions and, inward-directedly, a 'plain ego-act' (*yid-shes*), and an 'emotionally toned ego-act' (*nyon-yid*). These constitute the mind (*sems*) as comprising eight perception patterns." Taking the various explications together, *kun-gzhi'i rnam-par shes-pa* can be paraphrased as 'a perceptivity tending to distinct perceptual judgment, but as yet undetermined and being merely the dynamic aspect of a stratum that will allow all possible differentiations.' As Klong-chen rab-'byams-pa elaborates in his *Shing-rta chen-po*, pp. 208 f, each of the five senses is in mutual dependence with its field of operation, and this mutual dependence results in a certain feeling-tone. Specifically, it is the 'ego-act' that sets up the emotional 'poisons' that make all actions 'unwholesome'. This is so because the ego is unable to 'accept' things, but must of necessity 'interfere' with them and twist them according to its interests. The 'ego-act' (*yid*) fits everything that is perceived into its 'world'-pattern. Whatever 'I' perceive or think about is always 'my' world made up of the 'meanings' the things have for 'me'.

9) *kun-brtags*. This and the two subsequent terms (*gzhan-dbang* and *yongs-su grub-pa*) are introduced into Buddhist philosophy by the Yogācārins. As detailed in *Shing-rta chen-po*, pp. 212 f, *kun-brtags* sums up what we do when we want to talk about things. 'Things', here, are to be understood in a very broad sense, covering 'physical things' and 'physiological states' and so on. By convention, words stand for things, but words also denote and designate. The word 'pleasure' denotes all the particular feelings to which the word 'pleasure' is applicable, and it also designates those characteristics which something must have in order for the word 'pleasure' to be applicable to it. The words which both designate and denote are known as *rnam-grangs-pa'i kun-brtags*). There are also cases where we know what a certain term designates, while we still do not know what this term denotes. The term (or phrase) 'hare's horn', denotes nothing whatsoever, for there are no hare's horns. Words which do not denote are known as *mtshan-nyid chad-pa('i kun-brtags*). All of the *kun-brtags* have no closer relationship to things than have labels on bottles.

10) *gzhan-dbang*. This, too, is a summary term for certain experiences with which every one of us is familiar (see H. V. Guenther, *Buddhist Philosophy in Theory and Practice*, p. 99). The

distinction between 'pure' and 'impure' is intimately connected with aesthetic experiences as contrasted with our ordinary, interest-bound perception. The 'pure' relativity (the
fact that everything is relative to everything else as are
mountains to valleys and these, in turn, to the beholder) is
illustrated by 'Buddha-realms' and 'palaces of light'. These
certainly are not spatio-temporal objects of our ordinary perceiving capacity, nor are they any representations of something—a representation presupposes another thing, somehow
made to reappear under the guise of something else. Even the
world as we see it is not a duplicate of something else, but
merely a presence 'contaminated' ('impure') by what we intend it to be, and our intentions may have little to do with
the phenomenon itself. And what is worse, such intentions
quickly and easily lend themselves to theoretical reductions,
to the 'nothing but'. It may be easy to dismiss the 'Buddha-
realms' and the 'palaces of light' as something non-existing,
but it may be very difficult, if not impossible to state what this
means. How is it possible for a sheer presence to be something
when, in the same breath, this something is said to be non-
existent? To put the question in this way is merely to re-
state the intellectualistic prejudices of using representational
thought as the sole criterion of meaning. The fact that *gzhan-
dbang* is of two kinds, 'pure' and 'impure', points to perspectives displayed in experience, and one can move from one
perspective to another, as Klong-chen rab-'byams-pa points
out in his *Shing-rta chen-po*, p. 223, after a devastating critique of
the reductionism in purely intellectualist philosophy.

11) *yongs-su grub-pa.* As 'unchanging', the absoluteness of Being is
no part of any system of transitory differentiations and their
relativistic associations, but since it is nowhere else than in
what there is, its very presence inevitably leads us into a
paradoxical situation. We try to describe it only to find that it
cannot be described. Designation is made possible only by
using words denoting specific characteristics. Consequently,
recourse to descriptive terms brings out the differentiations
and characteristics, rather than what the presence is as such.
The use of the term *stong-pa*, which in non-technical language

corresponds to our 'empty', is not meant to be a defining characteristic of the absoluteness of Being, but points to the open texture and the inexplicable mixture of the apparently concrete and the thoroughly elusive, as is the reflection of the moon in water, and the utter spontaneity of this presence (see *Shing-rta chen-po*, p. 220). As the 'incontrovertible' it is the realization of the 'unchanging' absoluteness of Being, which permits us to see things in their 'Being' whereby they have changed over from their status (*gnas-'gyur*) of having been contaminated ('impure') by the demands made on them by ego-centered interests, to a 'pure' presence (*Shing-rta chen-po*, p. 223).

12) In Indian mythology the lord of the deceased and of the ghosts.

13) Klong-chen rab-'byams-pa here follows the account of *Abhidharmakośa*, III, 91.

14) Takṣaka is one of the serpents of divine extraction, well-known in Indian epic mythology.

15) The loss of pure awareness (*ma-rig-pa*) which initiates and, in a certain sense, is mind (*sems*), may be conceived of as a kind of self-estrangement in search of a 'self'. In this search it is driven on by 'motility' (*rlung*), which is the mind's readiness to find a place for itself (*sems*); the place which this mind finds is its re-incarnation, aided by the conditions that are provided by its parents.

Notes to Chapter Four

1) See also note 8 to Chapter Three. The term 'stratum' is used to preserve the distinction between *kun-gzhi* and *gzhi* ('ground' proper) in rDzogs-chen thought, and to mark it off from *sku* 'founding stratum'. On the difference between *kun-gzhi* and *chos-sku*, see Klong-chen rab-'byams-pa's *Theg-pa'i mchog rin-po-che'i mdzod*, vol. 1, p. 610, and *Tshig-don rin-po-che'i mdzod*, pp. 103 f, which are the basis for 'Jigs-med gling-pa's discussion in

his *rNam-mkhyen shing-rta*, pp. 648 ff, and Yon-tan rgya-mtsho's elaboration in his *Zab-don snang-byed nyi-ma'i 'od-zer*, pp. 446 ff.

2) This analysis of the idea of *kun-gzhi*, which is unique to rDzogs-chen thought, is based primarily on Klong-chen rab-'byams-pa's works, specifically, his *Theg-pa'i mchog rin-po-che'i mdzod*, vol. 1, pp. 598 ff; *Lung-gi gter-mdzod*, pp. 131a f (where on p. 132a he uses *lus-kyi kun-gzhi* 'stratum of embodiment' for the more generally used *bag-chags sna-tshogs-kyi kun-gzhi*); *Tshig-don rin-po-che'i mdzod*, pp. 105 ff. Substantially the same interpretation is found in Rig-'dzin rGod-kyi ldem-'phru-can's *dGongs-pa zang-thal*, vol. 2, p. 498; vol. 5, pp. 115 f; in 'Jigs-med gling-pa's *rNam-mkhyen shing-rta*, pp. 650 f; in Yon-tan rgya-mtsho's *Zab-don snang-byed nyi-ma'i 'od-zer*, pp. 447 f. The term *lus-kyi kun-gzhi*, used both by Klong-chen rab-'byams-pa, *loc. cit.*, p. 132a and by Rig-'dzin rGod-kyi ldem-'phru-can, *loc. cit.*, vol. 2, p. 498, in connection with *bag-chags(-sna-tshogs-kyi kun-gzhi)* indicates that we as 'embodied beings' do not so much *have* a body, as we *are* ongoing embodiments. Rig-'dzin rGod-kyi ldem-'phru-can continues:

> Out of the interaction of the cognate loss of pure awareness and the conceptually proliferating loss of pure awareness, there comes about the stratum of ingrained tendencies. When these tendencies gain in strength the process leading to Saṃsāra starts, and, when in the wake of the mistaken idea of a 'self' and an 'other' being two separate entities, both the external world as a container and the sentient beings as the contained essence, have simultaneously come into existence, then the stratum of embodiment has been set up by the eight perception-patterns. The body (as embodiment) is the site for various frustrations.

See also *Shing-rta chen-po*, p. 342.

The *sKu-i rgyud Padma 'khyil-ba* (in *rNying-ma rgyud-'bum*, vol. 5, p. 404, in *Vairocana rgyud-'bum*, vol. 8, p. 260) states: "Since the power of karma is predominant in the stratum of the tendencies (resulting in our) body, its span of life is uncertain."

3) The difference between *sbyor-ba don-gyi kun-gzhi* and *ye don-gyi kun-gzhi* is that the former focusses on the possibility of involvement with certain perspectives, while the latter points to the source from which this involvement stems.

4) *Shing-rta chen-po*, p. 276.

5) *rigs*. It is because of this affinity with Being that Being is realized. In his *Grub-pa'i mtha' rin-po-che'i mdzod*, pp. 161 ff, Klong-chen rab-'byams-pa states that " 'affinity with Being' is Being felt to be present in each living being as the thrust towards Being." Other terms for it are *khams*, 'man's physico-psychological make-up' or 'existentiality', and *de-bzhin gshegs-pa'i snying-po*, 'the very thrust of being towards Being'. Both these terms refer to the presence of Being in the concrete human existence, not in the sense that Being is something over and above man's existence, but as the challenge to find Being in his being. Therefore, in his *bDen-gnyis gsal-byed zla-ba'i sgon-me*, p. 280, Yon-tan rgya-mtsho equates *khams* with *rang-bzhin* ('actuality'), *gzhi* ('ground' proper), and *chos-nyid* ('meaningfulness'), where positive qualities or, more precisely, values become gradually manifest. Once this thrust has reached its climax, it is known as *byang-chub*, 'limpid clearness and consummate perspicacity', or *de-bzhin gshegs-pa*, 'the thrust having reached its climax'. Being is never something newly established; ordinarily, it has not been allowed to make itself felt and experienced in its richness. Once it is allowed to do so it is experienced as 'replete' while at the same time, since nothing of what detracted us from its experience can be found anymore, it is 'empty' (where 'being empty' does not imply an ontological status called 'emptiness'). Affinity with Being is both the 'ground' proper, that is, the absoluteness of Being which is not grounded in anything else, and the 'path' or the unfolding of Being.

This presence of Being is illustrated by nine analogies which distribute over a variety of personalities: In those who are overcome by passion, Being is present like a lotus flower in its calyx; in those who are overcome by aversion, like the honey in a flower surrounded by bees; in those who are overcome by dullness, like grain in chaff; and in those in whom the three emotional obstructions are present in equal distribution, like gold in ore. To extract either the lotus flower, or the honey, or the grain, or the gold, needs effort. In those who have reached a saintly status of either a Śrāvaka or a Pratye-kabuddha, but who are still in the clutches of the lack of pure awareness, Being is present like a treasure in the home of a pauper without his knowledge. In the Bodhisattvas who are still under the influence of the factors that can be eliminated by pure vision, Being is present like the germinating power in the seed of a mango fruit and like a precious Buddha-statue wrapped in dirty clothes. In the Bodhisattvas who are under the influence of the factors that will be eliminated by developing the pure vision through making it a living experience, Being is present like a future universal ruler in the womb of a low caste woman or like the taking shape of a gold statue from its material, the gold. See also *Shing-rta chen-po*, pp. 326 ff. The illustrations are first found in the *Ratnagotravibhāga Mahāyānottaratantraśāstra*, I, 99–132. A very detailed account of what can be eliminated by a pure vision and what by the cultivation of this vision, is given by Yon-tan rgya-mtsho in his *bDen-gyi gsal-byed zla-ba'i sgron-me*, pp. 251 ff.

6) *Shing-rta chen-po*, p. 311.

7) *Shing-rta chen-po*, p. 339.

8) *Shing-rta chen-po*, p. 210.

9) Obscuration by emotional vagaries and obscuration by notions about the knowable.

10) The five sense perceptions, the 'plain ego-act', and the 'emotionally toned ego-act'.

11) See note 4 to Chapter Three.

12) *chos-dbyings*. The term is synonymous with Mind-as-such (*sems-nyid*) in its sheer lucency, present as the thrust towards Being. It ranges from the 'ground' (Being), through the 'path' (its presentation and cultivation), to the goal (Being as pure meaningfulness). *Lung-gi gter-mdzod*, pp. 4ab. In *Bi-ma snying-thig*, part I, pp. 189 f, this term is explained as *chos* indicating

the ineffability of the facticity of Being, *dbyings* the pure actuality of Being, and its self-presentation (*snang-ba*) as all-encompassing responsiveness. The term comprises what we tend to indicate by (and divide into) Being-Experience-Continuum-Meaningfulness.

13) *ting-nge-'dzin.* This is a kind of experience in which the distinction between inner and outer has become irrelevant. Instead of dealing with serially isolable objects or traits of a self, it opens up a path to self-understanding in a holistic way.

14) *rtag-mtha'* and *chad-mtha'.* Both terms refer to a widely accepted, though unfounded belief: the former to the assumption that there is some 'eternal' entity before whatever is transitory came into existence; the latter to the assumption that whatever is, will continue as 'eternally' in a state of being-no-more.

15) The six transcending functions are active generosity, higher self-discipline, patient endurance, strenuous and sustained effort, contemplative attention, and appreciative discrimination. The former five make up the 'accumulation of merits', the last one that of 'knowledge' which as 'pristine cognitions' is existential rather than representational. They are 'transcending functions' because they enable the transition from one growth-level to another, provided that they are not concretized into ends in themselves.

16) *rnal-'byor.* In rDzogs-chen thought this term indicates a 'coming to rest by taking a deep breath'. *Bi-ma snying-thig,* part 1, p. 90. This coming to rest is effected by various techniques, referred to by the same term, all of them aiming at making man capable of finding himself by passing beyond his ego-centricity.

17) See also note 9.

18) The one is *chos-sku,* on which see note 7 to Chapter One and, in particular, Chapter Thirteen for Klong-chen rab-'byams-pa's interpretation. The other one is the 'founding stratum of presented meaning' (*gzugs-kyi sku*) which comprises both the 'founding stratum of an engagement in a world-horizon'

(*longs-sku*) and the various 'founding strata of concrete embodiments and bearers of meaning' (*sprul-sku*).

19) See also note 5 above. In his *Shing-rta chen-po*, p. 313 f, Klong-chen rab-'byams-pa shows that this 'affinity with Being' is inseparable from experience and that experience has both a prereflective-nonthematic side and a reflective-thematic side. It is the prereflective-nonthematic side that is referred to by the term 'naturally present affinity with Being' (*rang-bzhin-du gnas-pa'i rigs, rang-bzhin gnas-pa'i rigs*). Synonymous with it are such other terms as 'Mind-as-such' (*sems-nyid*), 'meaning-as-such' or 'meaningfulness of Being' (*chos-nyid*), 'founding stratum of the pure facticity of Being' (*ngo-bo-nyid-kyi sku*). It is the reflective-thematic side that is referred to by the term 'growing affinity with Being' (*rgyas-'gyur rigs*), with which the term 'affinity with Being which stems from its realization' (*bsgrub-pa-las byung-ba'i rigs*) is synonymous. Thus Klong-chen rab-'byams-pa says:

> If we make a distinction (in this affinity with Being), we have a 'naturally present affinity with Being', present in the sense that it has been present since a beginningless beginning, and an 'affinity with Being that stems from its realization' in view of the fact that the incidental obscurations of the former have been removed. In the naturally present affinity with Being there is this naturally present affinity in the prereflective-nonthematic aspect (*chos-nyid rang-bzhin-du gnas-pa'i rigs*), Mind-as-such, an open dimension, divested of all propositions about it, serving as the cause-factor for the release of the founding stratum of the pure facticity of Being. There is also the naturally present affinity in a reflective-thematic aspect (*chos-can rang-bzhin-du gnas-pa'i rigs*), serving as the cause-factor for the release of the founding strata of presented meaning. From the beginningless beginning (this affinity with Being) has been present in both the reflective-thematic (*chos-can*) and the prereflective-nonthematic (*chos-nyid*) aspect.

About the 'affinity with Being which stems from its realization' he says, on p. 314: "With reference to the former (the naturally present affinity), this is the cleansing (of the former from its incidental obscurations) by engaging in appropriate actions and appreciative discriminations which go hand in hand on the incidental 'path of learning' and involve such actions as activating the ethical impulse, as well as (by engaging) in the accumulation of merit and pristine cognitions." The activation of the ethical impulse is dealt with in detail in Chapter Eight, and the 'path of learning' which comprises the stages of preparation, application of what has been prepared, vision, and cultivation of the vision, in Chapter Six.

Any reflection on experience emerges from, refers to, and is 'founded' on the ongoing, continuous process of experience. Thus Klong-chen rab-'byams-pa states on pp. 314 ff:

From the spontaneously present reach and range of the naturally present affinity with Being, this founding stratum of the pure facticity of Being, Mind-as-such, which is like a jewel, there comes the reflective-thematic naturally present affinity with Being. Its providing the basis for the 'founding stratum of engagement in a world-horizon' (as exemplified by the symbol of) a universal ruler and for the 'founding stratum of embodiments of meaning', whose supreme bearer (the Buddha) is the former's self-presentation to those to be led (to the realization of the meaningfulness of Being), is not manifestly present during the period of an ordinary sentient being. This is because the naturally present affinity with Being is obscured by the pollution (of representational thinking), and its operation removes the pollution that obscures the 'founding stratum of presented meaning' by the accumulation of merits involving such operations as the activation of the ethical impulse. It removes the pollution that obscures the 'founding stratum of the pure facticity of Being', meaningfulness (*chos-nyid*) (as the prereflective-nonthematic aspect of experience) by attending to and cultivating the openness of Being through the accumulation of pristine cognitions. However, while the naturally present affinity with Being is like clear water, the affinity with Being which stems from its realization is like the various images reflected in the water, and (the water and the reflection in it) are related to each other as 'founding' and 'founded' present since the beginningless beginning. In this continuum ('ground' proper) the naturally present affinity with Being is like a knowable object, and the affinity with Being which stems from realization incidentally is like the knowing intellect, both related to each other as 'founding' and 'founded'. And while the prereflective-nonthematic and the reflective-thematic aspect of the naturally present affinity with Being are there as the cause-factor for release, they are not the result of the release. Furthermore, while the naturally present affinity with Being which stems from its realization is there as a force purifying the pollution, it is not there as the concrete cause-factor for the founding strata of meaning in the manner of cause and effect, as in the setting up of something new and different from it. Rather, it sets free in or brings to maturity on the Buddha-level the understanding that operates in the path of learning, generating the most excellent and superb capabilities.

20) As Klong-chen rab-'byams-pa points out in his *Shing-rta chen-po*, p. 399, these two are indivisible and not a juxtaposition of separable moments or entities: "Their indivisibility constitutes a wholesome existentiality as meaning since the beginningless beginning. Although in view of its unchangingness it may be termed naturally present affinity with Being and, in view of the fact that the capabilities grow and become manifest when the pollution has been removed, it may be termed growing affinity with Being, their common root is sheer lucency (in the) pristine cognition operating out of pure awareness."

21) They are, on the one hand, the accumulation of merits and knowledge as commonly dealt with in Mahāyāna; and, in the specific 'existential' approach, the practice of the Developing Stage and the Fulfillment Stage.

22) The ritual empowerment by 'jar' (symbolizing physical purity

since a jar is used for ablutions), 'mystery' (symbolizing the purity of the 'mystery' of communication), and by 'pristine cognitions that develop in the wake of the application of appreciative discrimination' (symbolizing the purity of the mental-spiritual processes), belong to the Developing Stage and represent the accumulation of merits, which also involve the rich imagery of maṇḍalas. The fourth empowerment belongs to the Fulfillment Stage and represents the accumulation of pristine cognitions. Here attention is focussed on sheer lucency with no propositions entering. See *Shing-rta chen-po*, pp. 349 f, and below, Chapter Nine.

23) Actions and attitudes (mind) are functionally correlated in such a manner that a variation in one ('action') functionally determines the variation in the other ('attitude'). Similarly, the 'two realities', one 'the conventionally accepted reality' (*kun-rdzob*), and the other, 'the absolutely real reality' (*don-dam*) are functionally correlated. But this correlation is not imposed from without, but is derived from and grounded in the 'material' itself to be studied—man's quest for the meaning of life. This again points to experience which comes before any reflection about it. Reflection is an explication of what is found in experience. Both the 'conventionally real' and the 'absolutely real' are found *in* experience. In his *Shing-rta chen-po*, pp. 696 ff, Klong-chen rab-'byams-pa makes it quite clear that experience is distinct from the act of reflection on it, yet it is a distinction without separation: "Everything, be this the world of appearance and the fictions about it, Saṃsāra and Nirvāṇa, may be claimed by the intellect (the action of reflection) to be different as good and evil, yet from the very beginning (*ye-nas*, i.e., before reflection has set in) everything has been pure like the bright sky, and hence is beyond the objectification by reflective thought claiming it to be pure, impure, dual, nondual, very pure." It is because of a distinction without separation that it is permissible to speak of 'functional correlation' as a way of explicating what is found in experience. In the same work, pp. 713 ff, Klong-chen rab-'byams-pa gives three different 'explications': the correlation as it seems to operate in the external world, the correlation as understood 'physiologi-

cally' by the Śrāvakas (p. 719), and the correlation as it is transcended in the progress towards Nirvāṇa (p. 722). A more psychological explication is given by Klong-chen rab-'byams-pa in his *Tshig-don rin-po-che'i mdzod*, pp. 47 f. Still another explication—the evolution of Saṃsāra, the karmic counterpart, and the return to 'experience'—is offered in *mKha'-'gro yang-tig*, part Ah, pp. 175 ff.

NOTES TO CHAPTER FIVE

1) Desire-attachment (*'dod-chags*), aversion-hatred (*zhe-sdang*), and dullness (*gti-mug*).

2) *don-gnyis*. All experience is tendential in that it means something for the experiencer, and insofar as something means something for someone it also constitutes a value. The value is not attributed to, but is inherent in what is experienced. There is here a kind of dynamic parallelism at work. To the extent that man comes closer to his Being, more integrated, and more appreciative of his value (*rang-don*), he is also more able to appreciate values in others (*gzhan-don*). Moreover, the realization of life's meaning as an individual and private enterprise (*rang-don*) communicates itself to others (*gzhan-don*), arousing them to realize life's meaning for themselves.

3) According to *Shing-rta chen-po*, p. 408, the guru (*bla-ma*) gives spiritual sustenance, the tutelary deity (*yi-dam*) assures realization, and the Ḍākas and Ḍākinīs remove the obstacles on the way towards self-growth.

4) See note 9 to Chapter Four.

5) *bar-do*. As a generic term it implies that at any moment man is in a transitional phase; in particular it refers to the period of reorganization of the elements taken over from a previous situation into a new one.

6) Two legendary persons noted for their endeavors in their search for life's meaning.

Notes to Chapter Six

1) The idea of 'Jewel' in connection with Buddha, Dharma, and Sangha has been elaborated in the *Ratnagotravibhāga Mahā-yanottaratantraśāstra*, I, 22, and its commentary, quoted in *Shing-rta chen-po*, pp. 436 f. Accordingly, Buddha, Dharma, and Sangha are 'Jewels' because (1) in the cycle of aeons they are not found by anyone in whom the wholesome and healthy has not taken root; (2) because they are flawless in every respect; (3) because they possess powers beyond imagination; (4) because they are an ornament to the world; (5) because they are the most precious; and (6) because they remain unchanged in value.

2) This is the traditional way of classifying the Buddhist texts according to their Sanskrit terms indicating stylistic genres. They distribute over the triple classification into Vinaya, Sūtra, and Abhidharma, according to Yon-tan rgya-mtsho in his *bDen-gnyis gsal-byed zla-ba'i sgron-me*, pp. 270 f, as follows:

Sūtra, Geya, Vyākaraṇa, Gāthā, Udāna: Hīnayāna Sūtra-piṭaka;
Nidāna, Avadāna, Ityukta: Hīnayāna Vinayapiṭaka;
Jātaka: Mahāyāna Vinayapiṭaka;
Vaipulya, Adbhutadharma: Mahāyāna Sūtrapiṭaka;
Upadeśa: Hīnayāna and Mahāyāna Abhidharmapiṭaka.

3) *thugs-rje.* This term covers a wide range of meaning in rDzogs-chen thought. Above all, it is operative only on the Buddha-level, and here 'Buddha' must be understood in its specific meaning of 'everything negative (in the widest sense of the word) having gone (*sangs*) and everything positive having expanded (*rgyas*)'. As such it is one of the vectorial connections in Being and operates in a variety of ways. In his *Tshig-don rin-po-che'i mdzod*, p. 94, Klong-chen rab-'byams-pa mentions five varieties: one belonging to the 'Buddha-level'; one engaging with its object; one exhorting and prompting; one performing various charismatic activities; one remaining unchanged with regard to those who have to be led and trained.

4) As Klong-chen rab-'byams-pa points out in his *Shing-rta chen-po*, p. 458, these countless levels are more like facets or refractions of the level of 'Light Everywhere'.

5) They are 'he who has entered the stream', 'he who will once again relapse into the realm of sensuous desires', 'he who will not relapse', and 'he who is becoming a saint'. Each of them also enjoys the fruit of his specific status and achievement. In this way there are 'four pairs'. See also Yon-tan rgya-mtsho, *bDen-gnyis gsal-byed zla-ba'i sgron-me*, p. 289.

6) 'Mystical inspirations' is a free translation of the technical term *rigs-'dzin,* also *rig-'dzin,* which refers to experiences ranging over the various phases of the 'path' and the 'spiritual levels'.

7) *lha*. This term, usually translated as 'god' without specifying in which sense this latter term is to be understood, also refers to the dynamic character of experience, both in its prereflective-nonthematic (*chos-nyid*) and reflective-thematic (*chos-can*) aspect. A detailed discussion of the wide-ranging significance of *lha* is found in Rong-zom Chos-kyi bzang-po's *Theg-pa chen-po'i tshul-la 'jug-pa mdo-tsam brjod-pa*, pp. 426 f. See also Yon-tan rgya-mtsho, *Zab-don snang-byed nyi-ma'i 'od-zer*, p. 54.

8) *mnyam-nyid*. This idea of sameness is not to be confused with the traditional conception of monadic sameness as an enduring substance. The emphasis here is on the experience of always already existing in a way that cannot be forced into or reduced to the categories of representational thinking. 'Sameness' stretches out infinitely into the past and reaches out infinitely into the future and is yet experienced in the now, inseparate and inseparable from past and future. Therefore this 'now' is not a special or particular, monadic event, otherwise 'sameness' would no longer obtain; hence 'no beginning', 'no end', 'no present', as Klong-chen rab-'byams-pa elaborates in his *Lung-gi gter-mdzod*, p. 19a.

9) Taking refuge is, in a certain sense, a prop. Once Being has been realized, no props are necessary because now the person can stand on his own feet. The literalist does not understand this because he confuses Being with some sort of being. The moment he lets the prop go he falls down.

10) The 'founding stratum of meaning' (*chos-sku*) underlying and making possible the 'founding stratum of meaningful engagement in a world-horizon' (*longs-sku*), and, out of it emerging, the 'founding stratum of embodiments of meaning concretely apprehendable' (*sprul-sku*).

Notes to Chapter Seven

1) For further explanation see also Chapter Thirteen.

2) See note 18 to Chapter Four.

3) See note 9 to Chapter Four.

4) In his *Shing-rta chen-po*, pp. 513 f, Klong-chen rab-'byams-pa specifies the identity of the goal, while at the same time emphasizing the difference of method of approach. "The epistemology-oriented disciplines accept the two accumulations as the generating cause-factor of the two founding strata of meaning, as is stated in the *Yuktiṣaṣṭikā*:

> Through this good and wholesome, all beings
> Accumulate merits and knowledge;
> May they obtain the two supreme values
> That come from merits and knowledge;

And, since the Mantrayāna claims that, for the removal of the two obscurations of the founding strata, the two accumulations must be experienced by the profound interaction of appropriate action and appreciative discrimination, and hence accept them as favorable conditions, both disciplines agree because they aim at realizing the openness of Being pervaded by and saturated with compassion."

Notes to Chapter Eight

1) On this term see note 19 to Chapter One.

2) In his *Shing-rta chen-po*, p. 682, Klong-chen rab-'byams-pa distinguishes these three contemplative attentions ('meditations', *bsam-gtan*) as follows:

Holistic experiences and realizations by those who have not entered upon the path (towards freedom), which involve the (state of) concentrated attention (to aesthetic form) (*bsam-gtan*) and to the (infinity feelings of the state of) formlessness (*gzugs-med*), are called 'contemplative attention indulged in by fools'. When by holistic experiences and realizations that come on the stages of preparation and application to those who have entered upon the path (towards freedom), the way towards freedom is traveled and the meaning and value of life (*don*) is laid bare, this is called 'contemplative attention laying bare the meaning and value of life'. The noble holistic experiences and realizations that come after the first spiritual level are called 'contemplative attentions that rejoice in what does not fail or in the having-arrived-there'.

In support he quotes *Laṅkāvatārasūtra*, II, 161, where, however, four contemplative attentions are mentioned.

In his *Yon-tan rin-po-che'i mdzod dga'-ba'i char*, p. 63, and his *bDen-gnyis shing-rta*, pp. 788 f, 'Jigs-med gling-pa closely follows Klong-chen rab-'byams-pa's interpretation. However, while Klong-chen rab-'byams-pa uses the term *de-bzhin-gshegs-dga'i bsam-gtan*, 'Jigs-med gling-pa uses *de-bzhin-gshegs-dge'i bsam-gtan* 'contemplative attention to the healthy and wholesome in the having-arrived-there'. The latter reading would correspond to the Sanskrit *tāthāgataṃ śubhaṃ*. Still, both authors recognize only three contemplative attentions as against the four in the *Laṅkāvatārasūtra* which they quote.

3) *Shing-rta chen-po*, pp. 681 f; *bDen-gnyis shing-rta*, p. 794.

4) In his *Shing-rta chen-po*, p. 680, Klong-chen rab-'byams-pa is quite emphatic that composure is not a blankness of the mind or a blocking of images. Rather it is a 'letting be', a 'not interfering with'.

5) *sems-dpa'*. Like *byang-chub* (see note 19 to Chapter One) this term also is a compound *sems* and *dpa'*. The term *sems* refers to the trend to objectify, to what becomes the reflective-thematic aspect of experience; the term *dpa'* points back to the non-

reflective-nonthematic aspect. This technical term has been explicated at length in the *sNang-srid kha-sbyor bdud-rtsi bcud-thigs 'khor-ba thog-mtha' gcod-pa'i rgyud phyi-ma* (in *rNying-ma rgyud-'bum*, vol. 6, p. 27).

6) According to *Shing-rta chen-po*, p. 560, they are: wheel, jewel, queen, minister, horse, elephant, commander-in-chief.

7) Ibid. They are: white mustard, *panicum dactylon*, wood-apple, vermilion powder, curds, bezoar (a kind of medicine), mirror, conch shell.

8) Ibid. They are: silk boots, cushion, carriage, bedding, throne, sword, lamb-skin.

9) The 'without' corresponds to material objects, the 'within' to the images of an inner vision, and the 'mystical' to the realm of pure experience. A most detailed analysis of these forms of worship is given by 'Gyur-med tshe-dbang mchog-grub in his *gSang-sngags nang-gi lam-rim rgya-cher 'grel-pa sangs-rgyas gnyis-pa'i dgongs-rgyan*, pp. 256–270.

10) They are symbolic forms through which the sensuous objects are experienced, representations of felt experiences in their intimacy and immediacy.

11) That is, settled determination and steady pursuance.

12) Ultimately this idea goes back to *Bodhicaryāvatāra*, III, 22. 'Jigs-med gling-pa elaborates it in his *Yon-tan rin-po-che'i mdzod dga'-ba'i char*, p. 46:

> From today on I have become spiritual sustenance for the
> living beings,
> Because I have become the elixir that overcomes the Lord
> of Death, an inexhaustible treasure,
> A gem dispelling poverty, a remedy alleviating disease,
> A walking-stick for the weary traveler on the road of
> fictitious being.

In his *bDen-gnyis shing-rta*, p. 543, he elaborates:

Elixir that overcomes the Lord of Death because, inasmuch as boundless merits accrue from this inner potential for limpid clearness and consummate perspicacity, a person having these merits cannot be overtaken by death unless his time has come; an inexhaustible treasure because an inexhaustible wealth of dispensation comes from it; a wish-fulfilling gem because poverty is dispelled; an excellent remedy because it alleviates all convulsions and emotion-induced diseases; and, since fictitious being is like a road going on and on for the living beings, then when they have become tired and lean on their walking-sticks so as to recover their breath, then will come capabilities beyond words, providing profitable sustenance to many other persons, when they rely on me.

13) They are, as Klong-chen rab-'byams-pa explains in his *Shing-rta chen-po*, pp. 619 ff:

A. Stealing the precious articles that are part of the Three Jewels; executing a monk who observes his rules; causing a novice to give up his training; committing the five heinous crimes (matricide, killing a saint, patricide, causing disunion among the Sangha, causing a Buddha to bleed); and holding wrong views;

B. Plundering a village, a cultivated valley, a town, a city, and a province;

C. Teaching the subject-matter of the open dimensions of Being to those who are intellectually not prepared for it; making a follower of the Mahāyāna forsake it; attaching oneself to the Mahāyāna while dismissing the obligations that go with one's status; following the Hīnayāna and proselytizing others into it; for the sake of gain extolling oneself and belittling others; speaking of one's alleged mystic experiences; appropriating donations to the Three Jewels; giving the property of one who practices inner calm to a person who recites texts for purpose of distraction.

D. Dismissing settled determination and steady pursuance.

See also *bDen-gnyis shing-rta*, pp. 553 ff, *bDen-gnyis gsal-byed zla-ba'i sgron-me*, pp. 435 f.

14) In his *Yon-tan rin-po-che'i mdzod dga'-ba'i char*, p. 61, 'Jigs-med gling-pa elaborates this idea as follows:

> Unregenerate people are fools:
> Fools are shrouded in clouds of evil.
> They extol themselves and broadcast the disgrace of others;
> The snake's tongue of their passions causes acute discomfort;
> Forever they scheme for glory and wealth, however shaky they may be;
> Discontented they affect the air of contentment;
> The spark of dissatisfaction is fanned into a flame by the slightest breeze;
> Like a monkey they create all kinds of mischief;
> Like a crocodile's, their belly is bloated with viciousness;
> Like a poisonous snake they destroy anyone they meet;
> Like fire they consume the tree of wholesomeness—
> Keep far away from such foolish friends.

15) See also above note 2.

16) *chos-nyid*, 'pure experience as meaningfulness of Being', is synonymous with *de-bzhin-nyid* 'just-this-ness', *dbyings rang-bzhin-gyis dag-pa* 'naturally pure continuum', *sems-nyid* 'Mind-(as-such)', *'od-gsal* 'sheer lucency'; *chos-can* 'reflected-on experience' comprises everything that is being said in concrete terms about the former. See *Shing-rta chen-po*, pp. 687 ff.

The cultivation and application of appreciative discrimination has thus to do with the distinction between the pre-reflective-nonthematic aspect of experience (also termed the absolutely real, *don-dam*) and the reflective-thematic aspect of experience (also termed the conventionally real, *kun-rdzob*).

As Klong-chen rab-'byams-pa points out on p. 700, these two are not separate entities. He has anticipated Calvin O. Schrag: "Reflection about or on experience is a movement which proceeds within experience" (*Experience and Being*, p. 45).

Notes to Chapter Nine

1) In his *rNam-mkhyen shing-rta*, pp. 4 f, 'Jigs-med gling-pa explains the term Vajrayāna by saying: "Since the very thrust towards Being remains unchanging and cannot be split or destroyed by something, Vajrayāna is posited as being the supreme pursuit," and in support of this explanation he quotes from the commentary on the Kālacakratantra: "Vajra means that it cannot be split nor be destroyed, and this also means spiritual pursuit, hence Vajrayāna. In it the Mantra and Pāramitā procedures are fused into the unity of effect and cause."

In his *Zab-don snang-byed nyi-ma'i 'od-zer*, p. 21, Yon-tan rgya-mtsho elaborates: "The encounter with the thrust towards bliss, the absolutely real indestructibility and meaningfulness of life, for which the Vajra is a symbol and analogy, by the help of the inner guide, overcomes all ideas about it being something 'out there' and proceeds unimpeded, and it can also not be reached by ideas about it being something 'in here', hence Vajra; and since this indestructibility is the main topic of discourse, one speaks of Vajrayāna."

There are two terms in Tibetan to indicate this thrust: *de-bzhin gshegs-pa'i snying-po* and *bde-bar gshegs-pa'i snying-po*; the former indicates the 'existential' implications of this thrust, the latter its 'affective' value, 'bliss'.

According to Padma-phrin-las snying-po in his *Lam-rim ye-shes snang-ba'i brjed-byang*, p. 25, the seven properties of the Vajra are distributed over the whole process of man's quest for life's meaning: "At the starting-point, the ground, as the open dimension of Being is not disrupted by obscurations through emotional vagaries and not undone by obscurations through what can be known in representational thinking; at the period of the path, the facticity of Being remains 'true', its actuality 'solid', and its response 'steady'. At the period of the climax it remains unassailable by obscurations through emotional vagaries and invincible by obscurations through what can be known in representational thinking."

2) In his *Theg-pa mtha'-dag-gi don gsal-bar byed-pa grub-pa'i mtha' rin-po-che'i mdzod*, p. 283 f, Klong-chen rab-'byams-pa explains the term *mantra* as follows: "*man* means 'mind as an ego-act (*yid*) taking this as a self', and *tra* means 'to protect', that is, to protect quickly and to protect easily. 'Quickly' means that in a single moment it conquers what opposes the transmutation of the emotions into pristine cognitions and 'easily' means that the sensuous objects become friends without there being any such frustrating exercises as mortification and so on."

In his *Theg-pa'i mchog rin-po-che'i mdzod*, vol. I, p. 130, Klong-chen rab-'byams-pa says succinctly: "It protects from emotional vagaries and speeds up the realization of limpid clearness and consummate perspicacity." Basically the same explanation is given by Yon-tan rgya-mtsho in his *Zab-don snang-byed nyi-ma'i 'od-zer*, p. 20. But in his *rNam-mkhyen shing-rta*, pp. 54 f, 'Jigs-med gling-pa gives the following interpretation: "*man* is the cognitive capacity, the appreciative discrimination that is cognizant of the thisness of Being; *traya* is to protect the world, or, protection is absolute compassion. The indivisibility of these two (appreciative of the openness of Being and compassion as its dynamic aspect) is *gsang-sngags* (*mantra*)." This explanation ultimately goes back to the definition of *mantra* in the *Thig-le kun-gsal chen-po'i rgyud* (in *rNying-ma rgyud-'bum*, vol. 5, p. 233): "The nature of *gsang-sngags* is Openness and Compassion."

3) This division is typical for rNying-ma thought. In his *Theg-pa'i mchog rin-po-che'i mdzod*, vol. 1, pp. 135 ff, Klong-chen rab-'byams-pa gives a very detailed account of each of these divisions. In general they share the common feature of referring back to immediate experience, rather than engaging in the reflective-thematic aspect of experience. The Mahā (*rgyud mahāyoga'i theg-pa*) is concerned with "the cultivation of the pristine cognitions, (the dynamic aspect) of sheer lucency which is both irradiative and 'nothing' (i.e., an utter openness), through the absolute unity of the (two) realities (i.e., the 'absolutely real' and the 'conventionally real', which in terms of experience constitute the prereflective-nonthematic side and the reflective-thematic side of experience) by way of three

holistic experiences and realizations (see below, notes 15–17) in connection with the primary importance (in this context) of the Developing Stage as appropriate action and technique" (p. 136).

The Anu (*lung anuyoga'i theg-pa*) deals with "the realization of the fact that the continuum (of experience) and (its) pristine cognition(s) are not two separate entities and that the unity defies any attempt to formulate it in propositions and does not reside in any limits (set up by propositions about experience) through the primary importance of appreciative discrimination belonging to the Fulfillment Stage" (pp. 140 f).

The Ati (*man-ngag rdzogs-pa chen-po*) is

self-existent pristine cognitiveness, which is not found as either Saṃsāra or Nirvāṇa, and having been free since the beginningless beginning is beyond acceptance and rejection. Once the spontaneous presence of its capabilities in its primordial and absolute purity as to any defects has been established as the foundation that is to be understood, because there is no ending to the operation of pristine cognitiveness free in every respect since it is not found anywhere as something, its cultivation is such that there cannot be any intentionally contrived cultivation because whatever arises in the self-existent pristine cognitiveness does so as the free play of pure meaningfulness. Since such non-purposive cultivation, absolutely free in itself, arises uncontrived as the flow of pristine cognitiveness (like) the current of a stream, its self-freedom in its cresting is like a wave of water; its receding by itself in its continuum is like mist in the sky; its wandering about in its own reach and range is like a whirlpool in the ocean; its presence in its self-manifestedness is overarchingly all-pervasive like the light in a lamp. (In view of the fact that this self-existent pristine cognitiveness) does not go beyond its 'commitments' of being non-existent (as something existent or non-existent), continual, spontaneous, and solitary, it is termed 'climax of the Vajrayāna'; it is the domain of accomplished mystics of highest intellectual acumen (pp. 144 f).

The four 'commitments' are the theme of Klong-chen rab-'byams-pa's *gNas-lugs rin-po-che'i mdzod* and his commentary on it, the *sDe-gsum snying-po'i don-'gsel gnas lugs rin-po-che'i mdzod*. The meaning of the terms *rgyud, lung, man-ngag*, by which the Mahā, Anu and Ati are specified, is elucidated by Klong-chen rab-'byams-pa in his *Zab-mo yang-tig*, part Wam, pp. 413 ff, as follows: *rgyud* means "self-existent pristine cognitiveness and its explication, arranged in the order of starting-point, path, and goal (like the strings of a lute) with all the necessary points being in tune" (p. 413); *lung* means "pure awareness and the trust in its explanation by the Teacher without adding or subtracting from it" (p. 425); and *man-ngag* means "the profound meaning of Buddhahood and its concise explication" (p. 427).

4) The Developing Stage is, for all practical purposes, a rediscovery of experience and a fresh vision, while the Fulfillment Stage is the relishing of the experience. For the psychological and philosophical implications, see below, note 13.

5) See note 7 to Chapter Six.

6) *Theg-pa'i mchog rin-po-che'i mdzod*, vol. I, pp. 282 f.

7) *Shing-rta chen-po*, p. 793; *Tshig-don rin-po-che'i mdzod*, pp. 197 f.

8) A more detailed account of this classification is offered by Klong-chen rab-'byams-pa in his *Theg-pa mtha'-dag-gi don gsal-bar byed-pa grub-pa'i mtha' rin-po-che'i mdzod*, pp. 290 f, and his *sNgags-kyi spyi-don tshangs-dbyangs 'brug-sgra*, pp. 21a f. The four ages (*yuga*) are common to both Buddhist and Hindu traditions.

9) Upā(ya) (Sanskrit: *ubhaya*, 'both') is another name for the Caryātantra group. This name is used because both ritual and contemplation are employed.

10) *thub-pa rgyud*. They are termed *rgyud* (*tantra*, 'existentiality') because they point to the involvement of the whole person in his quest for life's meaning, but they are not yet the inner process itself which is experienced in rDzogs-chen; hence they are still 'on the surface', 'external' (*phyi-pa*). See *Theg-pa*

mtha'-dag-gi-don gsal-bar byed-pa grub-pa'i mtha' rin-po-che'i mdzod,
p. 301.

In his *Theg-pa'i mchog rin-po-che'i mdzod,* vol. I, p. 169,
Klong-chen rab-'byams-pa defines *rgyud* as follows: "Because
it points out man's affinity with Being (*rigs*), because it makes
man be born in any form this affinity may take, and because it
continues wearily and uninterruptedly." On 'affinity with Being', see notes 5 and 19 to Chapter Four.

11) 'Meat' and 'nectar' are essentially 'symbolical' terms and their
use has a place in the imaginative technique under consideration. They are not 'literal' terms, although there is always a
'literal' core in every 'symbolical' term. On the 'symbolical'
aspect of these terms see 'Ba-ra-ba sGyal-mtshan dpal-bzang,
A Tibetan Encyclopedia of Buddhist Scholasticism, vol. 7, pp. 233 f.
Since in this context every term is both 'symbolical' and 'literal', it is a sign of dullness if a person only sees the 'literal'
aspect. This is what Klong-chen rab-'byams-pa wants to say.

12) See above note 3.

13) This transfiguration is both a discovery and recovery. Discovery means to find what has been there all the time, and
recovery is both a return to and renewal of health. The recovery from illness, from having gone astray into a fictitious
world of unfulfillable expectations, is, as Klong-chen rab-
'byams-pa points out in his *Shing-rta chen-po,* p. 760, the realization that

> What have been the five psychophysical constituents, the
> 'impure' and sham presence (of Being), have dissolved
> (*sangs*) and expanded (*rgyas*) into (and thus become Bud-
> dhahood in the symbolic forms of) the five 'male' poles of
> Being; what have been the five elemental forces, have dis-
> solved and expanded into (and thus become Buddhahood
> in the symbolic forms of) the five 'female' poles of Being;
> and what has been the whole assemblage of dividing con-
> cepts have dissolved and expanded into (and thus become
> Buddhahood in the symbolic form of) the 'Bodhisattva'-
> maṇḍala, which means that there is nothing whatsoever
> that is not Buddhahood (*sangs-rgyas*).

And this is, as he points out on the same page, 'Mind-as-such, sheer lucency'.

The term 'Bodhisattva', *byang-chub-sems-dpa'*, refers to an experience, not to a person. Its experiential meaning is explained in the *Rig-pa rang-shar chen-po'i rgyud* (in *rNying-ma rgyud-'bum*, vol. 10, p. 312): "*byang* is founding stratum of meaning (*chos-sku*), *chub* is founding stratum of meaningful engagement in a world-horizon (*longs-sku*) coming in five strata, *sems-dpa'* is to act for the living beings through the founding stratum of embodiments of meaning (*sprul-sku*), and this activity is present as pristine cognitions."

Since in all this we have to do with lived-through experiences, one point that emerges quite clearly is that experience has an intentional structure which is so aptly indicated by the term maṇḍala (*dkyil-'khor*, 'center-periphery'). These intentional structures act as connectives that pervade the whole of experience and underlie its varied permutations, such as 'embodiment' (*sku*), 'communication' (*gsung*), and 'noeticness' (*thugs*), each of them having a vectorial character. They are neither rooted in a Pure Ego nor in an eternal essence, but are embedded in experience itself which, as we have seen, is simultaneously prereflective-nonthematic and reflective-thematic. These considerations will clarify Klong-chen rab-'byams-pa's statement about the presence of three maṇḍalas: "In brief, everything that is visibly present is a maṇḍala of embodied meaning; everything that is audible is a maṇḍala of communication; and all cognitive processes are a maṇḍala of noeticness" (p. 761). And the nature of experience: "Whatever is present (appears) as manifold is the 'developed' (*bskyed*, that which has thematic significance); since this does not exist as such, it is 'the complete' (*rdzogs*, that which is non-thematically significant). The ground (i.e., experience) as the pivotal maṇḍala must be known as having nothing to do with a causative agent and a caused effect" (pp. 761 f). It is in experience that the thematic retains or, rather, reassumes its transparent 'divine' character because the crude concretizations set up by representational, objectifying, and reifying thought, on the one hand, have gone (*sangs*) and because, on the other hand, the open texture of experience has reasserted itself (*rgyas*), whereby the two movements, the prereflective-nonthematic and the reflective-thematic, are again reunited in the dynamics of experience and whereby the ground or starting-point, experience itself, has been made the foundation of man's journey towards the meaning of life. Thus, Klong-chen rab-'byams-pa sums up experience as the starting point:

> Since from the viewpoint of a presentational presence (*snang-tshod*, the thematic) the psychophysical constituents, the physico-spiritual make-up, the sensory world-picture, and all the rest has gone into and expanded as a divine actuality (*lha*), there is nothing good or bad about it, nor is there anything to accept or to reject; in view of this being an open texture (*stong-pa*, the non-thematic as meaningfulness), the fact that all propositions as to its existence or non-existence have subsided is the ground as a spontaneously present maṇḍala. Understanding experience in this way, by knowing the whole of appearance and the fictions about it—Saṃsāra and Nirvāṇa—to be a maṇḍala ('intentional structure'), whatever presents itself as a presence is preserved in pristine cognitions (pp. 762 f).

That the 'path' starts from the intentional structure of experience and passes through the images of the path which has an intentional structure of its own, to the climax of Buddhahood with its specific intentional structure, is also the theme of the latter part of Klong-chen rab-'byams-pa's *Padma dkar-po*, pp. 797 ff. See also his *Theg-pa'i mchog rin-po-che'i mdzod*, vol. 1, pp. 282 f.

14) *rdo-rje 'chang* is a symbolical term for the indivisible unity of the prereflective-nonthematic and the reflective-thematic in experience; *Zab-mo yang-tig*, part Wam, p. 217. *rdo-rje 'dzin* emphasizes the 'operational', reflective-thematic aspect of Being within Being; *Lung-gi gter-mdzod*, pp. 196b f. Both terms mean 'holding a Vajra', 'scepter-bearer'. In his *gSang-'grel phyogs-bcu'i mun-sel-gyi spyi-don 'od-gsal snying-po*, p. 156, Mipham 'Jam-dbyangs rnam-rgyal rgya-mtsho explains the latter term as "having the power to conquer the mire of Saṃsāra and Nirvāṇa."

15) This phase is termed *de-bzhin-nyid-kyi ting-nge-'dzin*, 'a holistic experience of just-so'; *Shing-rta chen-po*, p. 806.

16) This phase is termed *kun-tu snang-ba'i ting-nge-'dzin* 'a holistic experience of a total presence'; *Shin-rta chen-po*, p. 807.

17) This phase is termed *rgyu'i ting-nge-'dzin*, 'a holistic experience of what is going to be the substance-matter of the process'; *Shing-rta chen-po*, pp. 807 f.

18) The spikes refer to the four directions, the four intermediary directions, and to the zenith and the nadir; *Shing-rta chen-po*, p. 808.

19) A fabulous beast, half bird, half man.

    The architectural elements of the palace as the 'home of the mind' symbolize the various facets of the quest. Thus, for instance, the four gates are the four immeasurably great catalytic properties of Being; the four pediments, the four techniques of attentiveness and inspection; the eight cremation grounds, the eight cognitive patterns underlying the deadening forms of representational thinking; the roofing tiles, Mind-as-such; and so on. *Shing-rta chen-po*, pp. 814 ff.

20) *rigs lnga*: Vairocana at the center, Akṣobhya to the east, Ratnasambhava to the south, Amitābha to the west, and Amoghasiddhi to the north. Each presides over a world-horizon of meaning which is his affinity with Being (*rigs*).

    The male-female symbolism indicates the unitary character of the two components of experience, the 'male' polarity indicating the thematic ('apparent') significance, the 'female' polarity the nonthematic ('open') significance—the one cannot be without the other. The 'heroes' are the sensory perceptions by eye, ear, nose, and tongue as the four 'internal' ones, and the sensory capacities (organs) of eye, ear, nose, and tongue as the four 'external' ones. The 'heroines' are color-form, sound, fragrance, and flavor as the four 'internal' dancers, and the past, the present, the future, and the timelessness of meaningfulness as the four 'external' goddesses. The 'guardians' are the cognitive capacity in the animate organism, the animate organism proper, the 'objects' for this cognitive capacity in the organism, and the 'spread-out' world for this organism; their female counterparts are the experiences of the meaning of the fact that nothing whatsoever has any status of eternalism *a parte ante*, of eternalism *a parte post*, of a self, or of an essence (that is, an abiding quality). *Shing-rta chen-po*, pp. 823 f.

21) *thub-pa*. A term usually used for the historical Buddha. There is, however, in each life-form a *thub-pa*. Thus again, *thub-pa* is a 'symbolical' term for the capacity to transcend one's limitations in whichever form of life someone may find himself.

22) The importance of the *mantra*, be it a single syllable or a longer formula, lies in the fact that it attempts to recapture the source from which language has sprung. The *mantra* (*gsang-sngags*, 'hidden language'), on the one hand, prevents the person's mind from sallying forth into the categorical and deadening schemata of representational thought and his language from becoming mere words that pass from hand to hand like a coin of little value; on the other hand, it is a first utterance, the first act of a form-giving process that asserts nothing and yet initiates everything, thus enabling us to speak at all. It is as if a hidden reality has only just crystallized in it.

23) *rlung, sems, rtsa, thig-le*. *rlung* is a term of the movement represented by and taking place in the elemental forces; *sems* is the 'intending phase' in the direction of the subject-object division and thus is the noetic-noematic complex; *rtsa* is both 'structuring' and 'structured'; and *thig-le* is the 'psychic energy' as its first 'creative spark' which, in a sense, is 'a maṇḍala in the making'. These 'meanings' are, of course, only some aspects of what goes on in experience as a dynamic process.

24) *rdo-rje 'dzin*. See above, note 14.

Notes to Chapter Ten

1) *rig-pa'i ye-shes*. This term is unique to rDzogs-chen thought. Specifically, *rig-pa* is the 'charge', 'cognitiveness', 'readiness to respond (to Being)' in or of Being, and thus is inseparable from 'facticity', 'actuality', and 'responsiveness', which are the three vectors of Being or Experience. Its 'active' aspect is indicated by *ye-shes*, 'pristine cognitions', which are 'expressions' of the inherent creativity and dynamics of *rig-pa*. Therefore *ye-shes*

also participates in 'facticity' (open dimension of Being), 'actuality' (lucency as solicitation), and 'responsiveness' (as all-encompassing compassion). *mKha'-'gro yang-tig,* part Ah, p. 222; *Tshig-don rin-po-che'i mdzod,* pp. 98 ff.

2) The unity of the 'two truths' (*bden gnyis,* that is, the conventionally real and the absolutely real) is to be understood from the source from which these 'two' have sprung, that is, from experience itself. In his *Shing-rta chen-po,* p. 700, Klong-chen rab-'byams-pa states: "The two truths are not different like two horns; in the conventionally real phase, when one sees the reflection of the moon in the water, insofar as there is the reflection, this is the conventionally real; insofar as this reflection is not the moon, this is the absolutely real. The fact that both represent one fact insofar as there is the presence of the moon in the water of the well without existing there, is the indivisibility or unity of the two truths. About the intellect that understands it in this way, it is said that it understands the two truths."

The distinction that is made between a 'valid conventionally real' (*yang dag kun-rdzob*) and an 'invalid conventionally real' (*log-pa'i kun-rdzob*) again reflects the importance of experience and its primacy over objectifying thought. The experienced moonlight in a dark night is not an object for the astronomical and physical sciences. In the latter the moon and its light is represented by objectifying and reifying thought for dissection, instead of being apprehended in its presential immediacy. The absolutely real is 'Mind-as-such, sheer lucency', irreducible to the categories of representational thought. A further detailed account is given by Klong-chen rab-'byams-pa in his *Padma dkar-po,* pp. 799 ff.

3) *rtog-ge.* There are two varieties: The unregenerate person who will believe in any oddity because a 'reason' can always be found, and the philosopher who reduces everything to substances, essences and so on; idealism, with its regression to a transcendental subject, is as reductionist as realism with its postulation of objective essences. *Shing-rta chen-po,* pp. 887 f.

4) *kun-byed*. This term is a direct reference to *Chos-thams-cad rdzogs-pa chen-po byang-chub-kyi sems kun-byed rgyal-po* (in *rNying-ma rgyud-'bum*, vol. 1, p. 13):

> *kun* is all that is.
> What is meant by 'all that is'?
> The teacher and the teaching,
> The entourage, the place, and the time.
> *byed* is a learned personage (*mkhan-po*).
> Since it creates all—teacher, teaching,
> Entourage, place, and time—
> The self-existent pristine cognition is a learned personage.

The anthropomorphic imagery must not deceive us. The five 'constituents'—teacher, teaching, entourage, place, and time —clearly show that experience is configurative, and the experiencer is part of this context. Figuratively speaking, the experiencer creates (*byed*) his experience and knows (*mkhan-po*) it to be his experience.

5) This is here a play of words with *don* and *don-med*. *don* is the value of Being residing in the experiencer as the pivot (*don*) of experiences which he tends to externalize and project into a fictitious realm, into what is valueless and meaningless (*don-med*).

6) Written in the vein of Saraha's *Dohākośa*.

7) It is the ego (*yid*) that introduces the split in experience, while the mind (*sems*, the noetic-noematic complex as a mere 'in-tending') is like the beginning of a cloud formation in the sky and hence still an openness.

Notes to Chapter Eleven

1) *gnas-lugs*. This term emphasizes the primacy of experience in its primordiality, antedating the distinction between 'within' and 'without'. It has to be cultivated and can be cultivated only in such a way that the subject-object structure of representa-

tional thought with its *ad hoc* meanings (*chos*) is suspended so as to let this meaningfulness that is Being (*chos-nyid*) reassert itself and shine forth. Primordial experience and meaningfulness are synonymous. It is at a later stage, at the level of representational thinking, that 'meanings' are abstracted and its lucency is gradually lost in the murkiness of conceptual schemes.

2) *rang-grol*. Freedom is one of the distinguishing features of experience. Actually, freedom and experience are synonymous, and only when experience is split up by representational thinking starting from and 'falsifying' the thematic aspect of experience into objects as contrasted with a subject, is the contrast between freedom and bondage set up, and freedom confused with liberation. Whether we single out the prereflective-nonthematic aspect or the reflective-thematic, either operates in freedom through itself. A detailed discussion of the various nuances of freedom (*rang-grol, ye-grol, cer-grol, gcig-grol, mtha'-grol*) has been offered by Klong-chen rab-'byams-pa in his *Theg-pa'i rin-po-che'i mdzod*, vol. 2, pp. 263 ff; *Tshig-don rin-po-che'i mdzod*, pp. 266 ff. The illustration for this 'self-freedom' are clouds appearing in the sky and waves rolling in the ocean.

3) *gol-sa*. Primordial experience antedates space and time in the same way as it antedates subject and object, hence as Klong-chen rab-'byams-pa explains in his *Shing-rta chen-po*, p. 917: "Since one does not go anywhere, there is no place where to go astray; and since one does not look for anything, the seeing is not obscured." In particular, the 'places into which one may go astray' are the conceptual schemes of an eternalism *a parte ante* or an eternalism *a parte post*, and the concretizations of contemplative experiences. *Tshig-don rin-po-che'i mdzod*, pp. 308 f; *mKha'-'gro yang-tig*, part Ah, pp. 187 f.

4) *mtha'-grol*. The extremes are existence, non-existence, both together, neither. *Theg-pa'i mchog rin-po-che'i mdzod*, vol. 2, pp. 269 f; *Tshig-don rin-po-che'i mdzod*, pp. 271 f.

5) Although they may be dealt with in isolation, their effectiveness is guaranteed by their unity.

6) In his *Shing-rta chen-po*, p. 921, Klong-chen rab-'byams-pa illustrates this situation as follows: "A person of highest intellectual acumen need not cultivate contemplations for any amount of time since whatever he encounters is meaningfulness and hence there is nothing to combat, just as a person who has arrived at the island of gold will not find stones, even if he were searching for them."

7) In his *Shing-rta chen-po*, p. 922, Klong-chen rab-'byams-pa elaborates: "By composing himself in a state of unoriginatedness, a clarity undisturbed by depression and elation, and calm like the water in a well when the mud is not stirred, through his understanding of the vision of Being, a person of medium intelligence unites inner calm and wider perspective. When the dividing concepts have completely subsided, an understanding as vast as the sky arises."

8) In his *Shing-rta chen-po*, p. 922, Klong-chen rab-'byams-pa says: "When a person of low intelligence, whose mind is volatile and obstinate and, like a monkey, cannot be at rest for a moment, is infiltrated by an inner calm that is well-focussed on its object of interest, and has developed a taste for contemplation, then, in order to counter his restlessness, by cultivating a wider perspective which understands that all that is has no essence and is an utter openness, as well as that all that presents itself is like an apparition, he will understand what is meant by unoriginatedness."

9) They are: sitting cross-legged, joining the hands one on top of the other, keeping the back straight, turning the tongue up to the roof of the mouth, breathing slowly, lowering the eyes to the tip of the nose, and bending the neck slightly.

10) As Klong-chen rab-'byams-pa points out in his *Shing-rta chen-po*, pp. 924, it is not a matter of blocking or repressing the senses, but of refraining from 'seeing' the objects of our experience just as familiar 'things' or as rational 'contents' through preconceived 'forms'. It is rather a releasing of perception and thought from the compulsion for dominance, control, making demands, and permitting meanings to present themselves in the phenomena:

In addition to the fact that no violence is done to any object when it is not turned into this or that entity by dividing concepts, each object's qualities ('meanings') are allowed to rise, and, since what appears in observable qualities is not interfered with by dividing concepts, one speaks of a conceptless pristine cognition (*rnam-par mi-rtog-pa'i ye-shes*). If there is no (setting up of) observable qualities (noematic correlations), there also is no correlated (noetic) mind, and since there is no discursive elaboration since there has been no selection of a concept to be used, even conceptless pristine cognition ceases to exist as something.

11) Once perception has been freed from the compulsion for control, mind automatically becomes stable, which is to say that it is no longer torn by opposing trends. It is here that man's being as an embodying process (*lus*) of meaning emerges. This embodying process has nothing to do with the traditional category of existence, nor is it a finite existent. If Being is meaningfulness, then man's concrete existence (*lus*) embodies meaning and hence cannot be reduced to either a transcendental subject nor an eternal essence. Klong-chen rab-'byams-pa says in his *Shing-rta chen-po*, p. 926:

> If at that time one sticks to such notions as 'object' (anything that appears as an external material entity), or 'mind' (anything that is an internal immaterial cognition), Mind-as-such, co-existent with (such mentation), and a thrust towards the optimum level of Being is fettered and obscured. Therefore, one must not entertain the slightest ideas about Saṃsāra and Nirvāṇa, good and evil, and, in the last instance, should not have any craving for one's holistic experiences. When one does not entertain any ideas about substantiality or non-substantiality, and when there also is no other intentional thinking, all movements of concepts totally subside in the reach and range that is Being, Mind-as-such; and when mind does not move and remains steady, it is freed from Saṃsāra. Since there is then no belief in duality, no craving for a self and the other, the sublime founding stratum of meaning has become concretely em-

bodied, but immune to any propositions about it and defying any ideas about or verbalizations of it.

12) In his *Shing-rta chen-po*, p. 928, Klong-chen rab-'byams-pa elaborates: "Since the without and the within as the reflective-thematic aspect in experience (*chos-can*), illustrated by the eight analogies beginning with apparitionalness and their non-reflective-nonthematic aspect (*chos-nyid*), are not different from each other in their facticity of never having come into existence as such, presentational thereness and openness are seen as one feature.

13) *ye-grol*. Just as *rang-grol* refers to the character of freedom of experience, *ye-grol* indicates its freedom genealogically. Figuratively speaking, *rang-grol* means 'is free throughout', and *ye-grol* 'has been free throughout time out of mind'. For Klong-chen rab-'byams-pa's discussion of the problems connected with this term see the references given in note 2.

14) As Klong-chen rab-'byams-pa points out in his *Shing-rta chen-po*, p. 934, both are experienced as a unity.

15) *snang-ba'i ye-shes*. This term refers to the first stirring of pristine cognitions and marks the beginning of the journey to the realization of Being. *Shing-rta chen-po*, p. 935, 944.

16) *mched-pa'i ye-shes*. The phase following the 'dawn' when light spreads far and wide. *Shing-rta chen-po*, p. 907, 945 f. This phase corresponds to the 'path of application' leading to the 'path of seeing'.

17) *thob-pa'i ye-shes*. This is the phase of 'seeing', the having come to the first spiritual level of pure joy. *Shing-rta chen-po*, p. 939, 946.

18) This passage refers to the 'path of cultivation'. *Shing-rta chen-po*, p. 940.

19) *nye-bar thob-pa'i ye-shes*. It is the pristine cognition operating on the path of cultivation and removing all blemishes of the nine spiritual levels. *Shing-rta chen-po*, pp. 941 ff, 947. The first three of these consuming cognitions burn away the coarser obscu-

rations that prevent experience from being experienced in full. The last one is the realization of Buddhahood, the sheer lucency residing in the founding stratum of meaning.

20) Accumulation of merits and accumulation of knowledge (i.e., experiential, not cumulative).

21) They are the various stages of concentrative attention, from our normal 'consciousness' with its 'desires' and tasks-at-hand ranging over the four stages in the world of aesthetic forms and images, to the four stages in the world of formlessness with their feelings of infinitude.

Notes to Chapter Twelve

1) *Shing-rta chen-po*, p. 1014.

2) *Shing-rta chen-po*, p. 1021.

3) In his *Shing-rta chen-po*, p. 1005, Klong-chen rab-'byams-pa elaborates as follows:

> Since lack of control of body and mind prevents one from taking anything seriously, it is in opposition to the way to inner peace; since places where many people gather, such as the vicinities of cities, cause distraction, one fails in what one has to do; since taking pleasure in drowsiness, sluggishness, and idleness prevents one from achieving any work, to say nothing of gaining a holistic experience, it is a false friend; since exultation and self-reproach disturb the mind, they hinder a wider perspective; since many people and acquaintances are an occasion for many involvements and for attachment and aversion, they counteract concentration; since talkativeness diminishes any feeling of wholeness and hinders it to be born, and is the source for dissatisfaction and strife, it is by giving up all these hindrances that holistic experiences will naturally grow and that one will hold to the message of the Victorious One.

4) There are eleven ways of doing so, *Shing-rta chen-po*, p. 1020.

5) There are nine techniques involved. See *gSang-'grel phyogs-bcu'i mun-sel-gyi spyi-don 'od-gsal snying-po*, pp. 117 f.

Notes to Chapter Thirteen

1) The vectorial character of the founding strata, providing the primordial basis for meaning and supporting the experience which itself is vectorial by nature of facticity, immediacy, and responsiveness, and which therefore has both a prereflective-nonthematic aspect and a reflective-thematic aspect, is indicated by Klong-chen rab-'byams-pa in his *Shing-rta chen-po*, pp. 695 f, where the emphasis is on the prereflective-nonthematic aspect of the experience:

> Although the founding stratum of embodied meanings (*sprul-pa'i sku*) presents itself spontaneously through the (interaction between) the accumulation of merits and knowledge on the part of those to be trained, and through the compassion of Buddha, this stratum seems to step out of itself and change into something other than itself as far as the conceptual thought of those to be trained is concerned; but actually, there is no such stepping out of itself or changing into something other than itself. Although the image of a reflection of the moon in water seems to have the character of a stepping out of itself and changing into something other than itself due to a condition provided by a water vessel, there is no such stepping out of itself nor changing into something other than itself, in view of the fact that there is no moon as such. Similarly, although there seems to be an embodied stratum, it does not exist as such. The reason is that the founding stratum of meaning does not step out of itself nor change into something other than itself, and in it the three founding strata constitute a single fact to which nothing can be added nor anything be subtracted. Further, in the same way as the moon in the sky does not change in its capacity to create a reflection of itself in the water (under suitable conditions), but remains the moon facticity, so also the founding stratum of embodied meanings presents itself spontaneously out of the reach and range of the founding stratum of engagement in world-horizons, but it does not step out of itself nor change into something other than itself, because it actually is not found as such. Only as far as those to be trained are

concerned does there seem to occur a stepping out of itself and a changing into something other than itself.

It is this seeming change, the reflective-thematic occurring nevertheless in experience, that is the 'conventionally real'.

2) The three pristine cognitions pertaining to facticity, presentational immediacy, and integrative responsiveness are not three different kinds, but facets of the vectorial character of experience; *mKha'-'gro yang-tig*, part Ah, pp. 463 f. In his *Theg-pa'i mchog rin-po-che'i mdzod*, vol. 1, pp. 630 f, Klong-chen rab-'byams-pa states:

> The absolutely pure (*ka-dag*) pristine cognition pertaining to facticity is like the clear sky, beyond the limiting categories of existence and non-existence; the spontaneous (*lhun-grub*) pristine cognition pertaining to presentational immediacy, is present as creativity and source, because the capabilities (of Being) are complete since their beginningless beginning, and in its presential actuality, like a Wish-fulfilling Gem, it has nothing to do with such notions as substance and quality; the all-encompassing (*kun-khyab*) pristine cognition pertaining to responsiveness provides the root that will become the source (of interpretation) without existing in itself.

3) In his *Shing-rta chen-po*, p. 1044, Klong-chen rab-'byams-pa elaborates:

> When the eight perceptual patterns together with their foundation have become quiet and subside in the naturally pure reach and range Mind-as-such, sheer lucency, and the continuum of the experience of meaningfulness, then the continuum (which is pure experience), the primordial foundation, and pure awareness—in which the pristine cognitions (that have been the manifest operations of pure awareness) are going to subside—fuse and have only one flavor: this is the stainless natural purity. The purification from incidental stains is the incidentally achieved purity. Both purities mark the founding stratum of meaning.

4) *mi-'gyur rdo-rje'i sku*. In his *Theg-pa'i mchog rin-po-che'i mdzod*, vol. 2, p. 565, Klong-chen rab-'byams-pa gives further explanations: "One as pure awareness—the ground; one as

the stage of pure awareness—the path; returning to one as flawless, absolutely pure awareness—the goal; like the sky without limits, this founding stratum of unchangeability and indestructibility, being a thrust by pristine cognition in openness, and operating in the precious layer of spontaneity, is the founding stratum of Buddhahood from the first (to the last)." In support he quotes from the *Rig-pa rang-shar chen-po'i rgyud* (in *rNying-ma rgyud-'bum*, vol. 10, pp. 189 f), which also underlines the unity of facticity, immediacy, and responsiveness.

5) *mnyon-par byang-chub sku.* In *Shing-rta chen-po*, p. 1046, and *Theg-pa'i mchog rin-po-che'i mdzod*, vol. 2, p. 567, Klong-chen rab-'byams-pa defines it briefly as the climax of having dispelled what had to be dispelled and of having reached the deepest understanding of Being.

6) *zhi-ba chos-kyi sku.* In his *Shing-rta chen-po*, p. 1048, Klong-chen rab-'byams-pa elaborates:

> When in the reach and range of Mind-as-such or the continuum of experience, which is like the sky, pristine cognitions have become one in flavor with it, like the time of the new moon, the host of propositions has ceased, but an overall sensitivity remains; this is called 'having become latent but not blotted out', and it is a state of composure in which pristine cognition is internally lucent, and which is the vitalizing force for pristine cognitions to spread when they begin to shine outwardly. Although there is no duality of objective situation and owner of the objective situation, there is a very special conceptless pristine cognition, termed 'founding stratum of meaning (present as) calmness'.

> 'Overall sensitivity' (*thams-cad mkhyen-pa*) is explained by Klong-chen rab-'byams-pa in his *Theg-pa'i mchog rin-po-che'i mdzod*, vol. 2, pp. 19 f, as referring to "the inner lucency of meaningfulness (*chos-nyid*) or the facticity of experience," while 'sensitivity to details (*rnam-pa thams-cad mkhyen-pa*)' refers to the "outward glow of reflected-on experience (*chos-can*) or the detailed observable qualities." Here again the two movements in experience, the prereflective-nonthematic and the reflective-thematic, are clearly stated.

7) See note 19 to Chapter Nine.

8) According to the *sGyu-'phrul dra-ba ye-shes-kyi snying-po'i rgyud* (in *rNying-ma rgyud-'bum*, vol. 15, p. 311), the lions symbolize fearlessness, the elephant strength, the horses higher forms of cognition; the peacocks controlling power; the birds unobstructedness; sun and moon natural lucency, and the lotus flower undefilement. (For 'shang-shang', see note 19 to Chapter Nine.)

9) The 'peaceful' aspects are basically values of light in a process of 'externalization' from an 'inner glow'. Klong-chen rab-'byams-pa in his *Zab-mo yang-tig*, part Wam, p. 159, clearly distinguishes between the 'inner glow' (*mdangs*), a steady, intense lucency without effulgence, and the 'outward radiance' (*gdangs*), radiation. This radiance, as yet calm, becomes the 'angry' aspect. The 'peaceful' aspect is associated with the 'heart', the 'angry' one with the brain. *Bla-ma yang-tig*, part Wam, p. 246. Since the 'brain' is associated with the 'ego', this means, psychologically speaking, that the 'angry' aspects are refractions and deflections of the 'peaceful' aspects of psychic life.

10) See note 20 to Chapter Nine; 'Jigs-med gling-pa, *rNam-mkhyen shing-rta*, pp. 811 f; Yon-tan rgya-mtsho, *Zab-don snang-byed nyi-ma'i 'od-zer*, pp. 532 ff.

11) They are the *thub-pa* in each of the six forms of life. See note 21 to Chapter Nine.

12) They are Samantabhadra and Samantabhadrī (*kun-tu bzang-po, kun-tu bzang-mo*), the male-female polarity in unity.

13) These are the 'Buddhas' of the 'five affinities to Being', male and female, thus accounting for the number 10. Thus, $6 + 2 + 24 + 10 = 42$.

14) They are the heroes, heroines, gate-keepers and gate-keeperesses. See also note 9.

15) A detailed account is given in *mKha'-'gro yang-tig*, part Ah, pp. 206 ff; *rDzogs-pa chen-po dgongs-pa zang-thal*, vol. 4, pp. 12 ff.

16) These terms serve to emphasize the lustrous character of what in representational thought becomes mind, speech, body—in this order.

17) 'Og-min (Akaniṣṭha) is the realm of Vairocana; mNgon-dga' (Abhirati) that of Akṣobhya; dPal-ldan that of Ratnasambhava; Padma-brtsegs that of Amitābha; and Las-rab grub-pa that of Amoghasiddhi. See Yon-tan rgya-mtsho, *Zab-don snang-byed nyi-ma'i 'od-zer*, p. 550. In his *Shing-rta chen-po*, p. 1068, Klong-chen rab-'byams-pa has Vajrasattva instead of Akṣobhya. Vajrasattva is a symbol for the mirror-like pristine cognition as it is operative in the founding stratum of meaning. *Zab-mo yang-tig*, part Wam, p. 157. Specifically, Vajrasattva (*rdo-rje sems-dpa'*) is a term for experience as a dynamic and yet invariable process. As this, the term is explained at length by O-rgyan chos-'phel in his *dPal-gsang-bdag dgongs-rgyan-gyi spyi-don yang-gi bshad-pa'i zin-bris bla-ma'i man-ngag rin-chen 'phreng-ba*, pp. 446 ff.

18) *rang-don* and *gzhan-don*. The former term refers to the experience as experience in its completeness, the latter to the way as it becomes 'externalized' and, in so doing, refers back to itself. The *gzhan-don* thus serves as a way by which others (*gzhan*) will find themselves (*rang*) by overcoming the subject-object structure of representational thinking in the vividness of primordial experience.

19) This line is taken from *Mahāyānasūtrālankāra*, IX, 72. It qualifies the 'individualizing pristine cognition' not the 'self-accomplished one'. However, in his *Shing-rta chen-po*, p. 1072, Klong-chen rab-'byams-pa quotes the above passage in support of his definition of the 'individualizing pristine cognition'.

20) *thub-pa*. See above note 11.

21) See above note 18.

Selected
Bibliography

Collections

rNying-ma rgyud-'bum (Tantras of the Nyingma tradition). Ed. Jamyang Khentse, 36 vols.

The *rGyud-'bum* of Vairocana. Ed. Tashi Y. Tashigangpa. 8 vols. Leh, 1971.

Works in Western Languages

Guenther, Herbert V. *Buddhist Philosophy in Theory and Practice.* Baltimore: Penguin, 1971.

Roerich, George N. *The Blue Annals.* Calcutta, 1949–1953.

Schrag, Calvin O. *Experience and Being: Prolegomena to a Future Ontology.* Evanston: Northwestern Univ. Press, 1969.

Schuh, Dieter. *Untersuchungen zur Geschichte der tibetischen Kalenderrechnung.* Wiesbaden, 1973.

Zaner, Richard M. *The Way of Phenomenology: Criticism as a Philosophical Discipline.* Indianapolis & New York: Pegasus, 1970.

Individual Tibetan Works

Klong-chen rab-'byams-pa:
mKha'-'gro yang-tig (in *sNying-thig ya-bzhi*, vols. 4, 5, 6).

Grub-pa'i mtha' rin-po-che'i mdzod (full title: *Theg-pa mtha'-dag-gi don gsal-bar byed-pa grub-pa'i mtha' rin-po-che'i mdzod*). Ed. Dodrup Chen Rinpoche, Gangtok.

Ngal-gso skor-gsum. Ed. Dodrup Chen Rinpoche, Gangtok, 1973.

Ngal-gso skor-gsum-gyi spyi-don legs-bshad rgya-mtsho. Ed. Dodrup Chen Rinpoche, Gangtok, 1973.

Chos-dbyings rin-po-che'i mdzod. Ed. Dodrup Chen Rinpoche, Gangtok.

sNying-thig ya-bzhi. 11 vols. Reprinted by Trulku Tsewang, Jamyang & L. Tashi. New Delhi, 1970.

Theg-pa'i mchog rin-po-che'i mdzod. Ed. Dodrup Chen Rinpoche, Gangtok.

sDe-gsum snying-po'i don-'grel (commentary on *gNas-lugs rin-po-che'i mdzod*). Ed. Dodrup Chen Rinpoche, Gangtok.

gNas-lugs rin-po-che'i mdzod. Ed. Dodrup Chen Rinpoche, Gangtok.

Padma dkar-po (commentary on *Yid-bzhin-mdzod*). Ed. Dodrup Chen Rinpoche, Gangtok.

Padma dkar-po'i phreng-ba (full title: *rDzogs-pa chen-po Sems-nyid ngal-gso'i 'grel-pa shing-rta chen-po'i bsdus-don-gyi gnas rgya-cher dbye-ba Padma dkar-po'i phreng-ba*). Ed. Dodrup Chen Rinpoche, Gangtok.

Puṇḍarīka'i phreng-ba (full title: *rDzogs-pa chen po bsam-gtan ngal-gso'i bsdus-don Pundarika'i phreng-ba*). Ed. Dodrup Chen Rinpoche, Gangtok.

Bi-ma snying-thig (in *sNying-thig ya-bzhi*, vols. 7, 8, 9).

Bum-thang lha'i sbas-yul-gyi bkod-pa-la bsngags-pa me-tog skyed-tshal (Miscellaneous Writings [*gsun thor bu*] of Kun-mkhyen Klong-chen-pa Dri-med-'od-zer, vol. 1, pp. 235–245).

Byang-chub lam-bzang (full title: *rDzogs-pa chen-po Sems-nyid ngal-gso'i gnas-gsum dge-ba-gsum-gyi don-khrid Byang-chub lam-bzang*). Ed. Dodrup Chen Rinpoche, Gangtok.

Bla-ma yang-tig (in *sNying-thig ya-bzhi*, vol. 1).

Mandāraba'i phreng-ba (full title: *rDzogs-pa chen po sgyu-ma ngal-gso'i bsdus-don Mandaraba'i phreng-ba*). Ed. Dodrup Chen Rinpoche, Gangtok.

Man-ngag rin-po-che'i mdzod. Ed. Dodrup Chen Rinpoche, Gangtok.

Zab-mo yang-tig (in *sNying-thig ya-bzhi*, vols. 10, 11).

Tshig-don rin-po-che'i mdzod (full title: *gSang-ba bla-na-med-pa 'od-gsal rdo-rje snying-po'i gnas-gsum gsal-bar byed-pa'i Tshig-don rin-po-che'i mdzod*). Ed. Dodrup Chen Rinpoche, Gangtok.

Yid-bzhin-mdzod-kyi don-khrid zab-don rdo-rje snying-po. Ed. Dodrup Chen Rinpoche, Gangtok.

Yid-bzhin rin-po-che'i mdzod (full title: *Theg-pa chen-po'i man-ngag-gi bstan-bcos Yid-bzhin rin-po-che'i mdzod*). Ed. Dodrup Chen Rinpoche, Gangtok.

Rang-grol skor-gsum (Miscellaneous Writings [*gsun thor bu*] of Kun-mkhyen Klong-chen-pa Dri-med-'od-zer, vol. 2, pp. 178–318).

Lung-gi gter-mdzod (commentary on *Chos-dbyings rin-po-che'i mdzod*). Ed. Dodrup Chen Rinpoche, Gangtok.

Shing-rta chen-po (full title: *rDzogs-pa chen-po Sems-nyid ngal-gso'i 'grel-pa Shing-rta chen-po*). Ed. Dodrup Chen Rinpoche, Gangtok.

Shing-rta rnam-(par) dag-pa (full title: *rDzogs-pa chen-po bSam-gtan ngal-gso'i 'grel-pa Shing-rta rnam-par dag-pa*). Ed. Dodrup Chen Rinpoche, Gangtok.

Shing-rta bzang-po (full title: *rDzogs-pa chen-po sGyu-ma ngal-gso'i 'grel-pa Shing-rta bzang-po*). Ed. Dodrup᾽ Chen Rinpoche, Gangtok.

gSung thor-bu (Miscellaneous Writings [*gsun thor-bu*] of Kun-mkhyen Klong-chen-pa Dri-med-'od-zer). Reproduced by Sanje Dorje. 2 vols. Delhi, 1973.

'Gyur-med Tshe-dbang mchog-grub:

gSang-sngags nang-gi lam-rim rgya-cher 'grel-pa sangs-rgyas gnyis-pa'i dgongs-rgyan (in *Smanrtsis Shesrig Spendzod*, vol. 35). Reproduced by Padma-chos-ldan. Leh, 1972.

Chos-grags bzang-po:

Kun-mkhyen Dri-med 'od-zer-gyi rnam-thar mthong-ba don-ldan (in *sNying-thig ya-bzhi*, vol. 9, sec. Tsha).

'Jigs-med gling-pa:

bDen-gnyis shing-rta (full title: *Yon-tan rin-po-che'i mdzod-kyi rgya-cher 'grel-pa bDen-gnyis shing-rta*, in *Ngagyur Nyingmay Sungrab Series*, vol. 29). Gangtok, 1970.

rNam-mkhyen shing-rta (full title: *'Bras-bu'i theg-pa'i rgya-cher
'grel-pa rNam-mkhyen shing-rta*, in *Ngagyur Nyingmay Sungrab
Series*, vol. 30). Gangtok, 1971.
Yon-tan rin-po-che'i mdzod dga'-ba'i char in *Ngagyur Nyingmay
Sungrab Series*, vol. 30). Gangtok, 1971.

Padma-phrin-las-snying-po:
Lam-rim ye-shes snang-ba'i brjed-byang (in *Smanrtsis Shesrig Spendzod*, vol. 8). Leh, 1971.

dPal-sprul O-rgyan 'Jigs-med chos-kyi dbang-po:
*Kun-mkhyen Klong-chen rab-'byams-pa'i gsung-rab mdzod-bdun-la
blta-bar bskul-ba* (The Collected Works of —, vol. 1, pp.
149–158, in *Ngagyur Nyingmay Sungrab Series*, vol. 38).
Sems-nyid ngal-bso'i bsdus-don Padma dkar-po'i zil-mngar (The
Collected Works of —, vol. 2, pp. 349–399, in *Ngagyur
Nyingmay Sungrab Series*, vol. 39).

'Ba-ra-ba rGyal-mtshan dpal-bzang:
A Tibetan Encyclopedia of Buddhist Scholasticism (The collected
writings of —). Ed. Ngawang Gyaltsen & Ngawang Lungtok.
14 vols. Dehradun, 1970.

Mi-pham 'Jam-dbyangs rnam-rgyal rgya-mtsho:
Yid-bzhin-mdzod-kyi sa-bcad bsdus-don Kumuda'i phreng-ba. Ed.
Dodrup Chen Rinpoche, Gangtok.
Yid-bzhin rin-po-che'i mdzod-kyi dka'-gnad ci-rigs gsal-bar byed-pa.
Ed. Dodrup Chen Rinpoche, Gangtok.
gSang-'grel phyogs-bcu'i mun-sel-gyi spyi-don 'od-gsal snying-po. Ed.
Tarthang Tulku, Varanasi.

Yon-tan rgya-mtsho:
Nyi-ma'i 'od-zer (full title: *Yon-tan rin-po-che'i mdzod-kyi 'grel-pa
zab-don snang-byed Nyi-ma'i 'od-zer*, in *Ngagyur Nyingmay Sungrab Series*, vol. 27). Gangtok, 1971.
bDen-gnyis gsal-byed zla-ba'i sgron-me (see *Zla-ba'i sgron-me*).
Zab-don snang-byed nyi-ma'i 'od-zer (see *Nyi-ma'i 'od-zer*).
Zla-ba'i sgron-me (full title: *Yon-tan rin-po-che'i mdzod-kyi 'grel-pa
bDen-gnyis gsal-byed Zla-ba'i sgron-me*, in *Ngagyur Nyingmay
Sungrab Series*, vol. 26). Gangtok, 1969.

Rig-'dzin rGod-kyi ldem-'phru-can:
  rDzogs-pa chen-po dgongs-pa zang-thal (in *Smanrtsis Shesrig Spendzod*, vol. 60–64). 5 vols. Reproduced by Pema Choden. Leh,
  1973.

Rong-zom Chos-kyi bzang-po:
  Theg-pa chen-po'i tshul-la 'jug-pa mdo-tsam brjod-pa (Commentaries
  on the Guhyagarbha Tantra and other rare Nyingmapa texts
  from the library of Dudjom Rinpoche). Vol. 1, pp. 223–431.
  Published by Sanje Dorje. New Delhi, 1974.

O-rgyan chos-'phel:
  *dPal gsang-ba dgongs-rgyan-gyi spyi-don yang-gi bshad-pa'i zin-bris
  bla-ma'i man-ngag rin-chen 'phreng-ba* (Commentaries on the
  Guhyagarbha Tantra and other rare Nyingmapa texts from
  the library of Dudjom Rinpoche). Vol. 1, pp. 433–601.

Index

Technical Terms

Tibetan

Sanskrit

Names and Subjects

oneness, peaceful aspects of, 229
ontology, xvii, 26
open, 224
openness, 65, 169ff, 173ff, 213
  as mantra, 282 n.2
  as thereness, 173, 295 n.12
  other, 107, 220f, 301 n.17
    value in, 127, 273 n.2
    welfare of, 138

Padmasambhava, xiv
pain, 142
Pāramitā, xvi, 246, 281 n.1
passion, 55
past, 180, 196, 255 n.15
path, 51, 53, 70, 97, 152f, 277 n.2,
  286 n.13
  eightfold noble, 96f, 202, 244
  five, 64, 92ff, 101, 241ff
  proper, 251 n.7
  supreme, 86
  Vajrayāna, 12
  wrong, 121
patience, 68
patterns, six cognitive, 57, 59
people, worthy, 74f
perception, 24ff, 50, 167f, 204
  judgments of, 31
  objectifying, 206
  seven patterns of, 56
  visual, 59
perceptivity, stratum-bound, 32,
  50, 56, 57
perseverance, 201, 242
persons, 223
  three types of, 186, 293 n.6,7,8
  worthy, 74f
perspective, wider, 191, 195, 198.
  See also calm, inner
perspicacity, consummate. *See*
  clearness, limpid
Phyag-rgya-che, xvi
pivot, of involvement, 50, 291 n.5
playfulness, 250 n.3, 258 n.19
pleasure, 53, 262 n.9, 296 n.3
poisons, three, 54, 65, 262 n.8

polarity, male-female, 285 n.13,
  288 n.20, 300 n.12
potential, inner, 123f, 128f
  as deity, 150f
powers, five controlling, 202, 243
Pratyekabuddhas, 101, 235, 267
  n.5
predication, non-, 200
preparation, path of, 93, 201, 241f
presence, 24, 161, 287 n.13
  apparent, 146
  lucent, 55
  presentational, 218
present, 180, 196, 255 n.15
processes,
  actional perceptual and apper-
    ceptional, 50
  cognitive, 55, 56
project(s)-at-hand, 25ff, 50, 167
  ego-related, 28
properties, actional, 49f
pure, 224, 263 n.10
purpose, positive, 124
pursuance, steady, 129f, 278 n.11
pursuit,
  cause-dominated and goal-sus-
    tained, 91, 100, 102f, 121, 238
  existential, 157

Quietude, 66
quiescence, 190

Radiancy, 172
Ratnasambhava, 229, 233, 288
  n.20, 300 n.17
rDo-rje-'chang, 162, 287 n.14
rDzogs-chen, xvi, xviii, 24, 218,
  260 n.6
readiness, perceptual, 24
real, absolutely and conventionally, 272 n.23, 280 n.16, 290 n.2,
  298 n.1
realism, 290 n.3
realities, two, 68, 272 n.23, 282 n.3
reality, 94f, 162
realization, 277 n.2